CERTIFICATE

QUANTITATIVE STUDIES
(STATISTICS)

(i)

First edition August 1991

ISBN 0 86277 696 1

British Library Cataloguing-in-Publication Data

A catalogue record for this book
is available from the British Library

Published by

BPP Publishing Limited
Aldine House, Aldine Place
London W12 8AW

Printed in England by
DACOSTA PRINT
35/37 Queensland Road
London N7 7AH
(071) 700 1000

We are grateful to the Chartered Institute of Marketing, the Institute of
Chartered Secretaries and Administrators, the Chartered Association of
Certified Accountants and the Chartered Institute of Management Accountants
for permission to use past examination questions. The suggested solutions
have been prepared by BPP Publishing Limited.

CONTENTS

PREFACE

The Certificate awarded by the Chartered Institute of Marketing offers thorough and relevant coverage of key areas for marketers. Building on our expertise in producing comprehensive and up-to-date workbooks for the examination syllabuses of a number of professional bodies, BPP Publishing Limited have published a new range targeted directly at the CIM Certificate and Diploma qualifications.

The *Quantitative Studies* syllabus is demanding in its scope and treatment, and students will find the examination both challenging and rewarding. Written specifically for the syllabus, which is reproduced on page (vii), this *Quantitative Studies* text reflects both the syllabus content and the approach taken in recent examination papers, an analysis of which appears on page (ix).

The structure of the text follows the order of the syllabus itself and each of the eleven chapters covers a major area in a clear and user friendly style. Every chapter provides numerous examples and exercises and the student is encouraged to test acquired knowledge at the end of each chapter.Throughout the student is referred to illustrative questions, with full suggested solutions, on which to practice both knowledge and examination skills.

Students of the Certificate in Marketing should find this text an invaluable aid to examination success.

BPP Publishing
August 1991

INTRODUCTION

Syllabus

Aims and objectives

- To provide students with an introduction to statistical techniques which are widely used in business.

- To provide students with the knowledge and skills needed to apply quantitative techniques to business problems.

- To ensure that all marketing students have a working knowledge of sources of market research data and the methods which can be used to collect such data.

- To provide marketing practitioners with the quantitative skills necessary for forecasting.

By the end of their study students should be able:

(a) to produce and present statistical information;
(b) to interpret and use statistical information; and
(c) to undertake simple numerical calculations and explain the concepts and use of the various techniques.

Content

(a) *Collection and presentation of numerical information*

Secondary data
  Official sources of economic and business data

Primary data
  Methods of collecting data: survey, observation, experimentation
  Sampling methods
  Survey methods: interview, postal, telephone
  Questionnaire design

Presentation
  Tabulation
  Graphs
  Charts
  Diagrams

(b) *Frequency distribution*

Measures of location: mean, median, mode
Measures of dispersion: quartile deviation, standard deviation
Skewness: coefficient of variation

(c) *Relationships and forecasting*

Correlation and regression
  Product moment correlation coefficient
  Rank correlation coefficient
  Linear regression using the least squares method

INTRODUCTION

Time series analysis
Components of a time series: trend, cyclical, seasonal, random
Moving averages
Simple methods of forecasting

(d) *Index numbers*

Methods
Price relative methods
Aggregate methods
Problems involved in the use of index numbers

(e) *Probability and statistical inference*

A practical view of probability

Events and outcomes
Equally likely outcomes
Combination of events
Union of events
Conditional probability
Mutually exclusive events

Statistical inference
Confidence intervals and hypothesis testing for: a single mean, a single proportion

Hints and tips from the examiner

The following extract from the CIM Fact File makes useful reading.

'Adequate preparation is essential if students are to pass this paper. The examination is deliberately structured so that candidates have to undertake numerical aspects of the syllabus as well as explain the concepts and application of the various techniques.

The ability to interpret and explain is essential, so students should not only be able to calculate the arithmetical mean, but they should also know what its result measures and how it can be used either in business generally or marketing specifically.'

The format of the examination paper

The examination paper consists of eight questions, from which five must be selected. All questions carry 20 marks. Some statistical formulae are supplied for use in the examination and you will find a full list of these in the appendix to this text.

INTRODUCTION

Analysis of past papers

This brief analysis of the last five papers should help you to see the scope of recent examination questions.

June 1991

1. Using population census results in marketing decisions
2. Construct and interpret Lorenz curve
3. Correlation
4. Significance testing
5. Construction and use of retail price index
6. Arithmetic mean, standard deviation, median and quartile deviation
7. Draw graph or chart from tabulated data and write report
8   Time series analysis

December 1990

1. Report to summarise data; suitable diagram or graph required
2. Scatter diagram; calculate and comment on correlation coefficient
3. Write notes to describe four out of five statistical terms
4. Written question on the use of official statistics
5. Draw two charts to illustrate sales data
6. Ogive; calculate median and quartiles; comment
7. Calculations based on normal distribution
8. Calculate and comment on mean, standard deviation and mode

June 1990

1. Construct frequency distribution and histogram. Discuss bar chart
2. Index numbers
3. Written question on the use of statistics by a marketing department
4. Regression analysis
5. Sample selection and confidence intervals
6. Time series analysis
7. Calculate and comment on mean and standard deviation
8. Discuss problems in using questionnaires for collection of statistical data

December 1989

1. Calculate and explain mean, standard deviation and coefficient of variation
2. Index numbers
3. Scatter diagram and regression analysis
4. Calculate and explain median and quartile deviation
5. Significance testing
6. Write notes to explain four out of five statistical terms
7. Construct and discuss bar chart and pie diagram
8. Time series analysis

INTRODUCTION

June 1989

1. Construct grouped frequency distribution and histogram; calculate and comment on mean and standard deviation
2. Use an illustrative example to discuss stratified random sampling
3. Draw Z chart and interpret
4. Significance testing
5. Index numbers
6. Correlation and regression analysis
7. Write notes to comment on four out of five statistical terms
8. Time series analysis

How to use this text

Systematic approach

The study text is structured as far as possible to correspond with the order in which the syllabus itself is laid out and you should work through each part in order.

Each part of the text is divided into chapters which deal with the individual subjects in the syllabus. At the end of each chapter you will find a number of short questions which test your knowledge of the material which you have just read.

If you can provide complete answers to each of these short questions then you should try the relevant illustrative question(s) for the chapter. These are located towards the back of the text and the relevant question number(s) is indicated at the end of each chapter.

When you have checked your solution against ours and have understood the reasons for any differences then you are ready to proceed to the next chapter or part of the text.

This systematic approach will ensure that you have a thorough understanding of each aspect of the syllabus before you move on to a fresh one.

Calculators

You must have a calculator to study this syllabus effectively and we strongly recommend the use of a scientific calculator. Throughout this text we will be giving hints on the use of calculators and we will use a *Casio fx 100c* for demonstration purposes, since it is very widely used. You will find more information about how to choose a calculator at the beginning of chapter 4.

PART A
COLLECTION AND PRESENTATION OF
NUMERICAL INFORMATION

Chapter 1

COLLECTION OF DATA

This chapter covers the following topics.

1. Using statistics
2. Types of data
3. Questionnaire design
4. Sampling
5. Sources of published statistics

---

1. USING STATISTICS

The meaning of statistics

1.1 The word 'statistics' has three meanings.

(a) Firstly, it is used to describe a group of figures - for example, figures relating to a country's imports and exports are often referred to as 'trade statistics' and the figures kept by cricket commentators on past matches are called 'statistics'.

(b) Secondly, it is used as an abbreviation for 'statistical method' which means the methods by which information or data (or *numbers* obtained as a result of counting or measuring something) are presented. The importance of statistical method is that it enables a large mass of complex data to be condensed into a more readily understandable form.

(c) Thirdly, it has come to mean the way in which the information or data is interpreted, once it has been presented in a satisfactory form.

1.2 The subject called statistics therefore covers the collection of data, presenting it in a sensible fashion, and interpreting the data.

Advantages and limitations of statistics

1.3 The main advantage of statistics is that it offers some methods which can be used to make sense of numbers. In a business environment, for example, a manager may collect all sorts of data on production levels, or costs, or sales. On their own, the *numbers* making up this data are unlikely to mean very much. But by using statistics a manager can try to make sense out of the numbers, which in turn should assist in making sensible business decisions.

3

1.4   However, it is important to remember that nothing can be *proved* by statistics. It can be shown that something is extremely likely or extremely unlikely, but statistics deal with uncertain situations, and statistical results can rarely be 100% certain. For example, suppose light bulbs are produced by a factory in batches of 100. Using data on past batches, statistics might show that seven out of every batch of bulbs is faulty and fails to light up. But nobody could say for certain that there will *always* be seven faulty bulbs in a batch. Sometimes there will be less, and sometimes more. But at least statistics has given some sort of guidelines on how many bulbs are wasted, which can help a manager to estimate production costs.

2.   TYPES OF DATA

2.1   The information, or data, gathered for a particular purpose may be of several types. The first major distinction is between *attributes* and *variables*.

   (a)   An attribute is something an object has either got or not got. It cannot be measured. For example, an individual is either male or female. There is no measure of *how* male or *how* female somebody is - the sex of a person is an attribute. A person is one thing or the other.

   (b)   A variable is something which can be measured or counted. For example, the height of a person is a quantitative fact which can be measured according to some scale (for example feet and inches).

2.2   Data can be collected on either attributes or variables. For example, you could examine a sample of Londoners and count how many were male and how many female, or you could measure the heights of the people in the sample.

2.3   Variables can be further divided between discrete and continuous.

   (a)   *Discrete* variables can only be expressed in terms of whole numbers. The range of possible values is split into a series of steps. For example, the number of goals scored by a football team may be 0, 1, 2, 3 etc but cannot be $\frac{1}{2}$, $1\frac{1}{3}$ or $2\frac{1}{2}$. The value of a discrete variable is established by counting.

   (b)   *Continuous* variables may take on any value. They are measured rather than counted. For example, it may be considered sufficient to measure the height of a number of people to the nearest $\frac{1}{4}$ inch but there is no reason why the measurements should not be made to the nearest 1/1,000 inch or even 1/1,000,000 inch. Two people who are found to have the same height to the nearest $\frac{1}{4}$ inch could almost certainly be distinguished if more accurate measurements were taken.

Exercise

Look through the following list of surveys and decide whether each is collecting data on attributes, discrete variables, or continuous variables.

   (a)   A survey of statistics text books, to determine how many diagrams they contain.
   (b)   A survey of cans on a supermarket shelf, to determine whether or not each has a price sticker on it.

(c) A survey of athletes, to find out how long they take to run a mile.

(d) A survey of the results of an accounting examination, to determine what percentage marks the students obtain.

(e) A survey of the height of telegraph poles in England, to find out if there is any difference across the country.

Solution

(a) The 'number of diagrams in a textbook' is a *discrete variable*, because it can only be counted in whole number steps. You cannot, for example, have 26½ diagrams or 47.32 diagrams in a book.

(b) 'Whether or not a can possesses a sticker' is an *attribute*. It is not something which can be measured. A can either possesses the attribute or it does not.

(c) 'How long athletes take to run a mile' is a *continuous variable*, because the time recorded can in theory take any value. It does not have to be measured in steps, but could take any imaginable value - for example 4 minutes 2.0643 seconds. The measurement is only limited by the accuracy of the stop watch or electronic time keeper in use.

(d) 'The results of an accounting examination' is a *discrete variable*, taking whole number values between 0% and 100%. Possibly the discrete values might include half percent steps, if the examination is the sort where you could be awarded ½%. But it would not be possible to score, say, 62.32% or 55¼%, so the variable is not continuous.

(e) 'The height of telegraph poles' is a *continuous variable*. Rather like example (c) above, the height measurement is only limited by the accuracy of the measuring instruments being used.

Primary data

2.4 Primary data is data collected especially for the purpose of whatever survey is being conducted.

Examples of methods of collecting primary data are as follows.

(a) Observation.
(b) Experiment.
(c) Interviews.
(d) Questionnaires.

2.5 *Observation*
The investigator observes the situation in which he is interested and carries out measurements or counts that are relevant. This method is widely used in studying traffic flow, where the number of vehicles passing a given point in a given period of time is noted. In business it can be used to investigate queue lengths and the time that customers have to wait before they are attended to. Observation with sampling is widely used in quality control where regular samples are taken and the number of defective items is counted.

2.6 *Participant observation*

In this method, human populations are studied by joining them and observing their behaviour. Tony Wilkinson, a television reporter, used this method to investigate the lives of 'down and outs' living on the streets of London.

2.7 *Experiment*

In science an experiment involves two or more situations which are identical in every respect except for the one factor which is being studied. The outcomes are then noted. Essentially the same method is widely applicable in business, although the term 'experiment' might not be used and it is not possible to control all the other factors as precisely as in science. Examples would be retailing identical products with different packaging or trying different arrangements of goods in a shop.

2.8 *Interviews*

Interviews conducted without a questionnaire tend to be very wide ranging and open to interviewer bias (to be discussed later in this chapter). They tend to be very time consuming and are therefore expensive, and only small numbers of people can be interviewed in this way. It is rarely possible to draw generalised conclusions from such interviews but they may provide the investigator with insights which can then be studied using other methods.

2.9 *Questionnaires*

A questionnaire means that the questions which need to be answered for the survey are listed out and are either sent to a number of people (so that they can fill in their answers and send the questionnaire back) or are used by investigators to interview people (perhaps by approaching passers-by in the street and asking them the questions on the questionnaire).

Secondary data

2.10 *Secondary* data is data which has already been collected elsewhere, but which can be used or adapted for the survey being conducted.

2.11 Examples of secondary data are as follows.

(a) *Published statistics*: there is a huge mass of data published by various bodies. For example, the government publishes a great number of statistics through the Central Statistical Office (CSO). The EC and the United Nations also publish statistics. So do various newspapers and accountancy bodies.

(b) *Historical records*: the type of historical record used for a survey obviously depends on what survey is being carried out. An example is that an accountant producing an estimate of future company sales might use historical records within the company of past sales.

Comparison of primary and secondary data

2.12 Primary data is up to date and the investigator can decide exactly which population is to be surveyed, what methods will be used and what questions will be asked.

2.13 Secondary data may well have been collected some time ago and the population, the method and the questions may not be quite what the investigator wants. It may not even be possible to find out whether or not a reliable sampling method was used or the exact wording of the questions. Even sample size may not be known.

2.14 Primary data is therefore preferred, but it is costly and time consuming to obtain and so may not always be practical.

2.15 This does not mean that secondary data is without worth. Secondary data is usually essential if you want to compare the present position with that of previous years. Study of relevant secondary data can be valuable prior to conducting your own survey or for comparative purposes and it is essential for stratified random sampling, which will be discussed later in this chapter.

3. QUESTIONNAIRE DESIGN

Comparison of interviews and postal questionnaires

3.1 We are using the term 'postal' questionnaires to cover all methods in which the questionnaire is given to the respondent and returned to the investigator without personal contact. Such questionnaires could be posted but might for instance be left in pigeon holes or on desks and so on.

3.2 Postal questionnaires have the following advantages over personal interviews.

(a) The cost per person is likely to be less, so more people can be sampled.

(b) It is usually possible to ask more questions because the people completing the forms (respondents) can do so in their own time.

(c) All respondents are presented with questions in the same way. There is no opportunity for an interviewer to influence responses (interviewer bias) or to misrecord them.

(d) It may be easier to ask personal or embarrassing questions in a postal questionnaire than in a personal interview.

(e) The respondent may need to look up information for the questionnaire. This will be easier if the questionnaire is sent to their home or place of work.

3.3 On the other hand, the use of personal interviews does have certain advantages over the use of postal questionnaires.

(a) Large numbers of postal questionnaires may not be returned or returned only partly completed. This may lead to biased results if those replying are not representative of all people in the survey. Response rates are likely to be higher with personal interviews, and the interviewer can encourage people to answer all questions. Low response rates are a major problem with postal questionnaires.

(b) Misunderstanding is less likely with personal interviews because the interviewer can explain questions which the interviewee does not understand.

(c) Personal interviews are more suitable for deep or detailed questions to be asked, since the interviewer can take the time required with each interviewee to explain the implications of the question. Also, the interviewer can probe for further information and encourage the respondent to think deeper.

Measures to improve the response rate for postal questionnaires

3.4 (a) Provide a stamped and addressed envelope or a prominently sited box for the return of the questionnaire.

(b) Give a date by which you require the completed questionnaire.

(c) Consider providing an incentive such as a lottery number for those who return questionnaires on time.

Enumerators

3.5 A cheaper alternative to interviews is the use of an enumerator who will deliver the questionnaire and encourage the respondent to complete it. He will later visit the respondent again to collect the completed questionnaire and perhaps to help with the interpretation of difficult questions. This method results in a better response rate than for postal questionnaires.

Telephone surveys

3.6 Before we look in detail at how to design a questionnaire, we will discuss briefly the use of questionnaires in telephone surveys. There are a number of advantages and disadvantages in conducting telephone interviews.

Advantages

(a) The response is rapid.
(b) A wide geographical area can be covered fairly cheaply.
(c) It may be easier to ask sensitive or embarrassing questions.

Disadvantages

(a) A biased sample may result from the fact that a large proportion of people do not have telephones and many of those who do are ex-directory.
(b) It is not possible to use 'showcards' or pictures.
(c) The refusal rate is much higher than with face-to-face interviews.
(d) It is not possible to see the interviewee's expressions or to develop the rapport that is possible with personal interviews.
(e) The interview must be short, although it may be possible to split a long interview by ringing the respondents back.

Designing a questionnaire

3.7 When you are designing a questionnaire you should clarify the following points in advance.

(a) The target population. Who do you want to interview?

(b) The main items of information you want and what form it should be in for subsequent analysis.

(c) Any subsidiary information which would be of interest (for example so that you can compare the responses of men and women or old and young).

(d) Will the questionnaire be filled in by the respondent or by an interviewer. This determines how 'user-friendly' it needs to be.

3.8 The next step is to draft the key questions. Try them out on people similar to, but not from, your target population. If respondents cannot understand or relate to the questions, it is your problem not theirs. Rewrite the questions if necessary. After writing the questions, try to leave them for a day or two and then re-examine them.

3.9 Then consider each question in turn.

(a) Is it really necessary?

(b) Is it posed in a way that will provide the information and any subsequent analysis that you require?

(c) Will interviewers be able to simply read out the words, or will they need to 'ad lib', which might introduce bias?

(d) Is the question posed in a neutral, unbiased way or is it a 'leading' question which inclines towards a particular answer?

(e) Are respondents likely to find the question too personal or offensive? Can you reword it to reduce the risk of this happening?

(f) Is it unambiguous?

(g) Is the question worded in a way that the respondents will understand?

(h) *Open* questions are difficult to analyse. An open question might be worded like this.
'How did you travel to work today?'

The responses may be so numerous that analysis becomes onerous and time consuming. The designer of the questionnaire should instead try to offer a full range of possible responses to the question, perhaps like this.

'Please indicate how you travelled to work today.

By bus

By train

By private car

On foot

By bicycle/motorcycle

Other (please give details) . . . . '

The responses from this *closed* question will be much easier to analyse. However it is important to avoid putting such lists of responses in order of supposed popularity.

(i) Avoid questions that require respondents to perform calculations. Try to offer a list of options to remove or reduce this. For example offer options of annual, monthly or weekly earnings.

Designing the overall questionnaire

3.10 (a) If respondents have to complete the questionnaire themselves, it must be approachable and as short as possible. Consider the use of lines, boxes, different type faces and print sizes and small pictures. Use plenty of spacing. The questionnaire must not be 'squashed up'.

(b) Consider the use of tick boxes. Is it clear where ticks go or how to respond in each case? For analysis, will it be easy to transfer responses from the forms to a summary sheet or computer? Consider coding the answers.

(c) Explain the purpose of the survey at the beginning of the questionnaire and where possible guarantee confidentiality. Emphasise the date by which it must be returned.

(d) Start with quota control questions so that the interviewer can rapidly determine whether the interviewee is the right type of person. Quota control questions might for example identify whether the interviewee is employed or unemployed, under 40 or over 40 and so on. Such questions enable the interviewer to terminate worthless interviews as early as possible. We will return to quota sampling later in this chapter.

(e) Questions should be in logical order as far as possible, if difficult questions are necessary it may be more appropriate to put them at the end.

(f) At the end of the questionnaire, thank the respondent and make it clear what they should do with the completed questionnaire.

(g) Decide whether you wish to keep any record of interviews that fail (for example not willing to respond, not in quota and so on). If so, provide the interviewer with a form to note the failures and their reasons. Consider providing a space on the questionnaire for the interviewer to explain the termination of interviews.

4. SAMPLING

4.1 The term used in statistics to describe the total group of items under consideration is 'population'. In most practical situations the population under examination will be too large to carry out a complete survey and only a sample will be tested. A good example of this is a poll taken to try and gauge the results of an election. It is not possible to ask everyone of voting age how they are going to vote - it would take far too long and cost too much. So a sample of voters is taken, and the results from the sample are used to predict what is likely to happen in the whole population.

4.2 Occasionally a survey is small enough that 100% of the population can be looked at - for example, looking at the examination results of one class of students. When 100% of the population is looked at, it is called a *census*. This type of survey is quite rare, however, and usually the investigator has to choose some sort of sample.

4.3 You may think that using a sample is very much a compromise, but you should remember the following.

(a) In practice, a 100% survey (census) never achieves the completeness required.

(b) A census may require the use of semi-skilled investigators or postal questionnaires, resulting in a loss of accuracy in the data collected or a very low response rate.

(c) It can be shown mathematically that once a certain sample size has been collected, very little extra accuracy is gained by testing more items.

(d) It is possible to ask more questions with a sample.

(e) The higher costs of a census may exceed the value of the results.

(f) Things are always changing. Even if you took a census it could well be out of date by the time you had done it. So not even a 100% census is likely to be 100% correct.

(g) Some surveys result in the destruction of the objects being surveyed, for example lifetime testing of light bulbs. In such cases a census is not possible.

4.4 One of the most important requirements of data is that it should be *complete*. This does not mean that when an investigator is using a questionnaire, he should remember to ask all the questions on it! 'Complete' data means that the data covers all areas of the population to be examined. If this requirement is not met, then the sample will be biased.

4.5 For example suppose you wanted to survey the productivity of workers in a factory, and you went along every Monday and Tuesday for a few months to measure their output. Would this data be complete? The answer is no. You may well have gathered very thorough data on what happens on Mondays and Tuesdays, but you have missed out the rest of the week. It could be that the workers, keen and fresh after the weekend, work better at the start of the week than at the end. If this is the case, then your data will give you a misleadingly high picture of factory output. Your data is not complete, because it does not cover the whole population of factory output, and so could be biased.

Sample size

4.6 Whatever method we use to select a sample there is always the question: what size sample should we take? The solution to this problem uses complicated mathematical techniques which are not included in your syllabus.

4.7 In practice it is always sensible to take as big a sample as possible. But bear in mind that there are bound to be constraints on the time and money available for a survey, and also that the more work involved, the more likely it is that investigators will start making errors.

Random sampling

4.8   To ensure that the sample selected is free from bias, some form of *random* sampling must be used. A random or probability sample is one in which every population member has a known probability of being selected. In the majority of cases we require equal probabilities of selection.

4.9   *Simple random sampling*
       A simple random sample is selected, without any preliminary grouping of the population, in such a way that each population member has an equal chance of being included.

4.10   For example if you wanted to take a simple random sample of library books, it would not be good enough to pick them off the shelves, even if you picked them at random. Why not? Because the books which are out on loan stand no chance of being chosen. You would either have to make sure that all the books were on the shelves before taking your sample, or find some other way of sampling (for example by using the library index cards).

4.11   A simple random sample is not necessarily a perfect sample. For example you might pick what you believe to be a completely random selection of library books, and find that every one of them is a detective thriller! It might be a remote possibility, but it could happen. The only way to eliminate the possibility altogether is to take 100% sample (census) of the books - which, unless it is a tiny library, is impractical. Stratified sampling is used to partially overcome this problem of unrepresentative samples. We will return to stratified sampling later in this chapter.

Sampling frame

4.12   A sampling frame is simply a list, usually a numbered list, of all the items in the population. The idea is that once such a list has been made, all the items are numbered, and then it is easy to select a random sample.

4.13   For instance if you wanted to select a simple random sample of children from a school, it would be useful to have a list of names.

       1   J Absolam
       2   R Brown
       3   S Brown
       .....etc

       Now the numbers 1, 2, 3 .... can be used to help select the random sample.

4.14   Sometimes it is not possible to draw up a sampling frame. For example if you wanted to take a random sample of Americans, it would take rather too long to list all Americans! We will look at how we get round this sort of difficulty later in the chapter.

4.15   Assuming that a sampling frame *can* be drawn up, then a simple random sample can be picked from it by two main methods.

(a) The lottery method, for example picking numbers out of a hat.
(b) The use of random number tables. This method is to be preferred as it provides a high guarantee against bias.

4.16 Set out below is part of a typical random number table.

93716	16894	98953	73231
32886	59780	09958	18065
92052	06831	19640	99413
39510	35905	85244	35159
27699	06494	03152	19121
92962	61773	22109	78508
10274	12202	94205	50380
75867	20717	82037	10268
85783	47619	87481	37220

You should note the following points.

(a) The sample is found by selecting groups of random numbers with the same number of digits as the total population size. For example:

Total population size	Number of random digits
0 – 9	1
10 – 99	2
100 – 999	3 etc

The items selected for the sample are those corresponding to the random numbers selected.

(b) The starting point on the table should be selected at random (for example using a pin). After that, however, numbers must be selected in a consistent manner. In other words, you should use the table row by row or column by column. By jumping around the table from place to place personal bias may be introduced.

(c) In many practical situations it is more convenient to use a computer to select items at random, especially when a large sample is required. Most scientific calculators are now also able to generate random numbers.

Example

4.17 An investigator wishes to select a random sample from a population of 800 people. As there are three digits in 800 the random numbers will be selected in groups of three. Working along the first line of the table given earlier, the first few groups are as follows.

937   161   689   498   953   732

Numbers over 800 are discarded. The first four people in the sample will therefore be the 161st, 689th, 498th and 732nd.

Other random sampling methods

4.18 There are many other random sampling methods, the main ones are as follows.

   (a) Systematic sampling.
   (b) Stratified random sampling.
   (c) Cluster sampling.
   (d) Multistage sampling.

4.19 *Systematic sampling*
Systematic sampling may provide a good approximation to simple random sampling. It works by selecting every nth item after a random start. For example, if it was decided to select a sample of 20 from a population of 800, then every 40th (800 ÷ 20) item after a random start in the first 40 should be selected. The starting point could be found using the lottery method or random number tables. If (say) 23 was chosen, then the sample would include the following items.

   23rd,   63rd,   103rd,   143rd ...... 783rd.

Systematic sampling is used because it is easier than simple random sampling and does not require the sampling frame to be numbered.

4.20 *Stratified sampling*
In many situations stratified random sampling is the best method of choosing a sample. The population must be capable of being divided into strata (ie into bands or non-overlapping groups). A simple random sample is then taken from each stratum, with the sample size being proportional to the size of the stratum. Samples are most commonly stratified by gender, age or social class in order that they will represent the overall population in these respects.

4.21 Suppose we wanted to survey the spending habits of the students of a polytechnic. The student population could be divided up into several *strata*, the most obvious being the courses held at the polytechnic. Sampling is carried out by taking a random sample from each course, the number in each sample being proportional to the course size. For example, the size of the courses may be as follows.

   Course A   50
   Course B   50
   Course C   70
   Course D   80
                  250

If a sample of 25 is required, 10% of students from each course should be selected (because 25 is 10% of 250). So you would select a sample at random as follows.

   5 from course A
   5 from course B
   7 from course C
   8 from course D
   25

4.22 Stratified sampling is more difficult and time consuming than simple random sampling but it does result in more representative samples. There is no point in preparing a stratified sample if the various strata are all similar in their opinions or characteristics. For example if students on the various courses were likely to be similar, it might be better to stratify into age groups or some other groups by which differences could be fully represented.

4.23 It is not possible to sample from strata until the following points are known.

(a) At least approximately, how many people there are in each stratum, so that sample sizes can be calculated.

(b) Which stratum each individual belongs to.

Secondary data can be useful in providing information about the number of people in each stratum (for example the correct proportions of males and females). Within institutions such as colleges or workplaces, it is reasonably easy to obtain lists of people in the various strata, but no such lists exist for the general population. This is a serious problem if a stratified sample is required.

4.24 *Cluster sampling*
In order to save time and expense, the population might be divided into groups called clusters, each of which is (hopefully) representative of the entire population. Note that clusters are not the same as strata, which are chosen precisely because they are thought to differ from one another.

4.25 A small number of clusters is then randomly selected (generally in proportion to their size) and every member of the selected clusters is then surveyed.

4.26 For example a researcher might want to survey the opinions of people in a locality on the opening of, say, a new transport provision. If it is thought that opinions are unlikely to vary from one street to the next, the researcher might select just one street at random and then survey everyone living in it.

4.27 Clearly cluster sampling can result in more biased results than the other random sampling methods, since the selected cluster might in fact be markedly different from the general population. However it is relatively cheap and easy and therefore a larger sample might be possible.

4.28 *Multistage sampling*
Suppose we wanted to carry out market research over the whole of Britain. It is obviously impractical to draw up a sampling frame, so direct sampling would not be possible. In this case the sampling would have to proceed in stages.

4.29 For multistage sampling the country would be divided into a number of areas and a small sample of these would be selected at random. Each of the areas selected would then be subdivided into smaller units and a number of these is selected at random. This process is repeated as many times as necessary and finally a random sample of the relevant people living in each of the smallest units is made. A fair approximation to a random sample can be obtained.

4.30 For example we might choose a random sample of eight areas, and from each of these areas select a random sample of five towns. From each town, a random sample of 200 people might be selected so that the total sample size is 8 x 5 x 200 = 8,000 people.

4.31 Multistage sampling and cluster sampling are often associated. The first two stages in the previous example involved the selection of clusters and this would usually be the case with multistage sampling. The key difference is that in cluster sampling *every* member of the cluster is surveyed whereas in multistage sampling, further samples are taken from the cluster.

Non-random sampling

4.32 In many situations it is not possible or practical to use a random sample. For example it may not be possible to draw up a sampling frame or the investigators may wish to stratify and existing sampling frames may not permit that. In such cases, non-random sampling has to be used.

4.33 *Quota sampling*

In quota sampling, investigators are told to interview all the people they meet, up to certain quotas. The sample will (generally) be stratified so that they will have a quota for, say, young male manual workers and another for young male white collar workers and so on. The interviews will generally be carried out by the investigator asking people to complete the questionnaire in a shopping centre or similar public place.

4.34 For example we could use the figures in our polytechnic example in paragraph 4.21, but with the following additional information relating to the sex of students.

	Male	Female
Course A	30	20
Course B	40	10
Course C	60	10
Course D	50	30

An investigator's quota would be made up of 10% of each stratum, ie 10% of the 30 male students on course A, 10% of the 40 male students on course B, and so on. The 25 people selected by the investigator would be made up as follows.

	Male	Female	Total
Course A	3	2	5
Course B	4	1	5
Course C	6	1	7
Course D	5	3	8
			25

4.35 Using quota sampling, the investigator would interview the first three males he met from course A, the first two females he met from course A and so on.

4.36 A large degree of bias can be introduced accidentally. Whole sections of the population will have no possibility of being surveyed because their lives don't permit them to be in the right place at the right time. Additionally, many will be busy and will not have time to participate in the survey while they are out shopping.

4.37   The major advantage of quota sampling is that, although a fairly detailed knowledge of the characteristics of a population is required, it is not necessary to establish a sampling frame and it is possible to obtain representative samples by stratification. It is a very easy, cheap and quick survey method and this enables large samples to be taken. It is the method by which most market research and most opinion polls are carried out.

5.   SOURCES OF PUBLISHED STATISTICS

Using secondary data

5.1   You may be expected to identify the sources of certain published statistics. As you will probably be aware, the range of published economic, business and accounting data is very wide, and a comprehensive knowledge of sources is impracticable. In this chapter, the more well-known sources will be described. We will also discuss the sources which are of particular relevance to marketing.

5.2   All published statistics are a source of *secondary data*, which assist users in making further statistical analysis. Great care must be taken in using them, since the data may not be obtained or classified in precisely the same way as primary data collected *specifically* for the purpose of a statistical analysis.

5.3   Despite the general shortcomings of using secondary data there are many circumstances in which published statistics can be of great value. Many government statistics are compiled at least partly for the purpose of being used in further analysis and these are explained by way of notes so that users of the data know to what extent they are relevant to their needs and what level of confidence they can have in the results of their analyses.

Central Statistical Office

5.4   In the UK the government is the principal source of secondary statistical data. The government's statistical service is co-ordinated by the Central Statistical Office (CSO) which publishes an annual listing of all major government publications in the *Guide to official statistics*.

5.5   The European Community has a Statistical Office of the European Community (SOEC) which gathers statistics from each of the member countries. The SOEC has several statistical publications, including *Basic statistics of the community*.

5.6   The United Nations also publishes some statistics on the world economy (for example *Statistical yearbook*) and a *Yearbook of labour statistics* is published by the International Labour Organisation.

Obtaining secondary data

5.7   The CSO publish an invaluable pamphlet, entitled *Government statistics - a brief guide to sources*, which is available free from their press, publications and publicity department.

5.8   The pamphlet lists all main government publications with a brief summary of their contents. It also gives contact telephone numbers in government departments for the purpose of more detailed enquiries.

5.9   The Department of Trade and Industry runs the *Export market information centre* which provides comprehensive and up-to-date trade statistics for all countries, as well as many other publications of interest to exporters.

UK statistical publications

5.10   The most important statistical publications in the UK which you should be aware of are detailed in this section.

5.11   The *Annual abstract of statistics:* most government statistics of economic and business data are brought together into this main reference book, published by the CSO. Many government departments provide different items of data for this publication. Notes and definitions of the statistical data provided are contained in the book.

5.12   The *Monthly digest of statistics* is an abbreviated version of the Annual Abstract, but is published monthly. A January supplement provides definitions.

5.13   *Economic trends:* published monthly by the CSO gives statistics and graphs on topics which include the following.

   (a)   Production.
   (b)   Labour.
   (c)   External trade.
   (d)   Investment.
   (e)   Prices, wages and earnings.

5.14   *Department of employment gazette* published monthly by the Department of Employment. This provides monthly statistics on *labour* and on *prices*. Examples are as follows.

   (a)   Retail prices.
   (b)   Employment.
   (c)   Unemployment.
   (d)   Unfilled job vacancies.
   (e)   Wage rates.
   (f)   Overtime and short-time working.
   (g)   Stoppages at work.

5.15   The *Blue book on national income and expenditure* is published annually by the CSO, giving details of the following.

   (a)   Gross National Product (analysed into sections of the economy such as transport and communications, insurance, banking and finance, public administration and defence and so on).

(b) Gross National Income (analysed into income from self-employment, income from employment, profits of companies, income from abroad and so on).

(c) Gross National Expenditure (analysed into expenditure on capital goods, expenditure by consumers and by public authorities, imports and so on).

Important publications for marketing

5.16 The *Business monitor* series and *Business bulletins* contain detailed statistics on all areas of business activity including credit business, purchases by manufacturing industry, manufacturers' sales, import penetration, construction data, imports and exports analysed in terms of industries, retailing, wholesaling, service trades, computer trades and many other areas. They are generally produced monthly or quarterly.

5.17 The *Report on the census of production* is produced annually in the Business Monitor series, with separate parts for each industry. It includes data on total purchases, sales and stocks.

5.18 Two major consumer surveys produce reports annually detailing expenditure by different types of households. The *National food survey* reports on food consumption and expenditure whilst the *Family expenditure survey* shows income and a wide range of expenditure in great detail, including some regional analyses.

5.19 Information about potential customers or competitors can be obtained from the *UK Directory of manufacturing businesses* which is published in six volumes and is also available on magnetic tape.

Other published statistics

5.20 *The Financial Times*
The Financial Times and other newspapers or investment journals provide statistics about the stock market. Most well-known are the following indices.

(a) The FT-Actuaries All-Share Index (compiled jointly by the Financial Times, the Institute of Actuaries in London, and the Faculty of Actuaries in Edinburgh). This is an index of share prices quoted on the stock exchange.

(b) The FT Ordinary Share Index, which is an index of prices of 30 leading UK companies.

5.21 *The annual survey of published accounts*
The Institute of Chartered Accountants in England and Wales publishes a book which provides information and statistics about the contents of the published accounts of companies during the previous year.

5.22 *Bank reviews and trade associations*
Most major banks produce monthly or quarterly magazines containing articles and data on important economic topics.

5.23 Trade associations and most professional bodies also carry out research and compile statistics of interest to their members.

6. CONCLUSION

6.1 Statistics covers the collection, presentation and interpretation of data, but it cannot be used to *prove* anything. It can only indicate the likelihood (or otherwise) of a given situation or event.

6.2 Data can be collected on attributes or variables. Variables data can be further divided into discrete and continuous data.

6.3 The sources of data can be either primary or secondary.

6.4 Samples can be selected randomly (simple random, systematic, stratified, cluster or multistage sampling) or non randomly (quota sampling). Lottery or random numbers may be used for the random methods. Non-random sampling is used when random sampling is not feasible or practical (for example because a sampling frame does not exist or does not permit stratification).

6.5 Students are required to have a knowledge of the official sources of economic and business data, although testing such knowledge is difficult because of the extent of that material.

6.6 Reading about sources of secondary data cannot substitute for reading the actual publications and familiarising yourself with their contents, particularly those of special relevance to marketing.

6.7 Browsing through statistical publications may sound very dull but in fact it can provide a wealth of fascinating information which can enrich other areas of the marketing course and your working life, as well as helping you to prepare for your exam. You really should try it.

TEST YOUR KNOWLEDGE

The numbers in brackets refer to paragraphs of this chapter

1. What is the difference between an attribute and a variable? (2.1)

2. Distinguish between discrete and continuous variables. (2.3)

3. What is the difference between primary and secondary data? (2.4, 2.10, 2.12)

4. What are the advantages and disadvantages of postal questionnaires compared with personal interviews? (3.2, 3.3)

5. List five points that you would consider in selecting questions for a questionnaire. (3.9)

6. Why would a sample sometimes be preferable to a census? (4.3)

7. What is a sampling frame? (4.12 to 4.14)

8. What is multistage sampling and how does it differ from cluster sampling? (4.28, 4.31)

9. What is quota sampling? (4.33)

10. What is the name of the body which co-ordinates the UK government's publication of statistical data? (5.4)

11. What information is contained in the Blue Book? (5.15)

12. Name any six areas of business activity covered in the Business Monitor series. (5.16)

Now try illustrative question 1

Chapter 2

PRESENTATION OF DATA: TABLES AND CHARTS

This chapter covers the following topics.

1. Introduction and general guidelines
2. Tables and tabulation
3. Charts

---

1. INTRODUCTION AND GENERAL GUIDELINES

1.1 This chapter deals with the problem of conveying numerical information in reports and other written material. Many people are very nervous of numbers and will completely 'skip' text which includes a lot of numerical information. Even numerically confident readers will be put off by heavily numerical text. So it is generally preferable to separate numbers from text and to display them by means of either tables or charts.

1.2 There are several types of charts in the CIM syllabus which we will not cover in this particular chapter. These are the charts which are used as part of statistical analysis in order to facilitate decisions about what type of analysis is suitable and to make estimates. Such charts are of little value in communicating results because they are not attractive. We will introduce them individually in the chapters to which they are relevant.

General guidelines on tables and charts

1.3 The table or chart should be comprehensible without needing to refer back to the text so it needs the following.

(a) A title.
(b) The source of the data, if known.
(c) Clear headings or a key.

1.4 In using a chart or table, you are trying to communicate numerical information in a way that is appropriate to the readers. So you need to do the following.

(a) Think carefully beforehand about what exactly you are trying to communicate. Keep the chart or table as simple as possible within this brief.

(b) Think carefully about who is going to read it. Will he need the actual figures or will a visual representation be sufficient? If the figures are needed, a table will generally be preferable to a chart.

(c) Make the chart or table look attractive and approachable. Tables should be boxed and shading should be used where possible.

2. TABLES AND TABULATION

2.1 Tabulation means putting data into tables. A table is a matrix of data in rows and columns, with either the rows or the columns, or more probably both, having a title.

2.2 A table can only show two variables. For example, the resources required to produce items in a factory could be tabulated, with the columns representing the items produced and the rows representing the resources.

Resources	Product items				
	A	B	C	D	E
Material M	X	X	X	X	X
Material P	X	X	X	X	X
Labour grade 1	X	X	X	X	X
Labour grade 2	X	X	X	X	X
Supervision	X	X	X	X	X
Machine time	X	X	X	X	X

(The X's are put in to show where numbers would go in a completed table.)

2.3 To tabulate data you need to recognise what the rows and columns should represent, prepare them accordingly with suitable titles, and then insert the data into the appropriate place in the table.

2.4 Since tabulation is included in your syllabus, be prepared for an examination question that asks you to present data in tabular form.

Guidelines for tabulation

2.5 There are certain guidelines which you should apply when presenting data in tabular form.

(a) The table should be given a clear title.
(b) All columns should be clearly labelled.
(c) Where appropriate, there should be clear sub-totals.
(d) A total column may be presented. This would usually be the right-hand column.
(e) A total figure is often advisable at the bottom of each column of figures.
(f) Tables should not be packed with too much data so that the information presented is difficult to read.
(g) To eliminate unnecessary detail, rounding should be used.
(h) Always state the units being used.
(i) Consider grouping minor items into an 'others' category.
(j) Consider showing percentages.

2.6 *Tabulation: example.*
The expenditure of the Metropolitan Borough Council of Numac on school dinners for the year 19X0/X1 was £2,496,000 made up as follows.

Personnel: administration £108,800; meals supervision £195,200; kitchen staff £944,000.

Operating expenses: provisions £812,800; crockery and utensils £73,600; protective clothing £3,200; laundering £6,400.

Buildings: maintenance £32,000; fuel £83,200; cleaning £19,200; equipment and furniture £9,600; rent and rates £48,000.

Central establishment charges £160,000

During the year 3,200,000 school dinners were served.

You are required to present the foregoing information in the form of a table showing the following.

(a) The expenditure, item by item, and with subtotals for the separate categories of expenditure.
(b) The information specified for (a) expressed as costs per school dinner.

2.7 *Discussion and solution*
The two dimensions (ie rows and columns) to be represented in the table are as follows.

(a) Expenditure items.
(b) The amount of expenditure per item in total and as a cost per school dinner.

Expenditure items must be sub-analysed, but this forms part of the 'expenditure items' dimension. Sub totals are easily included, but it might make the table clearer if sub-total items are presented in a separate column to the main totals, as shown in the table.

2.8 When one dimension includes a larger number of items, it is often convenient to present these as the rows of the table. This makes better use of the space on the page.

2.9 The number of school dinners served is an important item of data but one which does not fit into the rows or columns of the table. It would therefore be appropriate to show it as a separate item, either just below the table heading or at the foot of the table.

2: PRESENTATION OF DATA: TABLES AND CHARTS

Metropolitan Borough Council of Numac
School dinner expenses 19X0/X1

Number of school dinners served in the year: 3,200,000

	Expenditure £	Expenditure £	Cost/school dinner pence	Cost/school dinner pence
Personnel				
Administration	108,800		3.4	
Meals supervision	195,200		6.1	
Kitchen	944,000		29.5	
Total		1,248,000		39.0
Operating expenses				
Provisions	812,800		25.4	
Crockery and utensils	73,600		2.3	
Protective clothing	3,200		0.1	
Laundering	6,400		0.2	
Total		896,000		28.0
Buildings				
Maintenance	32,000		1.0	
Fuel	83,200		2.6	
Cleaning	19,200		0.6	
Equipment and furniture	9,600		0.3	
Rent, rates etc	48,000		1.5	
Total		192,000		6.0
Central establishment charges		160,000		5.0
Grand total		2,496,000		78.0

3. CHARTS

Visual displays

3.1 Instead of presenting data in a table, it might be preferable to make a visual display in the form of a chart or a graph. The purpose of a chart is to convey the data in a way that will demonstrate its meaning or significance more clearly than a table of data would. Charts (or graphs) are not always more appropriate than tables, and the most suitable way of presenting data will depend on the following.

(a) What the data is intended to show. Visual displays usually make one or two points quite forcefully, whereas tables usually give more detailed information (ie detailed figures).

(b) Who is going to use the data. Some individuals might understand visual displays more readily than tabulated data. In general, the more nervous the reader is of numerical information, the more important it becomes to use attractive visual displays.

3.2 The types of chart that might be used to present data which you must know about are as follows.

(a) Pictograms.
(b) Pie charts.
(c) Bar charts.
(d) Band curves.
(e) Line charts.
(f) Statistical maps.

Pictograms

3.3 A pictogram (or picturegram) is a statistical diagram in which the data is represented by a recognisable picture or symbol. Examples are as follows.

(a) A pictogram showing the volume of sales of cars would represent the quantities of cars using pictures of cars.

Volume of car sales

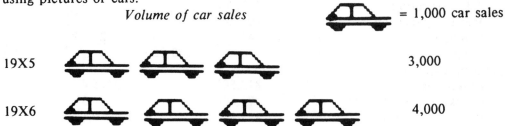

(b) A pictogram showing the number of employees at a factory would represent the quantities of employees using pictures of people.

Number of employees

In this example, each picture represents ten employees, and to represent a smaller quantity, a part-picture can be drawn. Here, there were 45 men employed in 19X6.

3.4 Notice too that different pictures can be used on the same pictogram to represent different elements of the data. Above, we have pictures of men and women. Other distinctions might be as follows.

(a) In a pictogram of hat sales, a distinction between export sales and domestic sales.

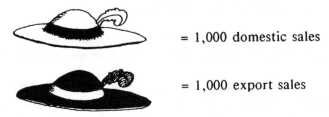

(b)   In a pictogram of methods of travelling to work, a distinction between different sorts of travel.

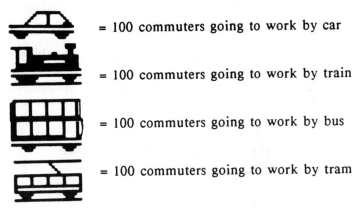

= 100 commuters going to work by car

= 100 commuters going to work by train

= 100 commuters going to work by bus

= 100 commuters going to work by tram

3.5   The guidelines for drawing a pictogram are as follows.

(a)   The symbols must be clear and simple.

(b)   The quantity of items that each symbol represents must be clearly shown in a key to the pictogram.

(c)   Bigger quantities should be shown by more symbols, not bigger symbols. For example, if sales of boxes of dishwashing powder double between 19X5 and 19X6, a pictogram should look like this.

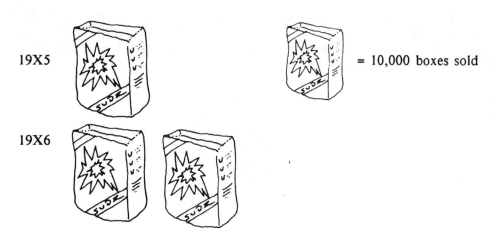

19X5

19X6

= 10,000 boxes sold

It should *not* look like this.

19X5   19X6

In this pictogram, the bigger symbol does not give a true impression of sales growth.

27

3.6 The advantage of pictograms is that they present data in a simple, readily understood way. Pictograms convey their message to the reader at a glance, and are consequently often used on television, for example in news items, and in advertisements.

3.7 The disadvantage of pictograms is that they can only convey a limited amount of data, and they lack precision. Each picture symbol must represent quite a large number of items, otherwise a pictogram would contain too many picture symbols. Using portions of a symbol to represent smaller quantities gives some extra precision, but not much. For example, if

 represents 1,000 men, then

 represents less than 1,000 men, but how many exactly? 400? 500? 600?

Pie charts

3.8 A pie chart, or circular diagram, is used to show pictorially the relative size of component elements of a total. It is called a pie chart because it is a circle, and so has the shape of a pie in a round pie dish (from a bird's eye view) and because the 'pie' is then cut into slices. Each slice represents a component part of the total, and the slices vary in size according to the relative size of each component part of the total.

3.9 To draw a pie chart accurately, you need to be able to draw a circle (using compasses perhaps). A circle consists of 360 degrees (360°), and so if a circle is divided into two equal halves, each half would consist of 180 degrees. If a circle were cut into four equal portions, each portion would contain 90 degrees.

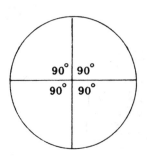

3.10 Pie charts usually involve drawing segments of various sizes and you need to be able to draw segment sizes fairly accurately. To do this you need a protractor which is semi-circular in shape and marks off degrees of a circle from 0 to 180. By putting the base line of the protractor across the middle of your pie chart circle you can mark off segment sizes accurately.

3.11 Working out segment sizes involves converting the component elements of the data into equivalent degrees of a circle. An example might help to illustrate this.

Example

3.12 The costs of production at factory A during March 19X2 were as follows.

	Factory A	
	£'000	%
Materials	70	35
Labour	30	15
Production overhead	90	45
Office costs	10	5
	200	100

Suppose that we wish to show the relative size of materials, labour, production overhead and office costs for the factory in a pie chart.

3.13 To convert the component elements into degrees of a circle, we take the appropriate percentage of 360°. For example, materials take up 35% of the costs of production at factory A. Therefore materials takes up 35% x 360° = 126° of the pie chart.

	Factory A	
	%	degrees
Materials	35	126
Labour	15	54
Production overhead	45	162
Office costs	5	18
	100	360

3.14 A pie chart could now be drawn as follows. A protractor is used to measure the degrees accurately to obtain the correct segment sizes.

Factory A

3.15 The advantages of pie charts are as follows.

(a)   They give a simple picture display of the relative size of component elements of a total value or amount.

(b)   They show quite clearly when one component is much bigger than others, and so perhaps more significant as an item.

(c)   Like pictograms, they are thought to be rather more attractive than most charts and hence to appeal to the widest range of readers.

3.16 The disadvantages of pie charts are as follows.

(a) They show only limited information, ie they are used to show the relative size of component elements in a total, and they have no other use.

(b) They involve calculating degrees of a circle and drawing segment sizes accurately, and this can be time-consuming. Pie charts cannot therefore be drawn quickly.

(c) It is often difficult to compare segment sizes easily. For example, suppose that pie charts are used to show the component elements of a company's sales.

19X6

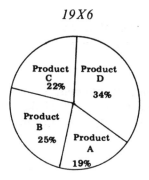

Without writing in the percentage figures, it would not be easy to see the difference between products B and C.

(d) If the number of components exceeds about six, the pie chart will look very cluttered and may be hard to follow.

(e) Pie charts can be used to compare the way that two totals are divided into components, but if one total is larger than the other, the areas of the pie charts should be in proportion to the totals. If this is not done, the wrong impression is given that the two totals are equal.

Bar charts

3.17 The bar chart is one of the most common methods of presenting data in a visual form. It is a chart in which data is shown in the form of bars whose heights are proportional to the magnitudes being displayed.

3.18 There are three main types of bar chart.

(a) Simple bar charts.
(b) Multiple bar charts.
(c) Component or stacked bar charts, including *percentage* component bar charts.

Please note that both multiple bar charts and component bar charts are at times called *compound* bar charts.

3.19 *Simple bar charts*
A simple bar chart is a chart consisting of one or more bars, in which the *length of the bar indicates the magnitude* of the data.

3.20 For example, suppose that a company's total sales for the years 19X1 to 19X6 are as follows.

Year	£'000
19X1	800
19X2	1,200
19X3	1,100
19X4	1,400
19X5	1,600
19X6	1,700

This data could be shown on a simple bar chart as follows.

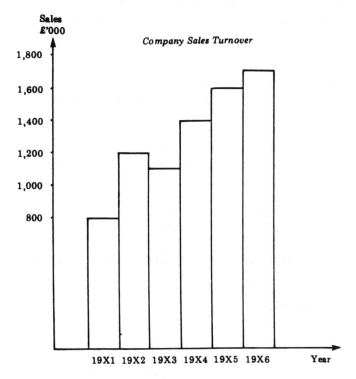

3.21 Each 'axis' of the chart must be clearly labelled, and to give the chart meaning, there must be a scale to indicate the magnitude of the data. Here, the 'y axis' (ie the vertical axis) indicates the scale for the amount of the sales turnover, and so readers of the bar chart can see not only that sales value on the whole has been rising year by year (with 19X3 being an exception) but also what the actual sales turnover has been each year.

3.22 Here are some important points on the construction of simple bar charts.

(a) The vertical axis should always start at zero. In the above example, the axis might have been started at 600 but this would have given a very wrong impression of the relative magnitudes.

(b) If it is reasonable to do so, the data is best presented in order of magnitude. In the above example the order could not be changed since we were showing sales from one year to the next. We could have changed the order if we were showing sales at the various branches of a firm.

(c) Shading should be used to make the chart more attractive and it is best if all bars are shaded in the same fashion.

(d) Small gaps may be used between bars.

(e) Bars may be drawn either vertically or horizontally.

3.23 Simple bar charts are used when there is only one single piece of information in each category ie per year in the above example. They serve two purposes.

(a) Showing the actual magnitude in each case.
(b) Comparing magnitudes, according to the length of each bar on the chart.

3.24 *Multiple bar chart*
A multiple bar chart is a bar chart in which two or more separate bars are used to present sub-divisions of data. For example, suppose that the output of a company, Rodd Ltd, in 19X6 to 19X8 is as follows.

	19X6 000 units	*19X7* 000 units	*19X8* 000 units
Product X	180	130	50
Product Y	90	110	170
Product Z	180	180	125

The data for output could be shown in a multiple bar chart as follows.

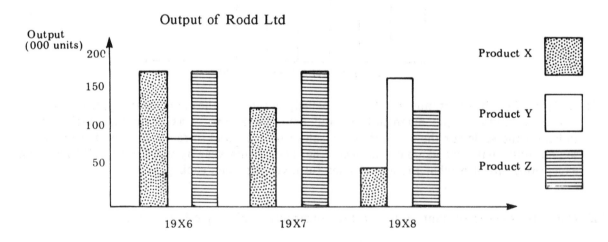

A multiple bar chart uses several bars for each item; in our example, the sales in each year are shown as three separate bars, one for each of the products.

3.25 Multiple bar charts are sometimes drawn with bars horizontal rather than vertical. Either way they present similar information to a component bar chart, with the following exceptions.

(a) Multiple bar charts do not show the grand total (in this example, the total amount of output each year of all three products) whereas a component bar chart does.

(b) Multiple bar charts illustrate the comparative magnitude of each component element more clearly perhaps than a component bar chart does.

3.26 For any table, there are always two possible multiple bar charts. In the above example the alternative would be to draw the three years' figures for product X as adjacent bars and then, after a gap, the three figures for Y and so on. This would show the trend for each product separately whilst the above chart shows the relative output of the products for each year.

3.27 *Component bar chart*
A component bar chart is a bar chart that gives a breakdown of the total amount into its component parts.

For example, suppose that sales of Charbart plc for the years 19X7 to 19X9 are as follows.

	19X7	19X8	19X9
	£'000	£'000	£'000
Product A	1,000	1,200	1,700
Product B	900	1,000	1,000
Product C	500	600	700
Total	2,400	2,800	3,400

3.28 A component bar chart would show the following.

(a) How total sales have changed from year to year.
(b) What are the component elements of each year's total.
(c) How the components have changed from year to year.

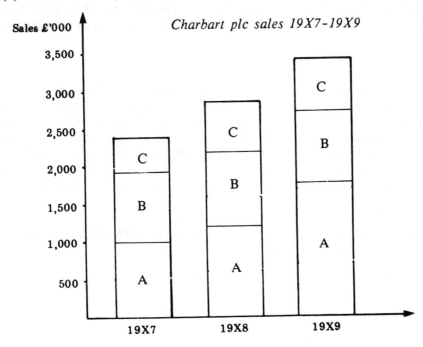

33

3.29 It is easiest to draw the bars if you have calculated cumulative subtotals beforehand.

	19X7 £'000	19X8 £'000	19X9 £'000
A	1,000	1,200	1,700
A + B	1,900	2,200	2,700
A + B + C	2,400	2,800	3,400

The total columns should be drawn first, so that the bars have neat side lines and then the horizontal lines drawn to coincide with the subtotals.

3.30 Here are some important points on the construction of component bar charts.

(a) It is generally possible to change the order of the components, showing them in order of magnitude with the major component at the bottom. The same order must be retained between bars.

(b) If shading is used or if component descriptions are lengthy, a key will be needed.

3.31 We could make the following comments on the chart in paragraph 3.28.

(a) Over the period from 19X7 to 19X9, total sales have shown a steady and marked increase.

(b) Sales have increased for each of the three products, with the most marked increase being that of product A from 19X8 to 19X9.

(c) Throughout the periods, the highest sales have been those of A, followed by B with product C selling markedly less than the other two.

3.32 *Percentage component bar chart*
A percentage component bar chart is like a pie chart, except that it is the shape of a bar instead of a circular pie, and component elements of the total are shown as a proportionate block of the bar.

3.33 The difference between a component bar chart and a percentage component bar chart is that with a component bar chart, the total length of the bar (and the length of each component element in it) indicates magnitude. A bigger amount is shown by a longer length of bar. With a percentage component bar chart, total magnitude is not shown. The total length of the bar is not relevant. If two or more bars are drawn on the chart, for comparison, the total length of each bar should be the same. The only varying lengths in a percentage component bar chart are the lengths of each component part, which vary according to the relative proportional size of the component.

3.34 For example, the information in the previous example of sales of Charbart plc could have been shown in a percentage component bar chart as follows.

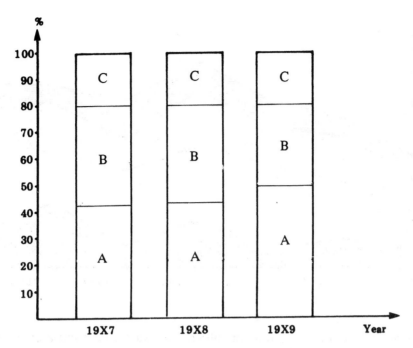

Charbart plc Sales analysis 19X7 - 19X9

Workings	19X7		19X8		19X9	
	Subtotal	%	Subtotal	%	Subtotal	%
A	1,000	42	1,200	43	1,700	50
A + B	1,900	79	2,200	79	2,700	79
A + B + C	2,400	100	2,800	100	3,400	100

3.35 *Comments on the above chart*

This chart shows, perhaps more clearly than a pie chart, that sales of C have remained a steady proportion of total sales, but the proportion of A in total sales has increased, while the proportion of B has fallen correspondingly.

Band curves

3.36 A band curve, also known as a layer graph, is a graph in which the total figure is broken down into its constituent parts.

For example, the costs of administration at the head office of Piper Walk Limited might be shown as follows.

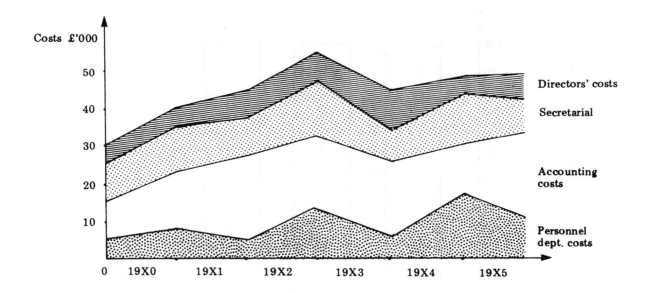

3.37 A band curve requires the calculation of subtotals in exactly the same manner as a component bar, but the subtotals are plotted and then joined 'horizontally' to create bands. Like a component bar chart it shows changes in the total costs and in the components and also shows the relative importance of the components.

3.38 A band chart differs from a component bar chart in the following ways.

(a) Its appearance is rather more 'mathematical' and this might be off-putting for some readers.

(b) Whilst a component bar chart could be used to compare, say, different branches or different countries, a band chart can only be used to compare different years.

Line chart

3.39 A line chart is similar to a bar chart but with lines instead of bars. The length of the line is proportional to the value represented. It is often used for discrete variables.

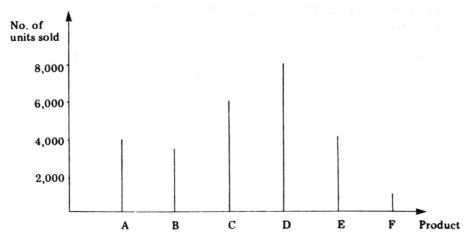

In general bar charts are preferable to line charts because they are more attractive but line charts can give a very quick and easy representation of data.

Statistical maps or cartograms

3.40 Statistical maps, or cartograms, may be used to display geographical data.

Unemployment in England and Wales 19X3

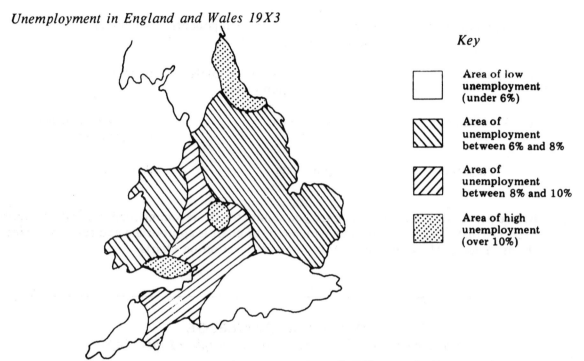

A key is usually necessary to explain the meaning of different shadings on the map.

4. CONCLUSION

4.1 Data can be presented in a variety of ways depending on who is going to use it and what aspect of the data needs to be emphasised. This chapter has looked at tables and at the types of chart that might be used to present data to ordinary readers.

4.2 *Summary*

	Type of display	*Data displayed*	*Type of reader*
(a)	Table	Full numerical information	Numerate
(b)	Pictogram	Single piece of information in each category	Innumerate
(c)	Pie	A total divided into its components	Relatively innumerate
(d)	Simple bar	Single piece of information in each category	Relatively innumerate

Type of display	Data displayed	Type of reader
(e) Multiple bar	Tabulated data where totals are not involved	Average
(f) Component bar	Several categories, each with a total divided into components	Average/numerate
(g) % component bar	Component bar with components shown as a % of the total	Numerate
(h) Band curve	Several years' data with totals divided into components	Numerate
(i) Line chart	As for simple bar	Not used in formal presentations
(j) Cartogram	Geographic data	Average

4.3 Before proceeding to the next chapter you should try the recommended illustrative questions to ensure that you can decide upon which type of chart is appropriate and can draw effective charts. Your CIM exam will probably have a question on charts.

TEST YOUR KNOWLEDGE
The numbers in brackets refer to paragraphs of this chapter

1. What are the general rules to be observed when presenting data in tabular form? (2.5)

2. What is the advantage of pictograms? (3.6)

3. What are the disadvantages of pie charts? (3.16)

4. Name the three types of bar chart. (3.18)

5. For what type of data might you use a band curve? (3.36)

Now try illustrative questions 2 and 3

Chapter 3

TECHNICAL CHARTS AND GRAPHS

This chapter covers the following topics.

1. Charts and graphs for decision making
2. Drawing graphs: basic rules
3. Z charts
4. Lorenz curves
5. Gantt charts
6. Semi-logarithmic graphs

---

1. CHARTS AND GRAPHS FOR DECISION MAKING

1.1 The charts and graphs dealt with in this chapter are used to display data, as were those of the previous chapter, but they are aimed at a very different audience. They are generally quite difficult to interpret unless the reader is familiar with their method of construction.

1.2 All of these charts have very specific functions in the decision-making process in business. They can all be viewed as aids to decision making.

2. DRAWING GRAPHS: BASIC RULES

What is a graph?

2.1 Graphs are a form of visual display of data. A graph shows, by means of either a straight line or a curve, the relationship between two items or 'variables'. In particular it shows how the value of one variable changes given a variation in the value of the other variable. For example, a graph might show the following.

(a) Changes in sales turnover over time.
(b) How a country's population changes over time.
(c) How total costs of production vary according to the number of units of output produced.

2.2 A graph has a horizontal axis, the x axis and a vertical axis, the y axis. The x axis is used to represent the independent variable and the y axis is used to represent the dependent variable. A dependent variable is one whose value depends on the value of the independent variable; in other words, the value of y depends on what the value of x happens to be.

2.3 For example, when plotting a graph of advertising expenditure against sales, the former is the independent variable as, presumably, a change in advertising will lead to a change in sales.

2.4 *Time* is always treated as the independent variable; when time is represented by the x axis on a graph, we have what is called a *time series*.

Some basic rules for drawing graphs

2.5 The general rules for plotting graphs can be summarised as follows.

(a) If the data to be plotted is derived from calculations rather than given in the question, make sure that there is a neat table in your working papers.

(b) The scales on each axis should be selected so as to use as much of the graph paper as possible. Do not cramp a graph into one corner. In some cases it is best not to start a scale at zero. This is perfectly acceptable as long as the scale adopted is clearly shown.

(c) Graphs should not be overcrowded with too many lines. They must always give a clear, neat impression.

(d) The axes must be clearly labelled with description and units.

(e) A graph must always be given a title, and where appropriate, a reference should be made to the source of data.

Example

2.6 Plot the graph for the relationship $y = 5 + 4x$ for the range of values $x = 0$ to $x = 10$.

Solution

2.7 In an example of this type, the first stage is to draw up a table for the formula. Although the problem mentions $x = 0$ to $x = 10$, it is not necessary to calculate values of y for $x = 1, 2, 3$ and so on. Start with a few values, calculating more only if it appears that this will lead to a smoother graph.

x	y
0	5
2	13
4	21
6	29
8	37
10	45

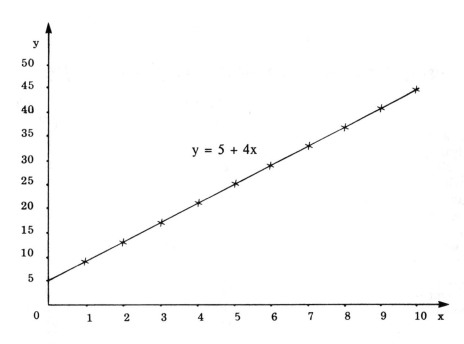

The equation $y = 5 + 4x$ gives a straight line. This is also true of all equations of the type $y = a + bx$. When plotting straight lines, it is only necessary to calculate two points and join them up, for example in the graph above, we could have plotted $x = 0$, $y = 5$ and $x = 10$, $y = 45$.

3.   Z CHARTS

3.1   A Z chart is a time series graph which can be extremely useful for presenting business data over a period of time. It can show the following.

(a) How results are changing from period to period.
(b) How they compare with the previous year.
(c) How they compare with budget for the year.

3.2   In order to produce a Z chart for a given year we need the monthly figures for that year and for the previous year.

3.3   The Z chart consists of three lines.

(a) The monthly figures plotted over the year.

(b) The cumulative monthly total over the year. The cumulative monthly total for, say, April is given by totalling the January, February, March and April figures.

(c) The annual moving total over the year. The annual moving total is the sum of the 12 monthly values for the 12 month period up to the end of the month under consideration.

Example

3.4   The sales figures for a certain company for 19X1 and 19X2 are as follows.

	19X1 sales £m	19X2 sales £m
January	7	8
February	7	8
March	8	8
April	7	9
May	9	8
June	8	8
July	8	7
August	7	8
September	6	9
October	7	6
November	8	9
December	8	9
	90	97

Solution

3.5   The first thing to do is to calculate the cumulative sales for 19X2 and the annual moving total for the year, using the data in the question.

	Sales 19X1 £m	Sales 19X2 £m	Cumulative sales 19X2 £m	Annual moving total £m
January	7	8	8	91
February	7	8	16	92
March	8	8	24	92
April	7	9	33	94
May	9	8	41	93
June	8	8	49	93
July	8	7	56	92
August	7	8	64	93
September	6	9	73	96
October	7	6	79	95
November	8	9	88	96
December	8	9	97	97

Note: the first figure in the annual moving total is arrived at by taking the sales for the year ending December 19X1, adding those for January 19X2 and subtracting those for January 19X1. This gives the sales for a 12 month period to the end of January 19X2: (90 + 8 - 7 = 91).

A similar approach is used for the rest of the year, by adding on the new 19X2 month and deducting the old 19X1 month.

Study the Z chart on the next page.

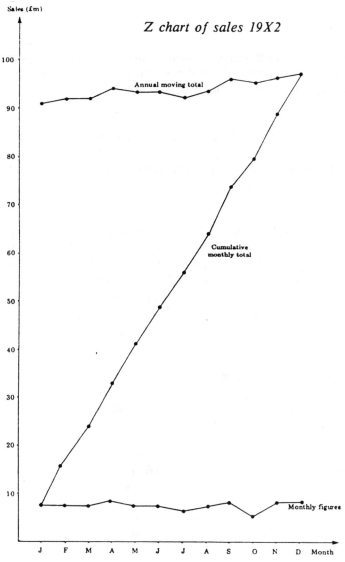

Z chart of sales 19X2

Interpretation of Z charts

3.6 The popularity of Z charts in practical applications derives from the wealth of information which such a seemingly simple graph contains. This can be summarised as follows.

(a) *Monthly totals:* the lower 'horizontal' section of the Z shows the monthly results at a glance. If there is a seasonal pattern it will be apparent here, as will be the results of special occurrences such as a strike or a promotional campaign.

(b) *Cumulative monthly totals:* the 'cross bar' section of the Z shows the total sales at each stage of the year. The chief purpose of this is to compare results with planned or budgeted performance. This section of the graph tends to be smoother than the lower section because monthly ups and downs tend to cancel out when totalled.

(c) *Annual moving totals:* the upper 'horizontal' section of the Z shows a comparison of current levels of performance with those of the previous year. If the line is rising then this year's monthly results are higher than the results of the corresponding months of last year. The opposite applies if the line is falling.

4. LORENZ CURVES

4.1 A Lorenz curve is a form of cumulative frequency curve, which measures one cumulative amount against another. It is common for both the x axis and the y axis to be shown in terms of percentages (each up to 100%) although this is not necessary.

4.2 A Lorenz curve, in effect, shows the degree of concentration that a distribution may have. A common application is the examination of the distribution of wealth. If the distribution between the population was completely even, then there is no concentration of wealth in the population.

4.3 If the cumulative value of one variable (income) were plotted against the cumulative frequency of the other (population) and if the distribution were completely even, then we would expect the graph to be a diagonal straight line. If the wealth is concentrated in the hands of a disproportionately small number of the population, then the cumulative graph would be a Lorenz curve and the measure of the inequality or degree of concentration of the distribution would be the divergence of the curve from the straight line or norm.

Example

4.4 The national wealth of Ruritania is spread as follows.

Wealth Roubles per person	No of people	Wealth 000s roubles
Under 500	13,000	5,200
$\geqslant$ 500 <1,000	16,000	12,800
$\geqslant$ 1,000 <5,000	16,000	48,000
$\geqslant$ 5,000 <40,000	2,000	50,000
$\geqslant$ 40,000	500	25,000
	47,500	141,000

4.5 What these figures mean is that 13,000 people each own less than 500 roubles, and they own 5.2m roubles altogether. Similarly, 16,000 people each own between 500 and 1,000 roubles, and they own 12.8m roubles altogether...and so on down the table.

4.6 From these figures the cumulative number of people and the cumulative wealth can be calculated.

No of people	Cumulative no of people	%	Wealth 000s roubles	Cumulative wealth 000s roubles	%
13,000	13,000	27	5,200	5,200	4
16,000	29,000	61	12,800	18,000	13
16,000	45,000	95	48,000	66,000	47
2,000	47,000	99	50,000	116,000	82
500	47,500	100	25,000	141,000	100

4.7 What these figures mean is that 13,000 people (27% of the population) own 5.2m roubles (4% of the country's wealth); 29,000 people (61% of the population) own 18m roubles (13% of the country's wealth); and so on, until the final line which says that 100% of the population own 100% of the country's wealth.

4.8 The graph is plotted from the percentage columns. It does not matter which axis is used for which percentage.

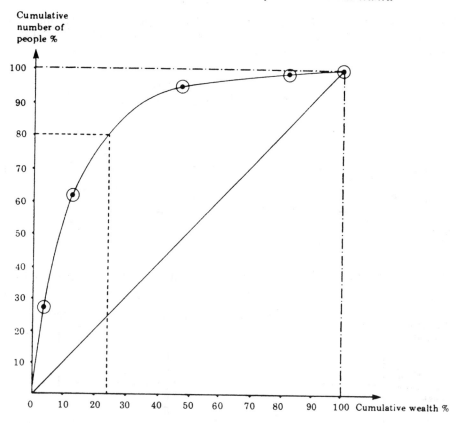

Lorenz curve showing the distribution of wealth in Ruritania

4.9 A straight line is also drawn to join the origin with the 100% cumulative value point. This is the line we would expect if there were no concentration of the wealth in the population, ie if everyone had the same wealth. It is drawn to show how much concentration or 'bend' there is in the actual Lorenz curve. The bigger the bend, the greater the concentration.

4.10 As explained earlier, this type of curve is drawn to show the degree of concentration. The further the curve is from the diagonal the greater is the concentration. In this case it appears that a large proportion of the wealth of Ruritania belongs to a fairly small section of the population. Reading off the graph, it can be seen that 80% of the population own only 25% of the wealth, or conversely that 20% of the population owns 75% of the wealth.

4.11 The main application of the Lorenz curve is for comparative purposes. For instance, in the example above researchers may wish to see whether in subsequent years the concentration of wealth in Ruritania changes. By plotting the Lorenz curves for subsequent years on the same graph it can be seen immediately whether the degree of concentration is increased (in which case the curve will be further from the diagonal) or decreased (in which case the curve will be nearer the diagonal).

4.12 In business the Lorenz curve is used to investigate the extent to which sales, labour or capital and so on are concentrated in the hands of relatively few firms.

5. GANTT CHARTS

5.1 A Gantt chart is a bar chart, scaled in units of time. It is sometimes used in business to indicate the progress which is planned, or has already been achieved, in the accomplishment of a job.

Gantt chart
Planned duration of project A

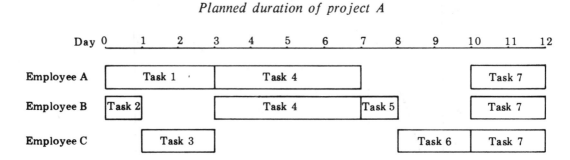

5.2 A Gantt chart can also be used to measure actual against budgeted achievement.

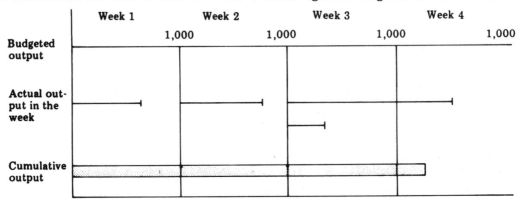

6. SEMI-LOGARITHMIC GRAPHS

6.1 In a semi-logarithmic graph (or log-linear graph), instead of plotting y against x, we first calculate the logarithm of y and then plot that against x.

6.2 This method is used to examine the rates at which prices or costs are increasing over a period of years. If costs (y) are plotted against years (x) the result is a curved graph which is very difficult to interpret. However, if the logarithm of the costs is plotted against years, the slope of the graph at each stage will relate to the rate of increase in costs. A high slope means a high increase and a low slope indicates a relatively lower rate of increase.

6.3   Suppose that costs are increasing at a constant annual rate.

The two alternative graphs will look like this.

(a) *Costs plotted against years*   (b) *Logarithm of costs plotted against years*

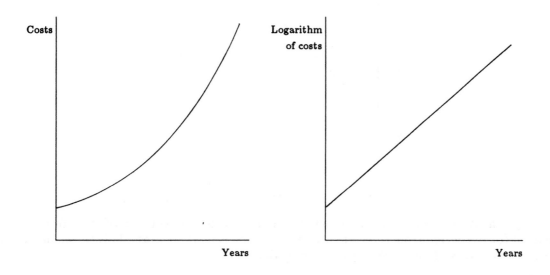

The graph using logarithms of costs shows clearly that the growth rate has remained constant.

Exercise

Draw a semi-logarithmic graph of the following data and interpret it. (The figures have been grossly exaggerated in order to illustrate the point.)

Time	1	2	3	4	5	6	7
Price	6	12	24	35	70	140	280

Solution

Time	1	2	3	4	5	6	7
Log of price	0.78	1.08	1.38	1.54	1.85	2.15	2.45

The logarithms are given by putting the value into your calculator and then pressing the log button, for example 6 |log| should give the result 0.78 to two decimal places.

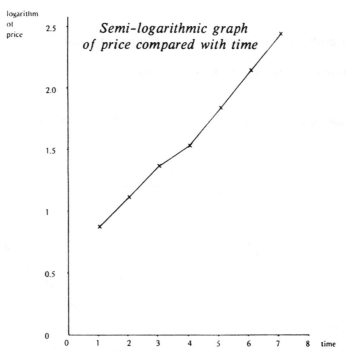

The graph has a constant slope, showing that there is a constant rate of growth in price, except for the period from time 3 to 4 when the slope is markedly less. This shows that there was a lower rate of increase in prices from time 3 to 4.

6.4   It is worth noting that due to rounding, you will rarely find that a semi-logarithmic graph results in a perfect straight line.

7.   CONCLUSION

7.1   The charts shown in this chapter are not very attractive but they are of great use in aiding decision making in business. Z charts have featured frequently in CIM examinations.

TEST YOUR KNOWLEDGE
The numbers in brackets refer to paragraphs of this chapter

1.   Which axis is used to represent the dependent variable? (2.2)

2.   What three lines are drawn on a Z chart? (3.3)

3.   What is the purpose of a Lorenz curve? (4.2)

4.   What is a Gantt chart? (5.1)

5.   What is the purpose of a semi-logarithmic graph? (6.2)

Now try illustrative questions 4, 5, and 6

PART B
FREQUENCY DISTRIBUTION

Chapter 4

DESCRIPTIVE STATISTICS FOR DISCRETE DATA

This chapter covers the following topics.

1. Introduction: calculators and mathematical notation
2. Frequency distributions
3. Averages
4. Measures of variability
5. Pictorial display of discrete distributions
6. Using a calculator in SD mode

---

1. INTRODUCTION: CALCULATORS AND MATHEMATICAL NOTATION

1.1 This is the point in the syllabus when you will have to start doing some calculations of a type that are new to you. We are going to operate on the assumption that you have probably forgotten all the mathematics that you ever knew and that perhaps it never was one of your strongest subjects. If at times we explain in detail processes that seem self-evident, we hope that you will bear with us. It seems better to err on the safe side!

Calculators

1.2 You must have a calculator to study this syllabus effectively and you may take any quiet, battery-operated calculator into the exam with you. It is important to note that if you use a programmable calculator you will be awarded full marks only if you show the method of working. Any basic calculator will suffice but we strongly recommend that you obtain a scientific calculator which will carry out statistical calculations. Don't wait until close to the exam before buying a new calculator. It is really important that you are completely familiar with the calculator that you use in the exam.

1.3 Throughout the text we are going to give hints on the use of calculators and we will use a *Casio fx100c* because this is very widely used. A more recent model than the 'c' would have virtually identical keys. In choosing a calculator, you should look for one that has *standard deviation* mode and, if possible, also *linear regression* mode.

Using a scientific calculator

1.4 If we give an instruction $\boxed{\text{MODE}}$ $\boxed{\bullet}$ it means first press the $\boxed{\text{MODE}}$ button and then the $\boxed{\bullet}$. Unlike with computers, you never press calculator buttons simultaneously.

1.5 Scientific calculators give priority first to functions, then to multiplication and division and only finally to addition and subtraction. For example if you punch into the calculator 1 $\boxed{+}$ 2 $\boxed{x}$ 3 $\boxed{=}$, it will firstly multiply the 2 and 3 and only then will it add the results to 1, giving a total of 7. Check this exercise on your own calculator. Many non-scientific ones will carry out operations in exactly the order in which they are punched in, so they would add the 1 and 2 first and then multiply the result by 3, giving a total of 9.

1.6 It is very important for you to find out at this stage, whether your calculator is 'scientific' or 'non-scientific' in the above sense. If it is non-scientific and you follow the instructions given in this text, you will keep getting the wrong answers!

1.7 *Clearing the calculator*
The 'all clear' button $\boxed{AC}$ will completely clear the entire calculation on which you are engaged whilst the 'clear' button $\boxed{C}$ will just clear the most recent number that you punched in. Try to get into a habit of generally using $\boxed{C}$ rather than $\boxed{AC}$.

Example

1.8 You are adding 3 + 4 + 5 but you make a mistake and punch 6 in place of the 4.

(a) 3 $\boxed{+}$ 6 realise error $\boxed{C}$ 4 $\boxed{+}$ 5 $\boxed{=}$ gives the correct result 12.

(b) 3 $\boxed{+}$ 6 $\boxed{+}$ realise error $\boxed{-}$ 6 $\boxed{+}$ 4 $\boxed{+}$ 5 $\boxed{=}$ would correct the error as would pressing $\boxed{AC}$ and starting again.

Memory

1.9 (a) The 'into memory' button $\boxed{MIN}$ wipes out the present memory contents and replaces it by the number displayed prior to pressing $\boxed{MIN}$. Thus 26 $\boxed{MIN}$ will replace memory contents by 26 and 0 $\boxed{MIN}$ will clear the memory altogether.

(b) $\boxed{M+}$ will add a number to the present memory contents and $\boxed{Shift}$ $\boxed{M+}$ will subtract from it. You will notice that the $\boxed{M+}$ button has M- written underneath it in orange. Functions written in orange always need the shift key to be pressed beforehand.

(c) $\boxed{MR}$ is the memory recall button and will display the memory contents.

Exercise

Put 30 into the memory and first add 20 to it and then subtract 10 from it. Check your result. Now clear the memory.

Solution

30 $\boxed{MIN}$ 20 $\boxed{M+}$ 10 $\boxed{SHIFT}$ $\boxed{M+}$ $\boxed{MR}$ 0 $\boxed{MIN}$

When you press MR it should show 40. At the very end the 'M' should disappear from the screen.

4: DESCRIPTIVE STATISTICS FOR DISCRETE DATA

1.10 We will introduce other calculator functions later in the text. Obtain a scientific calculator if you can but the really important thing is that, whatever calculator you have, you should aim to become thoroughly at ease using it.

Mathematical notation

1.11 Before we go any further we need to explain some of the mathematical notation which you will meet in this chaper.

(a) fx means f multiplied by x. We generally omit the multiplication sign.

(b) x^2 means x multiplied by x. x^n means x multiplied by itself n times, where n could be 2 or 3 or whatever.

(c) fx^2 means f multiplied by x^2. If we want to first multiply f by x and then square the result we use brackets $(fx)^2$.

1.12 *Sigma notation*

The symbol Σ is greek capital letter S and is pronounced 'sigma'. It means 'the sum of'. Hence Σx means the sum of the x's and it means that you need a column of figures entitled 'x' which you have to add up.

Exercise

In order to calculate $\Sigma fx / \Sigma f$, write down what columns you will need and what you will then do with them.

Solution

You need an fx column and an f column. You will then divide the total of the fx column by the total of the f column.

---

2. FREQUENCY DISTRIBUTIONS

2.1 When a survey is conducted the researcher is faced at the end with a large amount of data which needs to be sorted and analysed before any sense can be made of it.

Example

2.2 You have collected the following data in a survey.

Number of customers queuing at a checkout point on 50 occasions

1	5	1	4	5	4	3	5	5	2
3	3	4	3	4	5	7	6	2	3
4	6	5	7	3	5	4	3	4	5
6	4	7	5	6	3	5	4	5	6
4	5	3	7	6	8	3	6	4	5

Some terms that we use are as follows.

(a) The *variable* in any survey is the question that is being asked or the quantity that is being measured. In this case it is 'the number of customers queuing'.

(b) A *discrete* variable is one for which the answer must be a whole number, such as the number of customers. You will need to count something in order to obtain it.

(c) The *data* or the *observations* are all the answers obtained in the survey. In this case the observations are the 50 numbers shown. Although we have 50 observations, they are not all different.

(d) The *values* that a variable can take are the range of possible different answers that can be obtained. In our example the values are the whole numbers ranging from 1 to 8.

(e) The *frequency* of a value is the number of times it occurs and a *frequency distribution* is a list of values and their frequencies.

Exercise

Form the above data into a frequency distribution. Check your results against ours. You can use a 'tally' column if you wish but it isn't essential.

Solution

Number in queue (x)	Tally	Frequency (f)
1	//	2
2	//	2
3	⊬⊬⊬ ⊬⊬⊬	10
4	⊬⊬⊬ ⊬⊬⊬ /	11
5	⊬⊬⊬ ⊬⊬⊬ ///	13
6	⊬⊬⊬ //	7
7	////	4
8	/	1
		50

2.3 Even the very simple act of forming a frequency distribution enables you to begin to make sense of the results. Suppose your manager wanted an 'off the cuff' report at this point. Take a couple of minutes to think what you would say before reading on.

2.4 The above distribution shows that the queue size varies from one to eight people with an average of about five. On the majority of occasions there are between three and six people queuing. Interestingly there are no occasions when the checkout is not in use.

2.5   You might add to your report that the survey only counted the queue on 50 occasions and whilst you assume that it was conducted in a random, and therefore hopefully representative fashion, you do not have any definite information to that effect. So you cannot actually offer any guidance as to how reliable the results might be.

Descriptive statistics

2.6   If you repeated the above survey at, say, a hundred different retail outlets, it would not be practical to compare the results by making the above type of report. Statements such as 'the average is about five' would also not be sufficiently precise. To make such comparisons, you need to calculate various *descriptive statistics*. These are numbers calculated from the data which describe some important feature of it. The really essential descriptive statistics are the various averages and figures that tell us how variable the data is, called measures of variability.

3.   AVERAGES

3.1   An average is a representative figure that is used to give some impression of the size of all items in the set of data. The three main types of average are as follows.

(a)   The arithmetic mean.
(b)   The mode.
(c)   The median.

3.2   An average, whether it is a mean, median or mode, is a *measure of central tendency,* or middle value. By this we mean that a 'population' may range in values, but these values cluster around a central point. This central point, or average, may therefore be thought of as being a value which is in some way representative of the population as a whole. Phrases such as 'middle-of-the-road' and 'ordinary man-in-the-street' convey this idea of an average being representative of the whole.

3.3   The arithmetic mean is used far more often than the other two averages. In fact it is used so often that to the non-statistician, 'average' has come to mean the same as 'arithmetic mean'. But it is important to remember in statistics that the mode and the median are also types of averages.

The arithmetic mean

3.4   The arithmetic mean = $\dfrac{\text{sum of the observations}}{\text{number of observations}}$

Example

3.5   Suppose that the demand for a unit of product on each of 20 days was as follows.

3   12   7   17   3   14   9   6   11   10   1   4   19   7   15   6   9   12   12   8

The arithmetic mean of daily demand would be as follows.

$$\frac{\text{Sum of demand}}{\text{Number of days}} = \frac{185}{20} = 9.25 \text{ units per day}$$

The arithmetic mean is often written as $\bar{x}$ ('x bar'), and so in this example we would write:

$\bar{x}$ = 9.25 units per day

In our example, there is no day when demand is exactly 9.25 units. The arithmetic mean is merely an average representation of demand on each of the 20 days. It is the total demand shared out equally over the 20 days.

3.6   Let's return now to our example about queue sizes in paragraph 2.2. We could of course simply add the original 50 observations and then divide by 50, but it is easier to work from the frequency distribution which we prepared in the exercise at the end of paragraph 2.2

3.7   There are two 1's in the data, so they add up to 2. Likewise there are two 2's which add up to 4. There are ten 3's, so the 3's add up to 30 and so on. If you multiply each value by its frequency you obtain the total of the observations of that particular value. The method is therefore to calculate an fx column. The mean is then given by the total of that column (which is the same as the total of the original 50 observations) divided by 50.

3.8

Number in queue (x)	Frequency (f)	fx
1	2	2
2	2	4
3	10	30
4	11	44
5	13	65
6	7	42
7	4	28
8	1	8
	50	223

$$\text{The mean} = \frac{\text{total of fx column}}{\text{total frequency}} = \frac{223}{50} = 4.46 \text{ customers}$$

3.9   The following formula for the mean is given in the CIM exam.

$$\bar{x} = \frac{\Sigma fx}{\Sigma f}$$

If you are in any doubt about it, look back to paragraph 1.12 where we introduced sigma notation.

4: DESCRIPTIVE STATISTICS FOR DISCRETE DATA

The mode

3.10 The mode is an average which means 'the most frequently occurring value'. For example, if four sisters are aged 13, 13, 16 and 19, then the mode of their ages is 13, because 13 is the most frequently occurring value.

3.11 It is easy to pick out the mode from a frequency distribution since it is simply the value with the biggest frequency. In our example about queue sizes, the mode is five customers.

3.12 If a distribution has two adjacent values with the same highest frequency, the mode would be the average of those two values. For example suppose that 4 and 5 both had frequencies of 12. The mode would then be 4.5 customers.

3.13 If a distribution has several totally separate peaks it is called *multi-modal*. In this case it is not possible to find *the* mode, since there are several, and the mode would not then be a useful measure of central tendency.

The median

3.14 The third type of average is the *median*. The median is the value of the middle member of a distribution or array. The median of some ungrouped data is found by arranging the items in ascending or descending order of value, and selecting the item in the middle of the range.

3.15 For example suppose that demand per day for a particular item over a period of nine days was as follows.

Day	1	2	3	4	5	6	7	8	9
Demand	8	6	9	12	15	6	3	20	11

3.16 First, arrange the data values (ie the demand figures) into order as an array, in either ascending or descending order of value.

$$3 \quad 6 \quad 6 \quad 8 \quad 9 \quad 11 \quad 12 \quad 15 \quad 20$$

Then take the middle value, which in this case is the fifth one. The fifth value in this array is 9. So the median demand per day is 9.

3.17 What would have happened if there had been an even number of data values rather than an odd number? For example, suppose the demand per day data above had been extended to cover ten days as follows.

$$3 \quad 4 \quad 6 \quad 6 \quad 8 \quad 9 \quad 11 \quad 12 \quad 15 \quad 20$$

(ie the demand on day 10 was four items).

3.18 Now there is no single value in the middle of the array because the 5th and 6th items are equally in the middle, so instead we take the mid-way point between the 5th and 6th items. The median is $\frac{8+9}{2} = 8\frac{1}{2}$.

3.19 If there are n observations, the position of the median is $\frac{n+1}{2}$th when they are written in order of magnitude.

So in paragraph 3.16, n = 9 and the median is 10/2 = 5th whilst in paragraph 3.17, n = 10 and the median is 11/2 = 5½th. This means it is the average of the 5th and 6th item.

3.20 We will now return to our example of queue sizes.

Number in queue	Frequency	Cumulative frequency
(x)	(f)	(cum f)
1	2	2
2	2	4
3	10	14
4	11	25
5	13	38
6	7	45
7	4	49
8	1	50
	50	

The *cumulative frequency* of a value is the total frequency of all the values up to and including the value in question.

For example the cum.f of 4 is the total frequency of 1, 2, 3 and 4. There are two 1's, two 2's, ten 3's and eleven 4's so the cum.f of 4 is given by 2 + 2 + 10 + 11 = 25.

If we were to list the observations in order of magnitude, the very last of the 4's, before we started to write down the 5's, would be the 25th number.

3.21 The median's position is given by $\frac{n+1}{2} = \frac{50+1}{2} = 25\frac{1}{2}$.

So the median is the average of the 25th and 26th observations in order of magnitude. We know that the 25th observation is the last of the 4's and the 26th must be the first of the 5's, so the median is the average of 4 and 5.

Median = $\frac{4+5}{2}$ = 4.5 customers

3.22 Before we introduce any new ideas, it is important for you to work through an exercise for yourself. The only way to learn statistics is to *do* it, not just to read about it.

Exercise

Arrange the following data into a frequency distribution and calculate the mean, mode and median.

Number of units demanded over a 25 day period

4	6	6	8	5
7	5	5	6	6
6	6	7	4	7
5	8	7	5	6
9	6	6	6	5

Hint. It is very important to arrange the data in an orderly fashion. You need a column showing the number of units (x) and a column of frequencies (f). For the mean you need an fx column and for the median a column of cumulative frequencies.

Solution

Number of units (x)	Frequency (f)	fx	Cum.f
4	2	8	2
5	6	30	8
6	10	60	18
7	4	28	22
8	2	16	24
9	1	9	25
	25	151	

Arithmetic mean = $\dfrac{\Sigma fx}{\Sigma f}$ = $\dfrac{151}{25}$ = 6.04 units.

Mode = value with biggest frequency = 6 units.

Median is $\dfrac{25 + 1}{2}$ = $\dfrac{26}{2}$ = 13th observation in order of magnitude.

Hence median = 6 units.

(*Explanation:* the cum.f of 5 is 8. That means that the 8th observation is the last of the 5's. All the observations from 9th to 18th are 6's and hence the 13th observation is a 6.)

3.23 It is very important to master these basic ideas and techniques before going on with this chapter. If you found the exercise difficult, read through the preceding paragraphs and try the exercise again before reading on.

4. MEASURES OF VARIABILITY

4.1 Having arrived at an average or typical value for any data, it is essential to investigate the variability of the data around that value. Are the observations generally very close to the average or do they range quite widely either side of it? The answer to this question can be very important in business.

4.2 Suppose for instance that two branches of a firm both have much the same level of weekly demand but that in branch A the demand is very steady whilst in branch B it varies widely from one week to the next.

4.3 In branch B they will either need to hold greater stocks or they will lose customers. Either way, their profits will suffer. Additionally the staff at B will sometimes have too little to do whilst at other times they will be run off their feet. This is wasteful and bad for morale and probably would also lead to increased overtime payments.

4.4 The difference in variability would almost certainly mean that profits at B were much lower than at A despite their average demand being the same.

4.5 The measures of variability which you should be able to calculate are:

    (a) the range
    (b) the standard deviation
    (c) the coefficient of variation
    (d) the quartile deviation.

The range

4.6 The *range* is the number of values from the smallest to the largest in a distribution. In the queuing example, the number of customers ranges from one to eight, so the range is 8.

The standard deviation

4.7 The standard deviation is the most important and widely used measure of variability. It can be thought of as measuring the average distance of the observations from the mean but algebraically it is much more complicated.

4.8 The distance between an observation x and the mean $\bar{x}$ is given by $x - \bar{x}$, but if you calculated $x - \bar{x}$ for all the observations you would find that, when you added the resulting numbers, it would come to zero. This is because the positive and negative *deviations* always cancel out.

4.9 To get round this problem, the deviations $(x - \bar{x})$ are first squared and then averaged. The square root of the resulting value must then be taken to get back into the correct units. Here is an example.

4: DESCRIPTIVE STATISTICS FOR DISCRETE DATA

Example

4.10 Find the standard deviation of the numbers 2, 4, 6, 8, 10.

> *Step 1*   Find the mean $\bar{x}$ = total/5 = 30/5 = 6.
>
> *Step 2*   Find the deviations x - $\bar{x}$.
> 2 - 6, 4 - 6, 6 - 6, 8 - 6, 10 - 6
> ie -4, -2, 0, 2, 4
>
> Notice that they add to zero, as they always must.
>
> *Step 3*   Square the deviations
>
> 16, 4, 0, 4, 16
>
> *Step 4*   Average = total/5 = 40/5 = 8.
>
> *Step 5*   Take the square root.
>
> Standard deviation = $\sqrt{8}$ = 2.83.

4.11 This process can be very tedious but fortunately a formula is given in the CIM exam which simplifies it, but which at first sight looks rather daunting.

$$\text{Standard deviation (s)} = \sqrt{\frac{\Sigma f x^2}{\Sigma f} - \left(\frac{\Sigma f x}{\Sigma f}\right)^2}$$

4.12 To apply this formula, whenever you see sigma (Σ) it means that you need a column which you then total. The totals are then substituted into the formula. The columns you will need will be entitled f, fx and fx^2.

4.13 In the queuing example the columns would look like this.

Number in queue (x)	Frequency (f)	fx	fx^2
1	2	2	2
2	2	4	8
3	10	30	90
4	11	44	176
5	13	65	325
6	7	42	252
7	4	28	196
8	1	8	64
	$\Sigma f = 50$	$\Sigma f x = 223$	$\Sigma f x^2 = 1,113$

$$\text{mean } \bar{x} = \frac{\Sigma f x}{\Sigma f} = \frac{223}{50} = 4.46 \text{ customers}$$

standard deviation $s = \sqrt{\dfrac{\Sigma fx^2}{\Sigma f} - \left(\dfrac{\Sigma fx}{\Sigma f}\right)^2}$

Notice that the second term in this formula is the same as the mean squared.

$$s = \sqrt{\dfrac{1,113}{50} - 4.46^2}$$

$$= \sqrt{22.26 - 19.8916} = \sqrt{2.3684}$$

$$= 1.54 \text{ customers.}$$

A word of warning: when you calculate the standard deviation, be careful to keep plenty of accuracy until the very end. We have worked with four decimal places even though we intended to round to two at the end.

Exercise

Find the standard deviation of the number of units demanded over a 25 day period.

Number of units (x)	Frequency (f)
4	2
5	6
6	10
7	4
8	2
9	1
	25

Solution

x	f	fx	fx²
4	2	8	32
5	6	30	150
6	10	60	360
7	4	28	196
8	2	16	128
9	1	9	81
	25	151	947

$\bar{x} = \Sigma fx / \Sigma f = 151/25 = 6.04$ units

$$s = \sqrt{\dfrac{\Sigma fx^2}{\Sigma f} - \left(\dfrac{\Sigma fx}{\Sigma f}\right)^2} = \sqrt{\dfrac{947}{25} - 6.04^2}$$

$$= \sqrt{37.88 - 36.4816} = \sqrt{1.3984} = 1.18 \text{ units}$$

4.14 *Interpreting the standard deviation*
It is difficult to comment on the standard deviation of a single set of data, beyond saying that it is a measure of how variable the data is around the mean. If you have to compare two sets of data, the one with the largest standard deviation is the more variable. However, if the means of the two sets of data differ markedly, it is better to use the *coefficient of variation* to make comparisons.

The coefficient of variation

4.15 If a person's weight changed by, say, a stone, that would probably be regarded as a big change, whilst the same change in the weight of a locomotive would be totally insignificant.

4.16 It is best therefore to consider variability relative to the average level. The *coefficient of variation* does this by expressing the standard deviation as a percentage of the mean.

$$\text{Coefficient of variation} = \frac{\text{standard deviation}}{\text{mean}} \times 100$$

This formula is not given in your exam but it is worth remembering.

4.17 In our queuing example:

$\bar{x} = 4.46, s = 1.54$

Therefore coefficient of variation $= \dfrac{1.54}{4.46} \times 100 = 35\%$

4.18 The coefficient of variation should be used when comparing sets of data which either have markedly different sized means or are in different units.

Exercise

Compare the variability of prices of an item in Britain and the USA if

British mean   = £6, standard deviation   = £2
and USA mean   = $15, standard deviation   = $4.

Solution

British coefficient of variation $= \dfrac{2}{6} \times 100 = 33\%$

USA coefficient of variation $= \dfrac{4}{15} \times 100 = 27\%$

Therefore prices are more variable in Britain.

The quartile deviation

4.19 Just as the median divides a distribution into two halves, so the *quartiles* divide it into four equal parts, when the observations are written in order of magnitude.

4.20 For example daily demand is as follows (when written in ascending order)

(a) The middle value gives the median = 9

(b) The *lower quartile*, denoted by Q_1, is the average of the 2nd and 3rd values so $Q_1 = \dfrac{5 + 6}{2} = 5.5$.

(c) The *upper quartile*, denoted by Q_3, is the average of the 2nd and 3rd values from the top, so $Q_3 = \dfrac{12 + 15}{2} = 13.5$.

4.21 The quartile deviation $= \dfrac{Q_3 - Q_1}{2}$

This formula is not given in your exam but it is worth remembering. In the above example, $Q_3 - Q_1 = 13.5 - 5.5 = 8$ so the quartile deviation = 4.

4.22 Another name for the quartile deviation is the *semi-interquartile range*, which describes exactly how it is calculated. The interquartile range, $Q_3 - Q_1$, is the range of the middle half of the data and the quartile deviation is a half of that range.

4.23 You can interpret the quartile deviation as the average distance either side of the median within which the middle, most typical, half of the data lies.

5. PICTORIAL DISPLAY OF DISCRETE DISTRIBUTIONS

5.1 The types of distributions we have studied in this chapter could very easily be displayed by simple bar charts or pictograms, but in statistical reports a *frequency polygon* would generally be used.

5.2 A frequency polygon is a graph with frequencies shown on the vertical axis and values on the horizontal axis. It is important to remember that if a value has zero frequency the graph must go down to zero at that point. Remember also to give the graph a title and to label and clearly scale the axes.

Example

5.3 Illustrate the following data by means of a frequency polygon.

Number of cars sold per day (x)	1	2	3	4	5	6	7
Number of days (f)	8	12	10	5	3	0	2

Note that the graph is taken down to zero at 0 and 8 as well as at 6. It is customary to do this at the top and bottom of the data.

Number of cars sold per day over a 40 day period

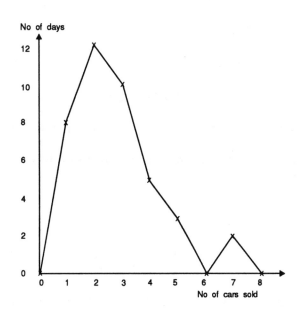

6.   USING A CALCULATOR IN SD MODE

6.1 If you have a scientific calculator it is very easy to calculate the mean and standard deviation by using *SD mode*. However in your exam you will be expected to tabulate the data and *show all workings* as we have done so far in this chapter. What you can do is to use SD mode as a very quick and easy check on your calculations.

Calculator modes

6.2 On the calculator there is a table showing the various modes. To select a particular mode you press ⌐MODE¬ followed by the number given in the table. The screen will display letters showing which mode is being used.

6.3   In general the calculator should be computation mode (mode 0) with normal types of numbers (mode 9). It will always be in one of the three trigonometrical modes, so either DEG, RAD or GRA will show on the screen and you cannot remove them. They are irrelevant in the context of your syllabus. You are unlikely to want to work with special types of numbers so if the screen shows either FIX or SCI return to normal numbers by pressing MODE 9 . If BASE-N shows on the screen, return to ordinary computation by pressing MODE 0. This is also how you get out of SD mode.

Using SD mode

6.4   *Step 1*   Put the calculator into SD mode   MODE   3

       Step 2   Clear any previous data   SHIFT   AC

       Step 3   *Input data* as follows:

                  first value x its frequency M+

                  then second value x its frequency M+

and so on through the data, not forgetting to press M+ at the very end.

If a frequency is 1 or if the data has not been shown as a frequency distribution, you can simply input value M+.

Queuing example

6.5

No of customers (x):	1	2	3	4	5	6	7	8
Frequency (f):	2	2	10	11	13	7	4	1

Input: 1 x 2 M+ 2 x 2 M+ ... and so on ... 7 x 4 M+ 8 M+ .

Step 4. Output: the keys 1 , 2 and 3 will provide various summations and statistics. Beneath these keys there are symbols in orange, which are obtained by first pressing the SHIFT key, and symbols in black for which you need to first press the K out key.

K out 3   gives total frequency (n) and is a useful check.
           In our example, n = 50.

K out 2   gives the total of the observations which is Σx, or Σfx for frequency distributions.
           Here we have $\Sigma fx = 223$.

If you look back to paragraph 4.13 you will see that this agrees with our previous calculation.

K out 1   gives Σx^2 or Σfx^2.
           In this case $\Sigma fx^2 = 1,113$.

SHIFT 1   gives the mean $\bar{x} = 4.46$ customers.

|SHIFT|2| gives the standard deviation s = 1.54 customers. On the calculator this is shown as '$x\sigma_n$'. 'σ' is greek lower case 's' and it is often used as an alternative symbol for the standard deviation. The 'x' preceding it means it is the standard deviation of values called x.

|SHIFT|3| gives a slightly larger figure, 1.55, and it provides an estimate of the standard deviation of the population from which the sample of 50 was taken. You do not need it in this course.

Please note that the output keys can be pressed in any order and as often as you wish. Each time they must be preceded either by |SHIFT| or |K out| .

Step 5. When you have finished with the data, clear it by pressing |SHIFT||AC| and return to computation mode if you have no further data to work on by pressing |MODE| |0|.

Exercise

Input the following data and check your results against those obtained in the exercise following paragraph 4.13.

Number of units (x):	4	5	6	7	8	9
Frequency (f):	2	6	10	4	2	1

Solution

Step 1: |MODE||3|

Step 2: |SHIFT||AC|

Step 3:   4 |x| 2 |M+| 5 |X| 6 |M+| ... and so on ... 9 |M+|

Step 4: |K out||3| n = 25

            |K out||2| Σfx = 151

            |K out||1| Σfx^2 = 947

            |SHIFT||1| $\bar{x}$ = 6.04 units

            |SHIFT||2| s = 1.18 units, to 2 decimal places.

---

7. CONCLUSION

7.1 The ideas and techniques introduced in this chapter are absolutely central to any statistics course. Before you go on to the next chapter, in which the same ideas and techniques will be applied to more complicated data, you should attempt the 'test your knowledge' questions and the illustrative questions for this chapter.

TEST YOUR KNOWLEDGE
The numbers in brackets refer to paragraphs of this chapter

1. What does 'Σ' mean? (1.12)

2. What is a discrete variable? (2.2)

3. What is a frequency distribution? (2.2)

4. What is meant by a 'measure of central tendency'? (3.2)

5. Define the mean, mode and median. (3.4, 3.10, 3.14)

6. What is meant by the 'cumulative frequency' of a value? (3.20)

7. Why are measures of variability important? (4.2 to 4.4)

8. State four measures of variability. (4.5)

9. When should the coefficient of variation be used? (4.18)

Now try illustrative questions 7 and 8

Chapter 5

CONTINUOUS AND GROUPED FREQUENCY DISTRIBUTIONS

> **This chapter covers the following topics.**
>
> 1. Introduction to continuous and grouped frequency distributions
> 2. Mean and standard deviation
> 3. Median and quartile deviation
> 4. Mode, histogram and range
> 5. Which statistics to use

1. INTRODUCTION TO CONTINUOUS AND GROUPED FREQUENCY DISTRIBUTIONS

1.1 In the previous chapter we dealt with simple, discrete frequency distributions in which each value was a whole number and had its own frequency.

1.2 In this chapter, the variable being investigated may be discrete or it may be *continuous*, which means that it is measured and may take decimal values. Equally values may be *grouped* together so that we only know the frequency of the group but not the separate frequencies of the values that make up the group.

Continuous variables

1.3 Variables such as time, length or weight are measured and their accuracy depends on the method of measurement used. If a time is stated as, say, 37 seconds, it is unlikely that the true time is exactly 37 seconds but that 37 is as close as we are able to measure it.

1.4 Most scientists, and indeed most statisticians, would interpret a time of 37 seconds as meaning that the true time was somewhere between 36.5 and 37.5 seconds. In other words, the time is closer to 37 than it is to either 36 or 38 seconds.

1.5 However in business statistics and more particularly in the CIM exams, a time of 37 seconds seems to be interpreted as being 37 or more but not as big as 38, in much the same way that a person is regarded as being 37 years old until the very instant that they become 38.

1.6 If in a frequency distribution we are told that the value 37 seconds has a frequency of 10, we shall interpret it as meaning that on ten occasions the time lay in the *interval* from 37 but less than 38. We cannot know exactly where in that interval each of the ten observations occurs.

5: CONTINUOUS AND GROUPED FREQUENCY DISTRIBUTIONS

Grouped frequency distributions

1.7 If the data consists of a very wide range of values, all with very small frequencies, it is customary to group values together into *classes* and to find the frequency of each class. This makes it easier to interpret the data. An example may illustrate this point.

1.8 Suppose that the output produced by each of 20 employees during one week was as follows, in units.

1,087	850	1,084	792
924	1,226	1,012	1,205
1,265	1,028	1,230	1,182
1,086	1,130	989	1,155
1,134	1,166	1,129	1,160

1.9 Imagine trying to comment on this data. The number of units produced ranges from 792 to 1,265 and most of the values in that range have zero frequency. None occur more than once. It is impossible to even hazard a guess as to what the average output might be or as to the range within which the big majority of employees fall. We need to group the data before we can begin to interpret it.

1.10 The range of output from the lowest to the highest producer is 473 units. This range could be divided into classes of say, 100 units and the number of employees producing output within each class could then be *grouped* into a single frequency, as follows.

Output Units	Tally marks	Number of employees (frequency)
700 - 799	/	1
800 - 899	/	1
900 - 999	//	2
1,000 - 1,099	⫽⫽⫽	5
1,100 - 1,199	⫽⫽⫽ //	7
1,200 - 1,299	////	4
		20

1.11 By grouping the data we have of course lost the original, exact figures. We can only say that output ranges from 700 to 1,299, not 792 to 1,265 as before. However we have gained an overview of the situation. We can see that average output is between 1,100 and 1,200 and that the vast majority of employees produce between 1,000 and 1,300 units per week.

Guidelines for grouping data

1.12 (a) Try to use between five and twelve classes if possible. With more than twelve classes it becomes difficult to interpret the data whilst with less than five classes too much accuracy is lost by grouping together wide ranges of values.

(b) Try to keep the class widths (ie the range of values within each class) equal if possible.

(c) It is generally easiest to select class widths of 10, 100 and so on and to select suitable 'round' numbers for the class limits. For example it is much easier to count the frequencies if your classes are 20-29, 30-39 and so on rather than, say, 23-32 and 33-42.

Example

1.13 A machine produces the following number of rejects in each successive period of five minutes.

16	21	26	24	11	24	17	25	26	13
27	24	26	3	27	23	24	15	22	22
12	22	29	21	18	22	28	25	7	17
22	28	19	23	23	22	3	19	13	31
23	28	24	9	20	33	30	23	20	8

Construct a grouped frequency distribution from this data, using:

(a) classes of 10, starting at 0;
(b) seven classes of equal width.

Solution

1.14 For the first part of the question we do not have to work out the starting point and size of classes because we have already been given that information.

No of rejects (Class)	Tally marks	Number of periods (frequency)
0 - 9	⫴⫴	5
10 - 19	⫴⫴ ⫴⫴ /	11
20 - 29	⫴⫴ ⫴⫴ ⫴⫴ ⫴⫴ ⫴⫴ ⫴⫴ /	31
30 - 39	///	3
		50

1.15 For the second part of the question we have to work out the classes for ourselves. The first thing to do is to look for the lowest and highest in the data: the smallest value in the table is 3, and the highest 33. This is a range of 30. Seven classes mean that the width of each class should be over 4 (because seven classes with width of 4 only gives a range of 7 x 4 = 28).

1.16 It might seem appropriate in this case to take a range of values 0 - 34 in groups of 5. The first class is 0 - 4, the second is 5 - 9, and so on. This is not the *only* way of creating classes but it is probably the best one in this case.

Class	Tally marks	Number of periods (frequency)
0 - 4	//	2
5 - 9	///	3
10 - 14	////	4
15 - 19	⫴⫴ //	7
20 - 24	⫴⫴ ⫴⫴ ⫴⫴ ⫴⫴	20
25 - 29	⫴⫴ ⫴⫴ /	11
30 - 34	///	3
		50

71

Grouped frequency distributions: continuous variables

1.17 In the previous examples there have always been gaps between the classes, such as 0-4 and 5-9, because discrete variables cannot take decimal values like, say, 4.2. However a continuous variable can take any value within its range and so such gaps cannot be left.

1.18 Suppose the previous data were measurements in millimetres (mm) rather than numbers of rejects. In place of the class of discrete values 0-4 we would need a continuous *interval* from 0 up to, but not including 5. The distribution would be listed like this.

Length (mm)	Frequency
0 and less than 5	2
5 and less than 10	3
10 and less than 15	4
15 and less than 20	7
20 and less than 25	20
25 and less than 30	11
30 and less than 35	3
	50

Descriptive statistics

1.19 Grouped distributions and continuous distributions share the very important feature that we cannot know exactly where in a class or interval the observations occur. This means that we have to *estimate* the various descriptive statistics rather than being able to calculate their values exactly as we did in the previous chapter.

1.20 It also means that grouped discrete distributions have to be treated as if they are continuous, and classes have to be converted into intervals, as we did in paragraph 1.18, even if the variable concerned is discrete. This is a very important point to note.

1.21 We will now introduce the new techniques used to estimate descriptive statistics for continuous or grouped data.

2. MEAN AND STANDARD DEVIATION

2.1 The formulae for the mean and standard deviation are exactly the same as those used previously.

$$\text{Mean}, \bar{x} = \frac{\Sigma fx}{\Sigma f}$$

$$\text{Standard deviation}, s = \sqrt{\frac{\Sigma fx^2}{\Sigma f} - \left(\frac{\Sigma fx}{\Sigma f}\right)^2}$$

The problem is that we no longer know the exact x values. We have to let x equal the *interval midpoint* in each case.

2.2 Clearly this will not give exactly the same values for the mean and standard deviation as we would obtain from the original ungrouped data. It will give reasonable approximations provided that within each interval the original values are spread around the interval midpoint in a balanced and symmetrical fashion.

Example

2.3 In a survey, the age distribution of television viewers of a certain programme was as follows.

Age (years)	Frequency
0 - 4	40
5 - 9	35
10 - 14	15
15 - 19	5
20 - 29	2
30 - 49	1
50 or more	2
	100

Find the mean and standard deviation.

2.4 *Preliminary comments*
Before we can find the interval midpoints, we have two things to do. Our first problem is that we have an *open interval* '50 or more'. We need to estimate an upper limit for it. Since the previous interval was of width 20 years, a sensible estimate seems to be 50-69. Our second problem is to convert the classes into continuous intervals and we will use the '0 but less than 5' type of interval.

2.5 In each case, the interval midpoint (x) is given by adding the lower and upper interval limits (for example 0 and 5) and dividing by 2.

2.6 This will give us a column entitled x and another entitled f. To decide what other columns we need, it is necessary to look back at the formulae given in paragraph 2.1. Whenever there is a sigma (Σ) in the formulae, you need a column, so we need fx and fx^2 columns.

Solution

2.7

Age years	Interval years	Midpoint (x)	Frequency (f)	fx	fx^2
0 - 4	0 and less than 5	2.5	40	100.0	250.00
5 - 9	5 and less than 10	7.5	35	262.5	1,968.75
10 - 14	10 and less than 15	12.5	15	187.5	2,343.75
15 - 19	15 and less than 20	17.5	5	87.5	1,531.25
20 - 29	20 and less than 30	25.0	2	50.0	1,250.00
30 - 49	30 and less than 50	40.0	1	40.0	1,600.00
50 - 69	50 and less than 70	60.0	2	120.0	7,200.00
			100	847.5	16,143.75

Mean age $= \dfrac{\Sigma fx}{\Sigma f} = \dfrac{847.5}{100} = 8.475 = \underline{8.5 \text{ years}}$ (to one decimal place)

$$\text{Standard deviation age} = \sqrt{\frac{\Sigma fx^2}{\Sigma f} - \left(\frac{\Sigma fx}{\Sigma f}\right)^2}$$

$$= \sqrt{\frac{16,143.75}{100} - 8.475^2}$$

$$= \sqrt{161.4375 - 71.8256}$$

$$= \sqrt{89.6119}$$

$$= \underline{9.5 \text{ years}} \text{ (to 1 decimal place)}$$

2.8 *Notes*

(a) Before you move on to the next paragraph it is a very good idea to work through all the above steps for yourself. Check out, say, the first row of figures. Are you happy with converting the class 0-4 into the interval '0 and less than 5'? The midpoint 2.5 is given by 0 $\boxed{+}$ 5 $\boxed{=}$ $\boxed{\div}$ 2 $\boxed{=}$. The fx value 100 is given by 40 $\boxed{\times}$ 2.5 $\boxed{=}$. The fx² value 250 is given either by f times x² ie 40 $\boxed{\times}$ 2.5 $\boxed{x^2}$ $\boxed{=}$ or by fx times x ie 100 $\boxed{\times}$ 2.5 $\boxed{=}$.

(b) Use your calculator in SD mode to check out the various totals, Σf, Σfx and Σfx^2 as well as the results $\bar{x}$ and s. Detailed instructions are given in section 6 of the previous chapter.

3. MEDIAN AND QUARTILE DEVIATION

3.1 The definitions of the median, quartiles and quartile deviation remain the same as they were in the previous chapter but with continuous or grouped data we can no longer be absolutely certain of their values.

3.2 The median is the middle value if the observations are listed in order of magnitude. Since we cannot be sure of the actual values of the observations, we have to translate this definition into saying that the median is the value whose cumulative frequency is half the total frequency.

The *cumulative frequency* of a value is the total frequency less than that value.

The *median* is the value whose cumulative frequency is n/2 where n is the total frequency.

The *lower quartile* (Q_1) is the value whose cumulative frequency is n/4.

The *upper quartile* (Q_3) is the value whose cumulative frequency is $\frac{3}{4}$n.

3.3 To obtain the median and quartiles we must first form the data into a *cumulative frequency distribution* and then graph cumulative frequency vertically against values horizontally. The resulting graph is called an *ogive* or cumulative frequency polygon. Here is an example to illustrate the process.

3.4 Age distribution of television viewers of a certain programme.

Age years	Frequency	Cumulative frequency		Value
0 and less than 5	40	40	less than	5
5 and less than 10	35	75	less than	10
10 and less than 15	15	90	less than	15
15 and less than 20	5	95	less than	20
20 and less than 30	2	97	less than	30
30 and less than 50	1	98	less than	50
50 and less than 70	2	100	less than	70
	100			

The cumulative frequency can only be calculated for the interval limits. There are 40 observations in the first interval. They must all be less than 5, so the cumulative frequency of 5 is 40. Similarly, in the first two intervals there are 40 + 35 = 75 observations and they must all be less than 10 and so on.

3.5 The very bottom interval limit (0 years in this case) has no observations less than itself, so its cumulative frequency must always be zero.

3.6 The *ogive* is a graph of cumulative frequency against values. Its vertical axis in this case must range from 0 to 100 and its horizontal axis must range across the intervals, in this case 0 to 70.

Ogive showing age distribution of viewers

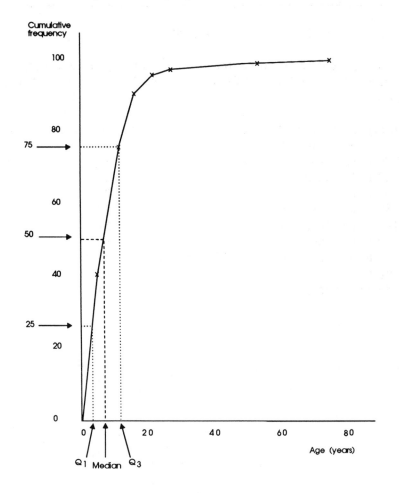

75

3.7 Having graphed the ogive, we can now use it to find the median and quartiles.

Cumulative frequency (cum f) of the median = total/2 = 100/2 = 50. We must first locate the cumulative frequency of 50 on the vertical axis and then read across to the graph and then down to the horizontal axis (as shown by the dashed line). The corresponding value on the horizontal axis is the estimate of the median. The estimate of the median is 6.5 years in this example.

3.8 To find the quartiles we similarly read across and down at the appropriate cumulative frequencies (shown by dotted lines).

Cum f of Q_1 = total/4 = 100/4 = 25 so Q_1 = 3.5 years.
Cum f of Q_3 = $\frac{3}{4}$ × total = $\frac{3}{4}$ × 100 = 75 so Q_3 = 10 years.

3.9 The median tells us that the average age of viewers is 7 years. We can now also calculate the *quartile deviation* or *semi-interquartile range*, $\frac{Q_3 - Q_1}{2}$, which provides a measure of how variable viewer's ages are.

$$\frac{Q_3 - Q_1}{2} = \frac{10 - 3.5}{2} = \frac{6.5}{2} = 3.25 \text{ years.}$$

3.10 Before we introduce any new techniques, you must practice the very important techniques introduced so far in this chapter by attempting the following exercise.

Exercise

Find the mean, the standard deviation, the median and the quartile deviation for the following data which relates to one of several factories owned by a freezer manufacturing company. Interpret your results.

Daily production of freezers	No of days
less than 20	1
20 to less than 40	10
40 to less than 60	14
60 to less than 80	27
80 to less than 100	39
100 to less than 120	51
120 to less than 140	40
140 to less than 160	25
160 to less than 180	10
180 and over	3

Solution

Production	midpoint (x)	frequency (f)	fx	fx²	cum f		value
0 - 20	10	1	10	100	1	less than	20
20 - 40	30	10	300	9,000	11	less than	40
40 - 60	50	14	700	35,000	25	less than	60
60 - 80	70	27	1,890	132,300	52	less than	80
80 - 100	90	39	3,510	315,900	91	less than	100
100 - 120	110	51	5,610	617,100	142	less than	120
120 - 140	130	40	5,200	676,000	182	less than	140
140 - 160	150	25	3,750	562,500	207	less than	160
160 - 180	170	10	1,700	289,000	217	less than	180
180 - 200	190	3	570	108,300	220	less than	200
		220	23,240	2,745,200			

Note that we have had to 'close' the open intervals at both ends in order to find the midpoints. Since all other intervals are of width 20 units, we have retained this width for the end intervals.

(a)   Mean $(\bar{x}) = \dfrac{\Sigma fx}{\Sigma f} = \dfrac{23,240}{220} = 105.6$ freezers.

$$\text{Standard deviation} = \sqrt{\frac{\Sigma fx^2}{\Sigma f} - \left(\frac{\Sigma fx}{\Sigma f}\right)^2} = \sqrt{\frac{\Sigma fx^2}{\Sigma f} - \bar{x}^2}$$

$$= \sqrt{\frac{2,745,200}{220} - 105.6364^2}$$

$$= \sqrt{12,478.1818 - 11,159.049}$$

$$= \sqrt{1,319.1328} = 36.3 \text{ freezers}$$

(b)   *Ogive showing production of freezers*

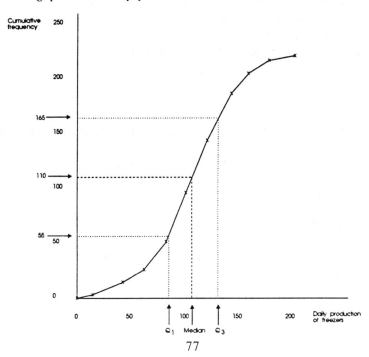

Cum f of median = $\frac{220}{2}$ = 110 so median = 107 freezers

Cum f of Q_1 = $\frac{220}{4}$ = 55 so Q_1 = 82 freezers

Cum f of Q_3 = $3 \times \frac{220}{4}$ = 165 so Q_3 = 132 freezers

(*Note:* the above values can only be approximate since they are obtained graphically. Don't worry if your values are two or three units different from ours.)

Quartile deviation = $\frac{Q_3 - Q_1}{2}$ = $\frac{132 - 82}{2}$ = 25 freezers.

(c) *Interpretation*

The mean and median are different types of averages and so both give us a typical or expected level of daily production of freezers. The mean of 105.6 is the total production of freezers shared out equally over the 220 days. The median tells us that production was 107 or less on half of all days.

Both the standard deviation and the quartile deviation are measures of the amount of variability from one day to the next. The standard deviation shows that there is an average variation of 36 freezers per day either side of the mean. The quartile deviation ignores the 25% of days when production is very low and the upper 25% when production is very high. It tells us that, for the middle 50% of days, production can be expected to range by up to 25 freezers either side of the median.

Calculation of the median

3.11 Instead of estimating the median graphically, it can be calculated using the following rather daunting formula which is given in your exam.

$$\text{Median} = L_1 + (L_2 - L_1)\left(\frac{n/2 - \Sigma f_1}{\Sigma f_2 - \Sigma f_1} \right)$$

where
L_1 = lower boundary of median class
L_2 = upper boundary of median class
n = total number of items
Σf_1 = cumulative frequency below median
Σf_2 = cumulative frequency above median

Example

3.12 Age distribution of television programme viewers (data used in paragraph 3.4)

Age (years)	Frequency	Cum f
0 and less than 5	40	40
5 and less than 10	35	75
10 and less than 15	15	90
15 and less than 20	5	95
20 and less than 30	2	97
30 and less than 50	1	98
50 and less than 70	2	100
	100	

Solution

3.13 *Step 1.*   Cum f of median = n/2 = 100/2 = 50. So median class is 5 to 10.

(There are 40 observations less than 5 and a total of 75 less than 10 so the 50th must lie between 5 and 10.)

3.14 *Step 2.*   It follows that

$L_1 = 5$ and $\Sigma f_1 = 40$ (the cum f of L_1)
$L_2 = 10$ and $\Sigma f_2 = 75$ (the cum f of L_2)
$n = 100$

3.15 *Step 3.*   Hence median

$$= L_1 + (L_2 - L_1)\left(\frac{n/2 - \Sigma f_1}{\Sigma f_2 - \Sigma f_1} \right)$$

$$= 5 + (10 - 5)\left(\frac{100/2 - 40}{75 - 40} \right)$$

$$= 5 + 5\left(\frac{50 - 40}{35} \right)$$

$$= 5 + \left(5 \times \frac{10}{35}\right) = 5 + 1.4$$

$$= 6.4 \text{ years (to one decimal place)}$$

3.16 Notice that this is very close to our graphical estimate of 6.5 years. The assumption in both cases is that the observations are uniformly spread over the median class.

Exercise

Calculate the median number of freezers produced per day using the data of the previous exercise following paragraph 3.10.

For your convenience, here are the key intervals needed for the calculation.

Production	Cum f
80 - 100	91
100 - 120	142
120 - 140	182

n = 220

Solution

Cum f of median = n/2 = 220/2 = 110
So median class is 100 - 120

(*Note:* this is because 110 lies between 91 and 142. The fact that it lies between 100 and 120 is incidental.)

$$L_1 = 100 \qquad \Sigma f_1 = 91 \qquad n = 220$$
$$L_2 = 120 \qquad \Sigma f_2 = 142$$

$$\text{Median} = L_1 + (L_2 - L_1)\left(\frac{n/2 - \Sigma f_1}{\Sigma f_2 - \Sigma f_1}\right)$$

$$= 100 + (120 - 100)\left(\frac{110 - 91}{142 - 91}\right)$$

$$= 100 + \left(20 \times \frac{19}{51}\right) = 100 + 7.5$$

$$= 107.5 \text{ freezers}$$

---

4. MODE, HISTOGRAM AND RANGE

4.1 The mode is the most frequent observation and we can easily pick out the interval in which it must lie, called the *modal interval*. As in the case of the median, the problem is to estimate whereabouts within this interval the mode actually lies. To do this we need to construct a chart called a histogram.

The histogram

4.2 A histogram is a series of adjacent rectangles rather like a bar chart. The horizontal axis shows the intervals of the distribution and the vertical axis shows the frequency of the intervals (or frequency density in cases where the intervals have different widths). The height of each rectangle corresponds to the frequency (or frequency density) of the interval which forms its base.

4.3 The mode is estimated from the histogram using a 'cross-over' construction that will be shown in each of the following examples.

4.4 *Example with equal interval widths*

No of rejects	Frequency
0 and less than 10	5
10 and less than 20	11
20 and less than 30	31
30 and less than 40	3
	50

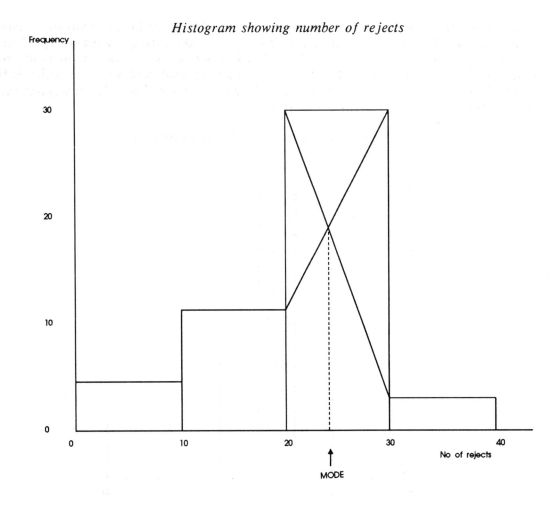

Histogram showing number of rejects

The estimate of the mode is 24.2 rejects.

4.5 *Unequal intervals*

If interval widths are unequal, the first step is to decide on a standard interval length for the distribution. Any sensible interval length, generally the one which occurs most often in the distribution, will suffice.

4.6 *Frequency density* is given by the frequency per standard interval. If a particular interval is twice the standard width, the frequency density of that interval is half its frequency. If its width is three times the standard, frequency density is given by frequency divided by three, and so on. The heights of the rectangles in the histogram show the frequency density in these cases.

4.7 *Example with unequal interval widths*

No of cars sold per week	Frequency	Frequency density
0 and less than 10	8	4
10 and less than 15	6	6
15 and less than 20	13	13
20 and less than 25	5	5
25 and less than 40	6	2
	38	

4.8 We have chosen a standard interval of width 5. The middle three intervals are all of standard width so their frequency densities are the same as their frequencies at 6, 13 and 5 respectively. The first interval is of width 10 which is two standard intervals, so its frequency density is frequency/2 ie 8/2 = 4. The last interval is of width 15 which is three standard intervals, so its frequency density is frequency/3 ie 6/3 = 2. The histogram for the above example will therefore look like this.

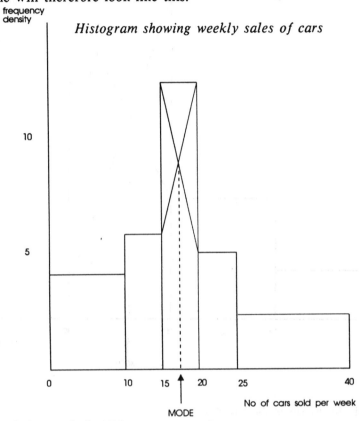

Histogram showing weekly sales of cars

The estimate of the mode is 17.3 cars per week.

The use of histograms

4.9 Histograms are not simply used in order to estimate the mode. They are of value in that they display the basic shape of the distribution, in the same way that a frequency polygon does for ungrouped data. A polygon can be obtained for grouped data by plotting frequency density on interval midpoints, but a histogram is better since it more clearly relates frequencies to intervals.

(a) They display the comparative frequency of occurrence of data items within each class interval, and so show which class intervals are the most frequently occurring and which are the least and so on.

(b) They indicate whether the range of values is wide or narrow, and whether most values occur in the middle of the range or whether the frequencies are more evenly spread.

5: CONTINUOUS AND GROUPED FREQUENCY DISTRIBUTIONS

For example:

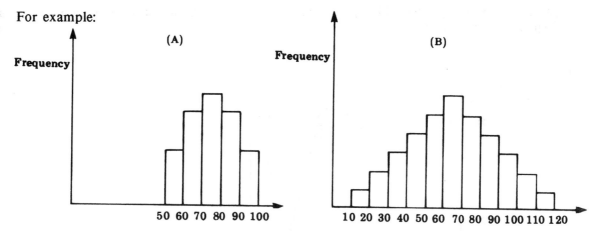

If these two histograms relate to the same items, we can see that histogram (A) has a narrower range of values than (B). Both have the most frequently occurring value somewhere in the middle of the range (70-80 with A and 60-70 with B).

Another example:

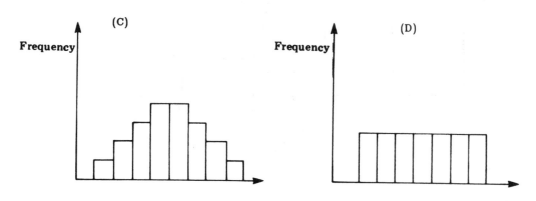

A comparison of these two histograms shows that the most frequently occurring values in histogram C are towards the middle of the range, whereas in histogram D, values occur with equal frequency across the entire range.

4.10 If in an exam you are asked to produce a histogram but the mode is not required, you should omit the construction used to estimate the mode.

Calculation of the mode

4.11 If a histogram is not specifically required then the mode can be estimated using proportions, in much the same way that we calculated the median. Unfortunately no formula is given for this in your exam. Here is an illustration of the method using the data about rejects.

4.12

No of rejects	Frequency
0 – 10	5
10 – 20	11
20 – 30	31
30 – 40	3

We do not need to graph the histogram accurately but it must be sketched and various quantities marked on it as shown.

4.13

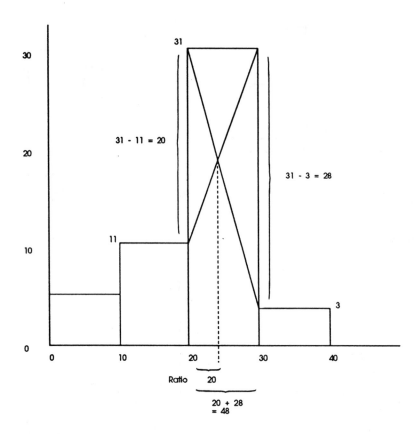

The mode is given by

20 plus $\dfrac{20}{48}$ths of the interval 20 to 30.

Mode $= 20 + \dfrac{20}{48} \times (30 - 20)$

$= 20 + \left(\dfrac{20}{48} \times 10 \right) = 20 + 4.2$

$= 24.2$ rejects

4.14 The *assumption* made in estimating the mode is that the observations in the most frequent interval will *not* be evenly spread across that interval. They are assumed to be located closer to the second most frequent interval in the proportions shown above.

5: CONTINUOUS AND GROUPED FREQUENCY DISTRIBUTIONS

The range

4.15 The range is another measure of variability with which you must be familiar. It shows the variation from the very bottom of the distribution to the very top.

Range = largest class limit minus smallest class limit.

4.16 In the previous example, the number of rejects ranged from 0 to 40 and the range = 40 - 0 = 40 rejects.

5. WHICH STATISTICS TO USE

Skewed data

5.1 If frequencies increase in a steady fashion to a central peak and then decrease in much the same way, the data is described as *symmetrical*.

If frequencies rise sharply and then tail off very slowly or, conversely, rise slowly and then drop away sharply, the data is described as *skewed*.

5.2 An important consequence of skewness is that the three averages take different values.

Symmetrical frequency distribution

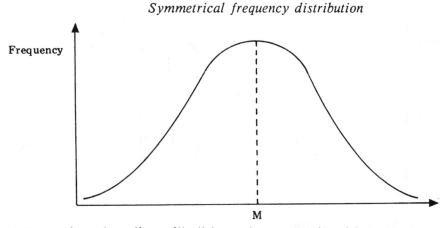

The mean, mode and median will all have the same value, M.

5.3 If a frequency distribution is *positively skewed* it will 'lean' towards the left hand side of the graph (ie be 'weighted towards' the left hand side, with a tail stretching out to the right).

It is important to note that the mean, median and mode now have different values.

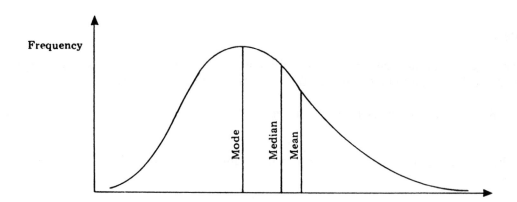

5.4 In a positively skewed distribution:

(a) the mode will be a lower value than the median; and
(b) the mean will be a higher value than the median.

5.5 If a frequency distribution is *negatively skewed*, it will 'lean' towards the right hand side of the graph, with a tail stretching out to the left.

Once again, the mean, median and mode will have different values.

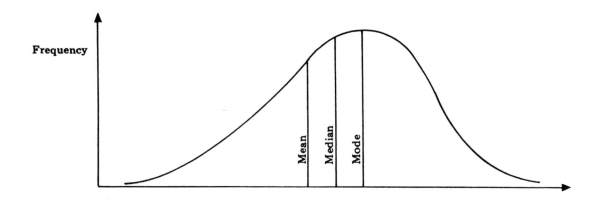

5.6 In a negatively skewed distribution:

(a) the mode will have a higher value than the median;
(b) the mean will have a lower value than the median.

5.7 As we have seen, for skewed distributions the mode, median and mean no longer have the same value. The mean and median are always on the side of the tail, the mean being further from the mode. The more the distribution is skewed, the more spread out will be the three averages.

A major use of histograms and frequency polygons is to show us whether or not the data is skewed.

5: CONTINUOUS AND GROUPED FREQUENCY DISTRIBUTIONS

Advantages and disadvantages of the various averages

5.8 *The arithmetic mean* gives the total shared out equally. Its advantages are that it is the most familiar average and is widely used, particularly in advanced mathematical statistics. It uses all the data, which means that all our knowledge of the situation is incorporated in its calculation.

Its disadvantages are that it is heavily distorted by skewed data, either overestimating or underestimating the typical level, and that its calculation requires us to guess the limits of any open intervals.

The assumption made in its estimation for grouped data is that the data is symmetrically distributed within each interval.

5.9 *The median* gives the middle value in order of magnitude.

Its advantages are that it is not distorted by skewness and its calculation is not affected by open intervals.

Its disadvantages are that it is.not very familiar, it does not have an exact algebraic formula so it is less used in advanced statistics and it does not use all the data.

The assumption made in its estimation for grouped data is that the observations are uniformly spread within its interval.

5.10 *The mode* gives the most common value.

Its disadvantages are that it is not very familiar, it is little used in advanced statistics, it does not use all the data and it is distorted by skewness.

Its advantages are that it is not affected by open intervals and it is the easiest of the averages to identify approximately.

The assumption made in its estimation for grouped data is that observations are unevenly spread over the modal class, clustering towards the class with the second highest frequency.

Advantages and disadvantages of the various measures of dispersion

5.11 *The standard deviation* attempts, via a rather complex procedure of squaring, averaging and square rooting, to measure average variability of the data about the mean.

Its advantages, disadvantages and the assumptions made in its estimation are identical to those of the mean.

5.12 *The quartile deviation* gives the average distance from the median to the quartiles. It can be said therefore to give the range, either side of the median, within which the middle half of the data lies.

Its advantages, disadvantages and assumptions are the same as for the median.

5.13 *The range* is the variation from the very bottom of the distribution to the very top.

Its only advantages are that it is very familiar and it gives a very easy and quick indication of variability.

It has many disadvantages. It relies totally on the two most extreme values, which are frequently the least reliable values in the data (due to errors such as misreading responses or respondents misunderstanding questions) and which have to be guessed if there are open intervals. It is distorted by skewness and it takes no account of the distribution of the data between the extremes.

5.14 Each of the three distributions shown below has the same range but they cannot really be said to show the same variability.

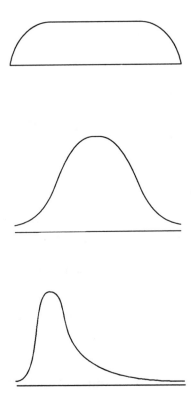

Which statistics to use

5.15 (a) The mode and range are used for an initial, very easy and quick exploration of the data.

   (b) The mode might also be used when an item is to be manufactured in one size only, in which case the single most common size might be preferred.

   (c) The median and quartile deviation should be used when data is skewed or when there are open intervals.

   (d) Otherwise the mean and standard deviation should be used.

5.16 Notwithstanding the above preferences, generally when we calculate statistics it is with a view to comparing them with other statistics such as those of previous years or of other firms. Like must be compared with like and this may leave us no option concerning which descriptive statistics to use. It would of course be correct to express our reservations about conclusions drawn from inappropriate statistics.

6. CONCLUSION

6.1 In this chapter and the previous one we have defined the three most important averages, the mean, median and mode, and we have shown how they are calculated or estimated.

6.2 Similarly we have dealt with the standard deviation, quartile deviation and the range which are all measures of how variable the data is.

6.3 We have shown how frequency data may be illustrated by a frequency polygon, a histogram or an ogive and how these charts may be used to estimate statistics.

6.4 In addition to knowing how to calculate the various statistics, we must know how to interpret them and what their shortcomings are.

6.5 In your exam it is virtually certain that there will be at least one, perhaps two, questions on these topics. It is essential that you try the illustrative questions before going on to the next chapter.

TEST YOUR KNOWLEDGE
The numbers in brackets refer to paragraphs of this chapter

1. State the guidelines for putting data into groups (1.12)

2. What are the x values used to estimate the mean in grouped data? (2.1)

3. What columns are required to calculate the standard deviation? (2.6)

4. What is an ogive? (3.3)

5. When and how is frequency density calculated? (4.6)

6. State two reasons why a histogram might be produced. (4.9)

7. Describe what is meant by 'positively skewed'. (5.3)

8. List the advantages and disadvantages of the mean. (5.8)

9. When is the median preferable to the mean? (5.15(c))

Now try illustrative questions 9 to 12

PART C
RELATIONSHIPS AND FORECASTING

Chapter 6

CORRELATION

This chapter covers the following topics.	

1. The meaning of correlation
2. The correlation coefficient
3. Rank correlation
4. Use of calculators in LR mode

1. THE MEANING OF CORRELATION

1.1 | Correlation is concerned with the extent to which the value of one 'variable' or item is related to or varies with the value of another variable.

If two items are correlated, then an increase in the value of one item will mean either an increase (positive correlation) or a decrease (negative correlation) in the value of the other item.

1.2 For example there may be a relationship between expenditure on advertising and the level of sales. If it is found that high sales correspond to periods of high expenditure on advertising, and that sales fall as advertising falls, then a positive correlation exists between the two.

1.3. Correlation means mutual dependence or inter-relationship. To investigate it we need several pairs of values, such as advertising expenditure and sales over several years. One of the variables will be called X and the other will be called Y. The variable called Y should be the one which you think is *dependent* on the other variable. In our example sales would be called Y since it is likely that they depend on advertising.

Scatter diagrams

1.4 The concept of correlation is perhaps most easily understood from a scatter diagram (scattergram or scattergraph) which is a graph with X plotted horizontally and Y vertically, resulting in a scatter of points.

1.5 Consider the following data.

	Advertising costs (£) X	Sales (£) Y
January	1,000	8,200
February	800	6,700
March	1,100	8,700
April	1,200	9,400
May	700	6,600
June	1,000	7,900
July	1,500	10,200
August	500	5,800
September	900	7,200
October	900	7,600
November	1,400	10,000
December	600	6,400

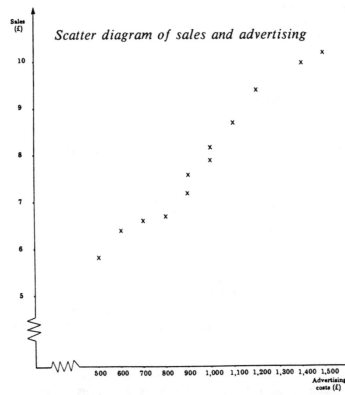

Scatter diagram of sales and advertising

1.6 It is clear from the scattergram that there is a strong relationship between advertising and sales. The strength of the correlation depends on how closely the scatter of points approximates to a straight line. In this case the correlation is not perfect but if we were to 'fit' a straight line to the data, none of the points would be very far from it. By 'fitting' a straight line, we mean drawing a line through the middle of the scatter of points, trying to follow the basic slope of the scatter and trying to keep a rough balance of points either side of the line.

1.7 Correlation, or the lack of it, can be judged from a scattergram as follows.

(a) The strength of the correlation depends on how closely the points in the scatter approximate to a straight line.

(b) Correlation is positive if Y increases as X increases and negative if Y decreases as X increases.

1.8 In our example of sales and advertising, we have a very strong positive correlation between advertising and sales. An example of negative correlation might be the relationship between sales of overcoats and daily temperature. We would expect overcoat sales to reduce when the weather is hot.

Degrees of correlation

1.9 There are three degrees of correlation as follows.

(a) Perfectly correlated.
(b) Partly correlated.
(c) Uncorrelated.

These may be illustrated by scatter diagrams.

1.10 *Perfect correlation*

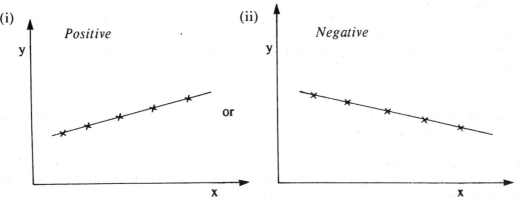

All the pairs of values lie on (or very nearly on) a straight line. An exact linear relationship exists between the two variables.

1.11 *Partly correlated*

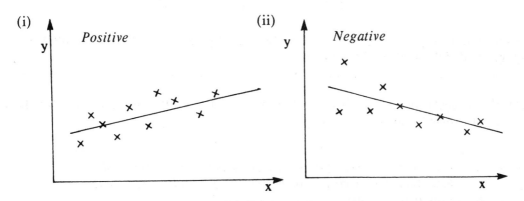

In (i), there is no exact relationship, but low values of x tend to be associated with low values of y, and high values of x with high values of y.

In (ii), again there is no exact relationship, but low values of x tend to be associated with high values of y and vice versa.

1.12 *Uncorrelated*

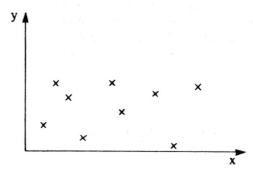

There is no clear trend up or down and the two variables are fairly obviously independent of each other, ie there is little or no correlation.

2.   THE CORRELATION COEFFICIENT

2.1   It is often hard to judge the degree of correlation from a scattergram since the appearance of the scatter is greatly influenced by the choice of scale and by the positioning of the axes. However the degree of correlation between two variables can be measured, and we can decide, using actual results or pairs of data, whether two variables are perfectly or partially correlated, and if they are partially correlated, whether there is a high or low degree of partial correlation.

2.2   This degree of correlation is measured by the *correlation coefficient* (also called the 'product moment correlation coefficient').

There are several formulae which could be used to calculate the correlation coefficient, although each formula should give the same value. We will use the most common formula, which is provided in the list of basic formulae in the examination.

2.3

$$\text{Correlation coefficient, } r = \frac{n\Sigma xy - \Sigma x\Sigma y}{\sqrt{[n\Sigma x^2 - (\Sigma x)^2][n\Sigma y^2 - (\Sigma y)^2]}}$$

where x and y represent pairs of data for two variables x and y, and n is the number of pairs of data used in the analysis.

2.4   The correlation coefficient must always fall between –1 and +1. If you get a value outside this range you have made a mistake.

$r = +1$ means that the variables are *perfectly positively correlated.*
$r = -1$ means that the variables are *perfectly negatively correlated.*
$r = 0$ means that the variables are *uncorrelated.*

Example

2.5 The cost of output at a factory is thought to be dependent on the number of units produced. Data has been collected for the number of units produced per month in the last six months, and their associated cost.

Month	Output in 000s of units (x)	Cost (£'000) (y)
1	2	9
2	3	11
3	1	7
4	4	13
5	3	11
6	5	15

Is there any correlation between output and cost?

Solution

2.6
$$r = \frac{n\Sigma xy - \Sigma x \Sigma y}{\sqrt{[n\Sigma x^2 - (\Sigma x)^2][n\Sigma y^2 - (\Sigma y)^2]}}$$

Where there is a Σ in the formula, we need a column entitled accordingly, so we need columns entitled xy, x, y, x^2 and y^2.

We need to find the values for the following.

(a) Σxy Multiply each value of x by its corresponding y value, so that there are six values for xy. Add up the six values to get the total.

(b) Σx Add up the six values of x to get a total. $(\Sigma x)^2$ will be the square of this total.

(c) Σy Add up the six values of y to get a total. $(\Sigma y)^2$ will be the square of this total.

(d) Σx^2 Find the square of each value of x, so that there are six values for x^2. Add up these values to get a total.

(e) Σy^2 Find the square of each value of y, so that there are six values for y^2. Add up these values to get a total.

Workings

x	y	xy	x^2	y^2
2	9	18	4	81
3	11	33	9	121
1	7	7	1	49
4	13	52	16	169
3	11	33	9	121
5	15	75	25	225
$\Sigma x = 18$	$\Sigma y = 66$	$\Sigma xy = 218$	$\Sigma x^2 = 64$	$\Sigma y^2 = 766$

$(\Sigma x)^2 = (18)^2 = 324$ $(\Sigma y)^2 = (66)^2 = 4,356$ n = 6

$$r = \frac{6(218) - (18)(66)}{\sqrt{[6(64) - 324][6(766) - 4,356]}}$$

$$= \frac{1,308 - 1,188}{\sqrt{(384 - 324)(4,596 - 4,356)}}$$

$$= \frac{120}{\sqrt{(60)(240)}} = \frac{120}{\sqrt{14,400}} = \frac{120}{120}$$

$$r = 1$$

2.7 There is *perfect positive correlation* between the volume of output at the factory and costs.

Exercise

You must learn to calculate the correlation coefficient with reasonable ease, and you should attempt the following exercise. Calculate the correlation coefficient for the data given in paragraph 1.5 of this chapter.

Solution

Advertising (£'00)	Sales (£'000)			
x	y	xy	x^2	y^2
10	8.2	82.0	100	67.24
8	6.7	53.6	64	44.89
11	8.7	95.7	121	75.69
12	9.4	112.8	144	88.36
7	6.6	46.2	49	43.56
10	7.9	79.0	100	62.41
15	10.2	153.0	225	104.04
5	5.8	29.0	25	33.64
9	7.2	64.8	81	51.84
9	7.6	68.4	81	57.76
14	10.0	140.0	196	100.00
6	6.4	38.4	36	40.96
$\Sigma x = 116$	$\Sigma y = 94.7$	$\Sigma xy = 962.9$	$\Sigma x^2 = 1,222$	$\Sigma y^2 = 770.39$

$$n = 12$$

$$r = \frac{12(962.9) - (116)(94.7)}{\sqrt{[12(1,222) - (116)(116)][12(770.39) - (94.7)(94.7)]}}$$

$$= \frac{569.6}{\sqrt{(1,208)(276.59)}} = \frac{569.6}{578.0}$$

$$r = + 0.985$$

This is close to +1 and indicates near-perfect positive correlation.

Correlation of a time series

2.8 Correlation exists in a time series if there is an inter-relationship between the period of time and the recorded value for that period of time, ie if there is a trend line. The correlation coefficient is calculated with time as the x variable although it is more convenient to use simplified values for x instead of year numbers. For example instead of having a series of years 1981 to 1987, we could have values for x from 1 (1981) to 7 (1987).

Example

2.9 Sales of product A between 19X1 and 19X5 were as follows.

Year	Units sold (000s)
19X1	20
19X2	18
19X3	15
19X4	14
19X5	11

Is there a trend in sales? In other words, is there any correlation between the year and the number of units sold?

Solution

2.10 Workings

Let 19X1 to 19X5 be years 0 to 4

Year	x	y	xy	x^2	y^2
19X1	0	20	0	0	400
19X2	1	18	18	1	324
19X3	2	15	30	4	225
19X4	3	14	42	9	196
19X5	4	11	44	16	121
	$\Sigma x = 10$	$\Sigma y = 78$	$\Sigma xy = 134$	$\Sigma x^2 = 30$	$\Sigma y^2 = 1,266$

$(\Sigma x)^2 = 100$ $(\Sigma y)^2 = 6,084$

n = 5

$$r = \frac{5(134) - (10)(78)}{\sqrt{[5(30) - 100][5(1,266) - 6,084]}}$$

$$= \frac{670 - 780}{\sqrt{(150 - 100)(6,330 - 6,084)}} \qquad = \frac{-110}{\sqrt{(50)(246)}}$$

$$= \frac{-110}{\sqrt{12,300}} \qquad = \frac{-110}{110.90536}$$

$$r = -0.992$$

2.11 There is partial negative correlation between the year of sale and units sold. The value of r is close to -1, therefore a high degree of correlation exists, although it is not quite perfect correlation. This means that there is a clear downward trend in sales, which is close to being a *straight* downward trend line.

Interpretation of r

2.12 The correlation coefficient, r, will be positive if y increases, and negative if y decreases, as x increases.

2.13 The numerical value of r varies between zero (no relationship) and 1 (perfect linear relationship). Intermediary values of r are best interpreted by means of r^2, the *coefficient of determination*.

The coefficient of determination indicates the proportion of changes in the value of y that can be predicted from changes in the value of x. If r = 0.985, r^2 = 0.97, which indicates that 97% of variations in the value of y (in our previous example, sales) can be predicted by changes in the value of x (in our example, advertising costs). This leaves only 3% of variations in y to be explained in other ways, or by other factors.

2.14 Here is a list of typical values of r and how we might describe the relationship.

Value of r	Value of r^2	Description of relationship
± 1	100%	perfect
± 0.9	81%	extremely strong
± 0.8	64%	very strong
± 0.7	49%	strong
± 0.5	25%	some relationship but not strong
below 0.5		only a weak relationship
0	0%	no relationship

2.15 *Values of r and scattergrams*

(a) If r = ± 1, the scattergram will show a perfect straight line.

(b) If r = ± 0.9, the points will lie in a narrow band either side of the 'line of best fit'.

(c) As r reduces in value, the band of points becomes wider.

(d) When r = 0, then the points will show no pattern at all.

Warnings about interpreting r

2.16 Low values of r mean that there is no linear relationship between x and y. There may be a strong curved relationship which only a scattergram will show. For example consider the following scattergram.

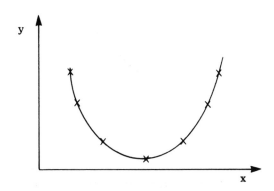

If the formula for r were used in a situation such as this, a low value of r would be obtained, suggesting that very little correlation exists, whereas in fact the two sets of variables are perfectly correlated by a non-linear relationship. There are methods of testing correlations of this type, but they are outside the scope of the syllabus.

2.17 High values of r do not mean that changes in the value of x *cause* changes in the value of y. If there is strong correlation, this does not mean that one thing causes another, only that one thing can be used to *predict* another with reasonable confidence in the likely accuracy of the prediction. For example there might be a high correlation between, say, sales of televisions and sales of cars since both will tend to reflect the general level of prosperity. It would be quite wrong to conclude that people buy cars because they possess televisions! Unexpected correlations often result from a third factor, such as the weather or the state of the economy, to which both variables relate.

> *The degree of correlation indicates 'power of prediction'* not cause and effect.

2.18 Too little data can result in misleading and unreliable results. With samples of less than ten pairs of values, only values of r very close to 1 can be relied upon at all. In this text, and also in your exam, small samples are generally used in order to make the examples simple.

> In an examination question you might be expected to conclude for small values of n that if r is greater than 0.9 or a higher negative value than -0.9, a high degree of positive or negative correlation appears to exist.

2.19 *Don't extrapolate*

'Extrapolation' means drawing conclusions beyond the range of the data. We cannot assume that the value of r still holds beyond the range of x values that we used in calculating it. Relationships are often approximately linear within a narrow range of x values but curved outside that range. Consider the following example.

6: CORRELATION

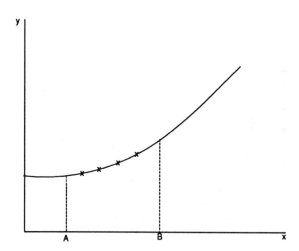

For x values between A and B the above curve is approximately linear and will give a high value of r but in general the relationship is curved.

3. RANK CORRELATION

Spearman's rank correlation coefficient R or r_s

3.1 The coefficient of correlation r that has been described is the most commonly used, and it is sometimes known as the Pearsonian correlation coefficient r, to distinguish it from another coefficient, Spearman's R.

> A rank correlation coefficient measures how well the *ranking* of values of one variable correlates with the ranking of values of another variable.

Ranking means putting items in order, 1st, 2nd, 3rd, 4th and so on. The difference between Spearman's correlation coefficient and the Pearsonian r is that it is not concerned with absolute values, only ranking.

3.2 Examples of ranking, and correlation between ranking, might be as follows.

(a) Asking two interviewees in a market survey to list six breakfast cereals in order of preference. The ranking given to the six cereals by each interviewee could then be correlated.

(b) Asking two panel members of a television rating panel to list ten television programmes in their order of preference.

(c) Comparing the rankings awarded by two different judges to songs in a song contest, or to competitors in a beauty competition or talent competition.

3.3 The examples might suggest to you that ranking and Spearman's correlation coefficient are applicable when we wish to compare *preferences*, or possibly characteristics or *attributes*.

3.4 Like the Pearsonian correlation coefficient, Spearman's rank correlation coefficient has a value ranging from -1 to +1. The formula is given in your exam and is as follows.

6: CORRELATION

$$R = 1 - \frac{6\Sigma d^2}{n(n^2-1)}$$

where R is the rank correlation coefficient
n is the number of items being ranked by two people in two different ways
d is the difference between one ranking and the other ranking for each item.
For example, if an item is first in one ranking and fourth in the other ranking, d would be either +3 or -3.

Example

3.5 In a survey of television viewers in Scotland and in Wales, seven television programmes were ranked as follows in order of preference.

TV Programme	Scotland	Wales
Coronation Street	1st	2nd
Neighbours	3rd	5th
ITN News	4th	4th
Playschool	2nd	6th
Songs of Praise	5th	1st
Panorama	7th	7th
Blue Peter	6th	3rd

How closely correlated are viewing preferences in Scotland and Wales, as measured by Spearman's rank correlation coefficient?

Solution

3.6

	Scotland rank	Wales rank	d	d^2
Coronation Street	1	2	-1	1
Neighbours	3	5	-2	4
ITN News	4	4	0	0
Playschool	2	6	-4	16
Songs of Praise	5	1	4	16
Panorama	7	7	0	0
Blue Peter	6	3	3	9
				46

n = 7

$$\text{Spearman's R} = 1 - \frac{6(46)}{7(7^2-1)} = 1 - \frac{276}{7(48)}$$

$$= 1 - 0.82$$
$$= 0.18$$

The correlation is very low.

103

Calculation note: when you list the values of d, you can omit the negative signs if you wish since they will vanish when you find d^2. If you do this, you should entitle the column |d| instead of d. The *modulus* of d (or indeed of any other number) is written as |d| and it means the numerical value of d with negative signs ignored.

The interpretation of R

3.7 R is interpreted in exactly the same way as r with the proviso that it measures the relationship between rankings and not between actual values of the variables.

Finding R for unranked data

3.8 First we have to rank the values in order of magnitude, calling the smallest number 1, the next number 2 and so on. If two values of x (or of y) are the same, we have to rank them equally. We give them the average of the ranks they would have had if they had been different. An example might help illustrate this process.

Example

3.9 Month	Advertising £	Rank	Sales units	Rank	|d|	d^2
January	1,000	7.5	8,200	8	0.5	0.25
February	800	4	6,700	4	0	0
March	1,100	9	8,700	9	0	0
April	1,200	10	9,400	10	0	0
May	700	3	6,600	3	0	0
June	1,000	7.5	7,900	7	0.5	0.25
July	1,500	12	10,200	12	0	0
August	500	1	5,800	1	0	0
September	900	5.5	7,200	5	0.5	0.25
October	900	5.5	7,600	6	0.5	0.25
November	1,400	11	10,000	11	0	0
December	600	2	6,400	2	0	0

$\Sigma d^2 = \underline{1.00}$

For advertising expenditures, August has the lowest value (£500) and is ranked 1. December is next with £600 and is ranked 2 and so on.

September and October have the same expenditure (£900). If they had been different, they would have been ranked 5th and 6th. Since they are equal, they both have the rank $\frac{5+6}{2} = 5.5$.

Similarly January and June would be 7th and 8th if they had been different, so we rank them both 7.5. There are no other *tied rankings* amongst the rest of the x or y values.

Solution

3.10 $\Sigma d^2 = 1.00$ $n = 12$

$$R = 1 - \frac{6\Sigma d^2}{n(n^2-1)} = 1 - \frac{6 \times 1.00}{12(144-1)}$$

$$= 1 - \frac{6}{12 \times 143} = 1 - \frac{6}{1,716} = 1 - 0.003$$

$$= 0.997$$

This result tallies very closely with the result $r = 0.985$ obtained in the exercise following paragraph 2.7 and shows an extremely strong positive relationship.

Which correlation coefficient to use

3.11 *For ranked data* R should be used since it will give exactly the same result as r and is a lot easier.

3.12 *For unranked data*, in general r should be used since information is lost about the actual values when we rank data and so r gives a more informed measure of the relationship than does R.

3.13 If the linearity of the actual values is important, as it is when we find the equation of the line of best fit and use it to make estimates, r must be used. This is dealt with in the next chapter.

3.14 If linearity is not important in that you want to investigate the relationship between the variables but have no interest in whether it is linear or curved, it might be easier to deliberately rank the data and calculate R.

4.   USE OF CALCULATORS IN LR MODE

4.1 Linear regression (LR) mode will provide all the Σ values you need in order to calculate r as well as the value of r itself. It could be very useful as a check on your calculations in the exam. It cannot be used to find R. Do not forget to show all your workings. Only use the calculator as a final check.

Method

4.2 *Step 1*   Put calculator into LR mode   MODE   2

   Step 2   Clear any previous data   SHIFT   AC

   Step 3   Input the data   x value [(---   y value M+

Example

4.3

x	y
2	9
3	11
1	7
4	13
3	11
5	15

Input: 2 [(---]   9 [M+]   3 [(---]   11 [M+]   and so on.

Step 4   Output

[K out]   [3]   gives n = 6, number of pairs of data

[K out]   [2]   gives $\Sigma x = 18$

[K out]   [1]   gives $\Sigma x^2 = 64$

[K out]   [4]   gives $\Sigma y^2 = 766$

[K out]   [5]   gives $\Sigma y = 66$

[K out]   [6]   gives $\Sigma xy = 218$

All of these symbols are shown in black beneath the relevant number buttons.

[SHIFT]   [9]   gives r = 1

The symbol r is shown beneath the [9] button in orange. SHIFT gives symbols written in orange whereas KOUT gives symbols written in black.

These results tally exactly with those obtained in paragraph 2.6 for the same data.

4.4   Remember that in your exam you will be expected to tabulate the data and to show all workings as we did in paragraph 2.6.

5.   CONCLUSION

5.1   We have seen how the linear relationship between the values of two variables can be investigated either by drawing a scattergram or by calculating a correlation coefficient.

5.2   Having calculated the correlation coefficient you should know how to interpret it and how to interpret the coefficient of determination. You should be aware of the various ways in which correlation coefficients can be misinterpreted.

5.3   The next stage is to calculate an equation which represents the relationship, provided that the variables are strongly correlated. This is described in the following chapter.

TEST YOUR KNOWLEDGE

The numbers in brackets refer to paragraphs of this chapter

1. Draw a sketch diagram to illustrate data which is

    (i)   perfectly positively correlated (1.10(i))
    (ii) partially negatively correlated (1.11(ii))
    (iii) uncorrelated. (1.12)

2. Explain the meaning of a calculated value of r = + 1. (2.4)

3. Interpret a calculated coefficient of determination r^2 = 0.97. (2.13)

4. What does a rank correlation coefficient measure? (3.1)

Now try illustrative questions 13 to 16

Chapter 7

REGRESSION LINES

This chapter covers the following topics.

1. The line of best fit
2. The method of least squares

---

1. THE LINE OF BEST FIT

1.1 If the relationship between two variables is linear then the line on which all pairs of values will lie must have an equation of the following form.

   y = a + bx

where a and b are constants. This equation can be drawn on a graph as shown below.

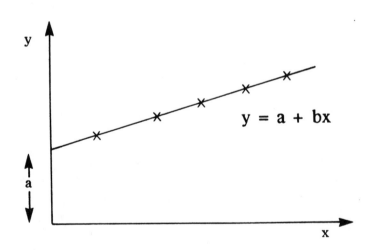

a is equal to the value of y when x = 0 and b is the gradient or slope of the line.

7: REGRESSION LINES

1.2 In the previous chapter on correlation, a scatter diagram of partly correlated variables was shown as follows.

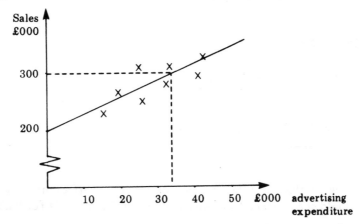

1.3 For example, a company may have discovered that there is a high degree of positive correlation between the amount of money spent each year on advertising, and the volume of sales turnover. The company's management may wish to use the relationship to forecast what level of sales might be expected if a given amount of money is allocated to the advertising budget for the coming year.

1.4 If they prepare a graph of advertising costs/sales turnover and draw in the line that seems to fit the points best, such an estimate can be made, for example if £35,000 is spent on advertising, sales of around £300,000 might be reasonably expected.

Obviously, this line could be drawn by eye after examining the points but this may not be very accurate. Regression analysis is concerned with finding the 'line of best fit', using a statistical method to give the most accurate estimate possible of the equation of the line.

Graphical method

1.5 It can be shown that the line of best fit must pass through the point represented by the arithmetic mean of the two sets of variables. Using this information the line of best fit can be drawn graphically.

   (a) Calculate the arithmetic means of the two sets of variables.
   (b) Plot the point corresponding to these figures on the scatter diagram.
   (c) Draw a line through this point lying as evenly as possible through the other points.

Although this method will be more accurate than drawing in the line by eye, it obviously suffers from the same drawback - the judgement of the person drawing the graph.

2. THE METHOD OF LEAST SQUARES

2.1 A 'line of best fit' of the two sets of data can be calculated by the method of least squares. This method is based on finding an equation for the line in the following form.

   $y = a + bx$

where a and b are 'constants' whose values are given by the following formulae, which are given in your exam.

2.2 | The best line is y = a + bx, where:

$$b = \frac{n\Sigma xy - \Sigma x\Sigma y}{n\Sigma x^2 - (\Sigma x)^2}$$

$$a = \bar{y} - b\bar{x} \quad ie \quad a = \frac{\Sigma y}{n} - \frac{b\Sigma x}{n}$$

where n is the number of 'pairs' of data.

2.3 If you refer back to the formula for the correlation coefficient, r, given in the previous chapter, you should see a marked similarity between the formula for b above and the formula for r.

2.4 The line determined by these equations represents *the regression of y upon x*. It is very important that x is the independent variable and y is the dependent variable, if we wish to forecast values of y from values of x. The regression line of x on y will be a different line, unless x and y are perfectly correlated.

First example: calculating a regression line

2.5 You are given the following data about output at a factory and costs of production over the past five months.

Month	Output (000s units) (x)	Costs (£'000) (y)
1	20	82
2	16	70
3	24	90
4	22	85
5	18	73

There is a high degree of correlation between output and costs, and so it is decided to forecast costs using the least squares method.

Required

(a) Calculate a formula to determine the expected level of costs, for any given volume of output.

(b) Predict total costs if output is 22,000 units.

Solution

2.6 *Workings*

x	y	xy	x^2
20	82	1,640	400
16	70	1,120	256
24	90	2,160	576
22	85	1,870	484
18	73	1,314	324
$\Sigma x = 100$	$\Sigma y = 400$	$\Sigma xy = 8,104$	$\Sigma x^2 = 2,040$

n = 5 (There are five pairs of data for x and y values)

$$b = \frac{n\Sigma xy - \Sigma x\Sigma y}{n\Sigma x^2 - (\Sigma x)^2}$$

$$= \frac{5(8,104) - (100)(400)}{5(2,040) - (100)^2}$$

$$= \frac{40,520 - 40,000}{10,200 - 10,000} = \frac{520}{200}$$

$$= 2.6$$

$$a = \bar{y} - b\bar{x}$$

$$= \frac{400}{5} - 2.6\left(\frac{100}{5}\right)$$

$$= 28$$

so y = 28 + 2.6x
where y = total cost, in £'000s
       x = output, in 000s units.

2.7 Thus, if the output is 22,000 units, we would expect costs to be, in £'000s:

28 + 2.6 (22)

= 85.2, ie £85,200.

Which variable to call y

2.8 (a) The dependent variable should be called y. In the previous example it is reasonable to assume that costs depend on the quantity of output, so costs were called y and output was called x.

(b) If you have to use the regression line to predict a value of one of the variables, then that variable must be called y. In the previous example we wanted to predict costs, so costs had to be called y.

(c) If you are asked to find, say, the regression line of costs on output, the first of the two variables to be mentioned (ie costs) must be y.

Exercise

Using the data on advertising and sales given in the exercise after paragraph 2.7 of the previous chapter, find the equation of the regression line of sales on advertising and predict the likely sales in a month when advertising expenditure is £950.

Solution

$$b = \frac{n\Sigma xy - \Sigma x\Sigma y}{n\Sigma x^2 - (\Sigma x)^2} \qquad a = \bar{y} - b\bar{x}$$

so we need columns entitled x, y, x^2 and xy. This has already been done in the previous chapter, giving

$n = 12$ $\quad \Sigma x = 116$ $\quad \Sigma y = 94.7$
$\quad\quad\quad \Sigma x^2 = 1,222$ $\quad \Sigma xy = 962.9$

so $\quad b = \dfrac{12 \times 962.9 - 116 \times 94.7}{12 \times 1,222 - 116^2} = \dfrac{569.6}{1,208}$

$\quad\quad = 0.4715$

and $a = \bar{y} - b\bar{x} = \dfrac{\Sigma y}{n} - b\dfrac{\Sigma x}{n}$

$\quad\quad = \dfrac{94.7}{12} - 0.4715 \times \dfrac{116}{12}$

$\quad\quad = 7.8917 - 4.5578$

$\quad\quad = 3.3339$

The regression equation is $y = a + bx$

ie $y = 3.33 + 0.47x$

where y gives sales in £'000 and x is advertising costs in £'00.

If advertising is £950 then x = 9.5 and the prediction of y is given by

$\quad y = 3.33 + 0.47 \times 9.5 = 7.795$

Hence predicted sales are £7,795 or £7,800 if we round to two significant figures.

2.9 The following points can be made about this exercise.

(a) In this exercise you were given that y = sales. You could usefully check however that, applying the criteria given in the previous paragraph, it is correct to call sales y.

(b) You may notice that in the calculation of 'b' we kept four decimal places of accuracy until after we had found 'a'. We then rounded to two decimal places. It is a good general rule to keep plenty of accuracy in the workings but then to round final answers to some extent.

(c) It is important to note the units being used. In our exercise a very frequent source of error would be to substitute $x = 950$ rather than $x = 9.5$.

Reliability of forecasts

2.10 If there is a perfect linear relationship between x and y (ie $r = \pm 1$) then we can predict y from any given value of x with absolute certainty. Otherwise there is an element of uncertainty about any prediction.

2.11 If correlation is high (for example $r = 0.9$) the actual values will all lie quite close to the regression line and so predictions should not be far out. If correlation is below about 0.7, predictions will only give a very rough guide as to the likely value of y.

2.12 As with any forecasting process, the amount of data available is very important. Even if correlation is high, if we have less than about ten pairs of values, we must regard any forecast as being somewhat unreliable.

2.13 When calculating a line of best fit, there will be a range of values for x. In the example in paragraphs 2.5 to 2.6, the line $y = 28 + 2.6x$ was predicted from data with output values ranging from $x = 16$ to $x = 24$. Depending on the degree of correlation between x and y, we might safely use the estimated line of best fit to predict values for y in the future, provided that the value of x remains within the range 16 to 24. We would be on less 'safe' ground if we used the formula to predict a value for y when $x = 10$, or 30, or any other value outside the range 16 to 24, because we would have to assume that the trend line applies outside the range of x values used to establish the line in the first place.

(a) *Interpolation* means using a line of best fit to predict a value within the two extreme points of the observed range.
(b) *Extrapolation* means using a line of best fit to predict a value outside the two extreme points.

2.14 When linear regression analysis is used for forecasting a time series (ie when the x values represent time) this assumption - ie that the trend line can be extrapolated into the future – must be adopted. It might not necessarily be a good assumption to make!

> When asked to comment on the reliability of a forecast you should consider the following.
>
> (a) The correlation.
> (b) The sample size.
> (c) Whether the forecast was obtained by interpolation.
>
> High correlation, a large set of data and interpolation are all necessary in order to obtain very reliable forecasts.

The meaning of 'least squares'

2.15 The term 'squares' in 'least squares regression analysis' refers to the squares of the differences between actual values and predicted values given by the regression line of best fit. 'Least squares' means that the line of best fit that is calculated is the one that minimises the total amount of the 'squared differences' between actual values used to calculate the line and the corresponding values on the estimated line.

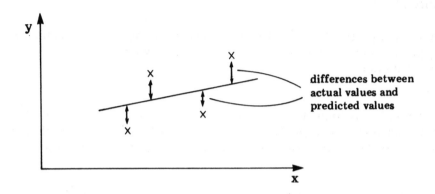

The line of regression is calculated so that the sum of the squares of these differences is kept to a minimum; hence the term 'least squares'.

2.16 There are three expressions all of which are used to describe the regression line.

(a) Regression line.
(b) Line of best fit.
(c) Least squares line.

2.17 In an exam you should assume that the equation of the line is to be calculated rather than obtained graphically from a scattergram unless the latter is specifically requested.

The interpretation of 'a' and 'b'

2.18 In the example of paragraph 2.5 we obtained the equation $y = 28 + 2.6x$ where $y = $ cost in £'000 and $x = $ output in 000's units. Thus $a = 28$ and $b = 2.6$.

2.19 If $x = 0$ (ie there is no output), $y = 28$ (ie cost is £28,000). In general 'a' is the value of y when $x = 0$. However care must be taken in this interpretation since $x = 0$ is often outside the range of the data, as it is in the example mentioned. The estimate that $y = 28$ must therefore be regarded as not very reliable.

2.20 If x increases from 0 to 2, y will increase by 2.6 and this same increase will occur whenever x increases by two units. In general 'b' is the increase in y corresponding to a unit increase in x.

2.21 In the above example therefore:

a = 28 tells us that fixed costs are £28,000
b = 2.6 tells us that costs increase by £2,600 for each extra thousand units produced.

Exercise

If $y = 3.33 + 0.47x$ where y = sales in £'000 and x = advertising costs in £'00, interpret the values of 'a' and 'b'.

Solution

a = 3.33 is the value of y when x = 0. Hence it is the value of sales in £'000 when there is no expenditure on advertising.

b = 0.47 is the increase in sales in £'000 for each increase of 1 in x, ie for each increase of £100 in advertising.

We can therefore say that if there is no expenditure on advertising, sales will be £3,330 in the period and each increase of £100 in advertising expenditure will be associated with an increase of £470 in sales.

However we must warn that x = 0 is outside the range of the data (which is that of the exercise following paragraph 2.8) and hence the figure of £3,330 cannot be relied upon.

Graphing the regression line

2.22 Sometimes in exams students are required to produce a scattergram, to calculate the regression equation and then to plot it on the graph.

2.23 Consider the example $y = 28 + 2.6x$, where y is cost in £'000 and x is output in 000s units and where x ranges from 16 to 24.

Choose any two convenient values of x within the range of the data and calculate the y values to which they correspond.

2.24 If x = 16, $y = 28 + 2.6 \times 16 = 69.6$
If x = 20, $y = 28 + 2.6 \times 20 = 80$

You can now plot these two points and the regression line is given by joining them.

Using a calculator in LR mode

2.25 Full instructions for working in LR mode were given in the previous chapter on correlation. The summations you require to find 'a' and 'b' are Σx, Σy, Σx^2 and Σxy and these can be obtained as previously stated.

2.26 The formula given in your exam is $a = \bar{y} - b\bar{x}$. If you wish you can check your values of $\bar{x}$ and $\bar{y}$ by pressing [SHIFT][1] and [SHIFT][4].

2.27 You can check your values of 'a' and 'b' by pressing [SHIFT][7] and [SHIFT][8] under which you will see A and B written in orange.

2.28 Suppose you wish to predict the value of y for, say, x = 20. This is given by pressing 20 followed by [---)]] . Under this button you will see $\hat{y}$, pronounced 'y cap', written in blue. $\hat{y}$ is the symbol we use for estimates of y. Estimates are always indicated by putting a 'cap' on them. For example, the estimate of a mean μ would be written as $\hat{\mu}$.

Second example: calculating a regression line (time series)

2.29 Sales of product B over the seven year period 19X1 to 19X7 were as follows.

Year	Sales of B (in 000s)
19X1	22
19X2	25
19X3	24
19X4	26
19X5	29
19X6	28
19X7	30

There is high correlation between time and the volume of sales. Calculate the trend line of sales.

Solution

2.30 *Workings*   n = 7

Year	x	y	xy	x²
19X1	0	22	0	0
19X2	1	25	25	1
19X3	2	24	48	4
19X4	3	26	78	9
19X5	4	29	116	16
19X6	5	28	140	25
19X7	6	30	180	36
	$\Sigma x = 21$	$\Sigma y = 184$	$\Sigma xy = 587$	$\Sigma x^2 = 91$

Where $y = a + bx$

$$b = \frac{7(587) - (21)(184)}{7(91) - (21)(21)}$$

$$= \frac{245}{196}$$

$$b = 1.25$$

$$a = \frac{184}{7} - \frac{1.25\,(21)}{7}$$

$$= 22.5357, \text{ say } 22.5$$

$$y = 22.5 + 1.25x \text{ where } x = 0 \text{ in 19X1, } x = 1 \text{ in 19X2 and so on.}$$

2.31 Using this trend line, predicted sales in 19X8 (x = 7) would be, in 000s units,

$$22.5 + (1.25)(7) = 31.25$$

Similarly, for 19X9 (x = 8) predicted sales would be, in 000s units,

$$22.5 + (1.25)(8) = 32.50$$

2.32 The actual sales and the trend could be shown on a time series graph as follows.

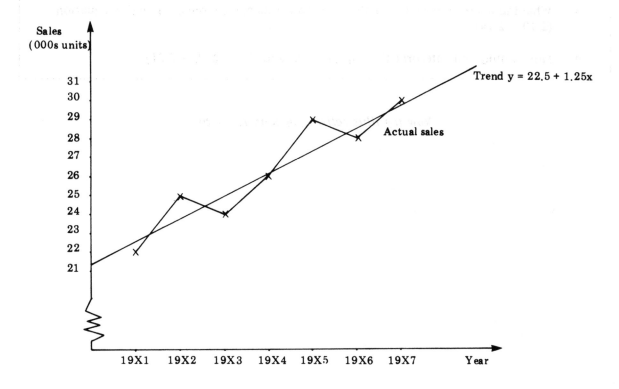

3. CONCLUSION

3.1 We have now seen the following.

(a) How the degree of correlation between two variables can be measured by the correlation coefficient.

(b) How a line of best fit can be calculated by regression analysis.

3.2 Mathematically, there is a very close link between regression analysis and correlation. Regression analysis is concerned with quantifying the *nature of the relationship between* two variables, whereas correlation is concerned with the *degree* of that relationship.

3.3 It is extremely important that you should master the techniques of scatter diagrams, measuring correlation and calculating a line of best fit by the least squares method. You are strongly advised to attempt the illustrative questions for this chapter. It is virtually certain that there will be a question on correlation or regression in your exam.

TEST YOUR KNOWLEDGE

The numbers in brackets refer to paragraphs of this chapter

1. How could you obtain a regression line graphically? (1.5)

2. How do you decide which variable to call y? (2.8)

3. What factors influence the reliability of forecasts made from a regression equation? (2.10 - 2.14)

4. How would you interpret the values of 'a' and 'b'? (2.18 - 2.21)

Now try illustrative questions 17 to 20

Chapter 8

TIME SERIES ANALYSIS

This chapter covers the following topics.

1. Introduction to time series
2. Components of a time series
3. Analysing a time series
4. Time series models
5. Forecasting
6. Seasonal adjustment

---

1. INTRODUCTION TO TIME SERIES

1.1 A time series is a series of figures or values recorded over time. Examples of a time series are as follows.

(a) Output at a factory each day for the last month.
(b) Monthly sales over the last two years.
(c) Total costs per annum for the last ten years.
(d) The Retail Price Index each month for the last ten years.
(e) The number of people employed by a company each year for the last 20 years.

1.2 A graph of a time series is called a historigram. The following time series can be shown as a historigram.

Year	*Sales* £'000
19X1	20
19X2	21
19X3	24
19X4	23
19X5	27
19X6	30
19X7	28

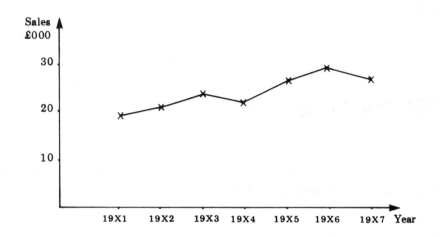

The horizontal, 'x' axis is always chosen to represent time, and the vertical axis represents the values of the data recorded.

2. COMPONENTS OF A TIME SERIES

2.1 There are several features of a time series which it may be necessary to identify. These are as follows.

(a) A trend.
(b) Seasonal variations or fluctuations.
(c) Cycles, or cyclical variations.
(d) Non-recurring, random variations. These may be caused by unforeseen circumstances, such as a political change in the government of the country, a war, the collapse of a company, technological change, a fire and so on.

Trend

2.2 A trend is the underlying long-term movement over time in the values of the data recorded. In the following examples of time series, there are three types of trend.

	Output per hour (units)	Cost per unit £	Number of employees
19X4	30	1.00	100
19X5	24	1.08	103
19X6	26	1.20	96
19X7	22	1.15	102
19X8	21	1.18	103
19X9	17	1.25	98
	(A)	(B)	(C)

(a) In time series (A) there is a *downward* trend in the output per hour over the six year period. Output per hour did not fall every year, because it went up between 19X5 and 19X6, but the long-term movement is clearly a downward one.

(b) In time series (B) there is an *upward* trend in the cost per unit. Although unit costs went down in 19X7 from a higher level in 19X6, the basic movement over time is one of rising costs.

(c)   In time series (C) there is no clear movement up or down, and the number of employees remained fairly constant around the 100 level. The trend is therefore a *static*, or level one.

2.3   A trend may be of great significance to a manager who will want to know whether the company's results are on an improving or a worsening trend. The difficulty is to isolate a trend from the other temporary factors causing variations in results over time.

Seasonal variations

2.4   Seasonal variations are short-term fluctuations in recorded values, due to different circumstances which prevail and affect results at different times of the year, days of the week, time of day, etc. Examples are as follows.

(a)   The sales of ice cream will be higher in summer than in winter, and sales of overcoats will be higher in autumn than in spring.

(b)   Shops might expect higher volumes of sales before Christmas, or in their winter and summer sales.

(c)   Sales might be higher on a Friday and Saturday than on a Monday.

(d)   The telephone network may be heavily used at certain times of the day (for example mid-morning and mid-afternoon) and much less used at other times (for example in the middle of the night).

2.5   'Seasonal' is a term which may appear to refer to the seasons of the year, but its meaning in time series analysis is somewhat broader, as the examples given above should illustrate.

Example: trend and seasonal variations

2.6   The number of customers served by a company of travel agents over the past four years has been as follows.

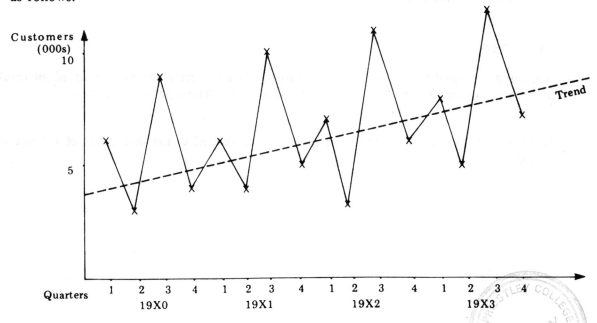

In this example, there would appear to be large seasonal fluctuations in demand, but there is also a basic upward trend in the total volume of customers.

Cyclical variations

2.7 Cyclical variations are medium-term changes in results caused by factors or circumstances which prevail for a while, then go away, and then come back again in a repetitive cycle. 'Cycles' have been compared to the ups and downs of 'wave' movements, and in business they are commonly associated with economic cycles, and successive booms and slumps in the economy. Economic cycles may come and go every few years, and variations caused by cyclical variations are therefore longer term than seasonal variations.

3. ANALYSING A TIME SERIES

3.1 The main problem we are concerned with in time series analysis is how to identify the trend, seasonal variations, cyclical variations and random one-off causes in a set of results over a period of time.

3.2 You need to be aware of cyclical and random variations, but the most common problem in a time series analysis is the separation of seasonal variations and a basic trend.

3.3 There are three principal methods of separating a trend from seasonal variations.

   (a) *Inspection:* the trend line can be drawn by 'eye' on a graph in such a way that it appears to lie evenly between the recorded points.

   (b) *Regression analysis by the least squares method:* this is a statistical technique to calculate the 'line of best fit'. This method, described in the previous chapter, makes the assumption that the trend line, whether up or down, is a straight line. (This technique is also used in forecasting future results, in combination with moving average analysis).

   (c) *Moving averages:* this method attempts to remove seasonal (or cyclical) variations by a process of averaging.

Moving averages

3.4 A moving average is an average, taken at the end of each successive time period, of the result of a fixed number of previous periods including the current period just ended.

3.5 Since it is an average of several time periods, it is related to the mid-point of the overall period.

Example: moving averages

3.6

Year	Sales (units)
19X0	390
19X1	380
19X2	460
19X3	450
19X4	470
19X5	440
19X6	500

Required

Take a moving average of the annual sales in a period of:

(a)   3 years;
(b)   5 years.

Solution

3.7   (a)   (i)   Average sales in the three year period 19X0 to 19X2 were

$$\left(\frac{390 + 380 + 460}{3} \right) = \frac{1,230}{3} = 410$$

This average relates to the middle year of the overall period, ie to 19X1.

(ii)   Similarly, average sales in the three year period 19X1 to 19X3 were

$$\left(\frac{380 + 460 + 450}{3} \right) = \frac{1,290}{3} = 430$$

This average relates to the mid-period of the three years, ie to 19X2.

(iii)   The average sales would also be taken of the period 19X2 to 19X4, 19X3 to 19X5 and 19X4 to 19X6, to give the following.

Year	Sales	Moving total of 3 years' sales	Moving average of 3 years' sales (÷ 3)
19X0	390		
19X1	380	1,230	410
19X2	460	1,290	430
19X3	450	1,380	460
19X4	470	1,360	450.3
19X5	440	1,410	470
19X6	500		

Points to note

1.   The moving average series has five values relating to the years 19X1 to 19X5. The original series has seven values from 19X0 to 19X6.

    2.   There is an upward trend in sales, which is perhaps more noticeable from the series of moving averages than from the original series of *actual* sales each year.

(b) (i)   Average sales over the first five years were: $\dfrac{(390 + 380 + 460 + 450 + 470)}{5} = 430$

This relates to the middle year of the period, 19X2.

    (ii)   Similarly, average sales from 19X1 to 19X5 were 440, and from 19X2 to 19X6 were 464.

(iii)

Year	Sales	Moving total of 5 years' sales	Moving average of 5 years' sales ($\div$ 5)
19X0	390		
19X1	380		
19X2	460	2,150	430
19X3	450	2,200	440
19X4	470	2,320	464
19X5	440		
19X6	500		

Points to note

1.   The series of moving averages has only three values for the years 19X2 - 19X4, even though the most recent year is 19X6.

2.   The upward trend in sales is again perhaps more noticeable in the moving average series than in the original series of actual annual sales.

3.8   Before leaving this example, it is necessary to consider another important point, namely: which would be more appropriate, the three year or five year moving average? The answer to this question is that the moving average which is most appropriate will depend on the circumstances and the nature of the time series. In particular, note the following points.

(a)   A moving average which takes an average of the results in many time periods will represent results over a longer term than a moving average of two or three periods.

(b)   On the other hand, with a moving average of results of many time periods, the last expression in the series will be 'out of date' by several periods. In our example, the three year moving average gave us an average for 19X5 whilst the five year moving average gave a more out of date final value relating to 19X4.

(c)   When there is a known cycle where seasonal variations occur, for example of days in the week or of seasons in the year, the most suitable moving average would be one which covers one full cycle.

Moving averages, trend and seasonal variations

3.9   Moving averages can be used to isolate a basic trend from seasonal variations. Suppose, for example, that output at a factory appears to vary with the day of the week. Output over the last three weeks has been as follows.

	Week 1 '000 units	Week 2 '000 units	Week 3 '000 units
Monday	80	82	84
Tuesday	104	110	116
Wednesday	94	97	100
Thursday	120	125	130
Friday	62	64	66

The trend in output is upwards, although ups and downs due to the day of the week should be apparent. Moving averages will enable the trend and seasonal variations to be measured.

3.10 A moving average of five days' output would be taken, as follows.

		Moving total of 5 days' sales	Moving average of 5 days' sales	
Week 1	Monday		-	
	Tuesday		-	
	Wednesday	460	92.0	(Average of Monday Week 1 to Friday Week 1)
	Thursday	462	92.4	(Average of Tuesday Week 1 to Monday Week 2)
	Friday	468	93.6	(Average of Wednesday Week 1 to Tuesday Week 2)
Week 2	Monday	471	94.2	(........ etc)
	Tuesday	476	95.2	
	Wednesday	478	95.6	
	Thursday	480	96.0	
	Friday	486	97.2	
Week 3	Monday	489	97.8	
	Tuesday	494	98.8	
	Wednesday	496	99.2	
	Thursday		-	
	Friday		-	

3.11 The moving averages indicate an upward trend in daily output. This upward trend is fairly consistent, but if it were drawn on a graph, it would not (quite) be a straight line.

Actual results fluctuate up and down according to the day of the week; and the difference between the actual result on any one day and the trend average for that day will be the seasonal variation for the day.

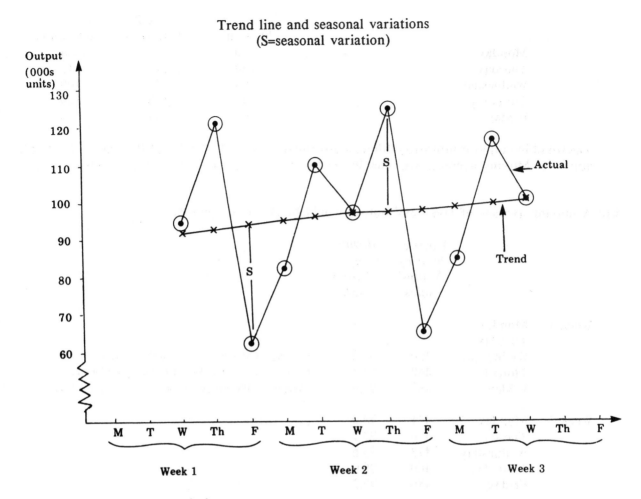

Trend line and seasonal variations
(S=seasonal variation)

Estimating the seasonal variation

3.12 In our example, the seasonal variation on each day would be as follows.

		Actual	Trend	'Seasonal variation'
Week 1	Wednesday	94	92.0	+ 2.0
	Thursday	120	92.4	+ 27.6
	Friday	62	93.6	− 31.6
Week 2	Monday	82	94.2	− 12.2
	Tuesday	110	95.2	+ 14.8
	Wednesday	97	95.6	+ 1.4
	Thursday	125	96.0	+ 29.0
	Friday	64	97.2	− 33.2
Week 3	Monday	84	97.8	− 13.8
	Tuesday	116	98.8	+ 17.2
	Wednesday	100	99.2	+ 0.8

Summary of seasonal variations

3.13	Monday	Tuesday	Wednesday	Thursday	Friday
Week 1			+ 2.0	+ 27.6	- 31.6
Week 2	- 12.2	+ 14.8	+ 1.4	+ 29.0	- 33.2
Week 3	- 13.8	+ 17.2	+ 0.8		
Average	- 13.0	+ 16.0	+ 1.4	+ 28.3	- 32.4

The variation between the actual results on any one particular day and the trend line average is not the same from week to week, but an average of this variation can be taken.

3.14 Our estimate of the 'seasonal' or daily variation is almost complete, but there is one more important step to take. Variations around the basic trend line should cancel each other out, and add up to 0. At the moment, they do not.

	Monday	Tuesday	Wednesday	Thursday	Friday	Total
Estimated daily variation	- 13.00	+ 16.00	+ 1.40	+ 28.30	- 32.40	+ 0.3
Adjustment to reduce total variation to 0	- 0.06	- 0.06	- 0.06	- 0.06	- 0.06	- 0.3
Final estimate of daily variation	- 13.06	+ 15.94	+ 1.34	+ 28.24	- 32.46	0

This might be rounded up or down as follows.
Monday -13; Tuesday +16; Wednesday +1; Thursday +28; Friday -32; Total 0.

3.15 The adjustment carried out above can be summarised as follows.

(a) The average seasonal variations are totalled. Suppose their total is X.
(b) Divide X by the number of 'seasons' involved (ie five days in this case).
(c) Subtract the result from the average seasonal variations.
(d) In the above case the daily variations total to 0.3 which gives 0.06 when divided by 5. This quantity is then subtracted from the average daily variation.

3.16 The resulting adjusted average seasonal variations are called the seasonal *components* or seasonal *effects*.

Moving averages of an even number of results

3.17 In the previous examples, moving averages were taken of the results in an *odd* number of time periods, and the average then related to the mid-point of the overall period.

3.18 If a moving average were taken of results in an *even* number of time periods, the basic technique would be the same, but the mid-point of the overall period would not relate to a single period. For example, if an average were taken of the following four results the average would relate to the mid-point of the period, ie between summer and autumn.

Spring	120	
Summer	90	average 115
Autumn	180	
Winter	70	

3.19 The trend line average figures need to relate to a particular time period, otherwise seasonal variations cannot be calculated. To overcome this difficulty, we take a moving average of the moving average. An example will illustrate this technique.

Example

3.20 Calculate a moving average trend line of the following results, and estimate the seasonal variations.

Year	Quarter	Volume of sales '000s units
19X5	1	600
	2	840
	3	420
	4	720
19X6	1	640
	2	860
	3	420
	4	740
19X7	1	670
	2	900
	3	430
	4	760

Solution

3.21 A moving average of four quarters will be used, since the volume of sales would appear to depend on the season of the year, and one year has four quarterly results. The moving average of four quarters does not relate to any specific time point. It always falls between two quarters. It is therefore easiest to tabulate these calculations if you leave a blank line between quarters.

Year	Quarter	Actual volume of sales	Moving total of 4 quarters' sales	Moving average of 4	Mid-point of 2 moving averages	Seasonal variation
		000s units (A)	000s units (B)	000s units (B ÷ 4)	TREND LINE (C)	(A) - (C)
19X5	1	600				
	2	840				
			2,580	645.0		
	3	420			650	- 230.00
			2,620	655.0		
	4	720			657.5	+ 62.50
			2,640	660.0		
19X6	1	640			660	- 20.00
			2,640	660.0		
	2	860			662.5	+ 197.50
			2,660	665.0		
	3	420			668.75	- 248.75
			2,690	672.5		
	4	740			677.5	+ 62.50
			2,730	682.5		
19X7	1	670			683.75	- 13.75
			2,740	685.0		
	2	900			687.5	+ 212.50
			2,760	690.0		
	3	430				
	4	760				

3.22 The double averaging process, which results in the trend values corresponding to time points, is called *centering* and the trend is a *centered* moving average.

3.23 In practice the 'moving average of 4' column would generally be omitted. We included it in this case to illustrate the double averaging process. In future we will calculate column C directly from column B by adding the moving totals in pairs and dividing the result by 8. This is equivalent to dividing first by 4 and then by 2.

3.24 Seasonal variations are calculated by the method previously described.

	1st Quarter	2nd Quarter	3rd Quarter	4th Quarter	Total
19X5			-230.0	+62.5	
19X6	-20	+197.5	-248.75	+62.5	
19X7	-13.75	+212.5			
Average variation	-16.875	+205.0	-239.375	+62.5	+11.25
Adjust total variation to nil*	- 2.75	- 2.75	- 3.0	- 2.75	-11.25
Estimated seasonal variation	-19.625	+202.25	-242.375	+59.75	0.00
Round to one decimal place	-19.6	+202.2	-242.4	+59.8	0.00
or rounded to the nearest whole number	-20	+202	-242	+60	0

3.25 The adjustment of -11.25 (*) should be divided equally between the four seasons, ie -2.8125 to each quarter's variation. However, a variation to four decimal places would be too exact, and in this solution the adjustments have been allocated as -11/4 = -2.75 to each quarter, with the balancing -0.25 added to the quarter with the largest seasonal variation. Even then, the resulting seasonal variations are stated to more decimal places than the moving average or trend line, and this gives a false impression of accuracy. This is why it is sensible to round the seasonal variations, as shown, to one decimal place or even the nearest whole number.

4. TIME SERIES MODELS

The additive model

4.1 In all the analyses so far in this chapter we have assumed that the value of sales for any quarter, say, is made up of a number of components. For quarterly data those components are the trend, the seasonal component and a residual or random component caused by unpredictable factors.

4.2 We have also assumed that, give or take a little bit of random variation, the actual sales figure at any point will be given by adding the seasonal component to the trend. If the seasonal component is negative this means that we subtract from the trend.

4.3 For example if the trend is 650 and the seasonal component is 100, this means that on average sales should be 100 more than the trend in this quarter. In other words, sales should be about 750.

4.4 This additive model can be summarised as follows.

Actual value = trend + seasonal component + residual component.

More complicated additive models might also include a cyclical component to take account of a longer term economic cycle, and a daily component to allow for the fact that sales vary on different days of the week.

Residuals

4.5 A residual is the difference between:

(a) the value we would predict from the model, namely trend plus seasonal component; and
(b) the actual value.

4.6 The residual is therefore the difference 'left over' which is not explained by the trend line and the seasonal variation. The residual gives some indication of how much actual results were affected by factors other than the trend line and seasonal variations. Large residuals would reduce the reliability of any forecast made and would cast doubts on whether the model being used fits in well with what actually happens.

4.7 In our example we would have the following.

Year	Quarter	Moving average trend	Seasonal variation (to 1 decimal place)	'Prediction'	Actual sales	Residual ('unexplained variance')
1	3rd	650	-242.4	407.6	420	+12.4
	4th	657.5	+ 59.8	717.3	720	+ 2.7
2	1st	660	- 19.6	640.4	640	- 0.4
	2nd	662.5	+202.2	864.7	860	- 4.7
	3rd	668.75	-242.4	426.4	420	- 6.4
	4th	677.5	+ 59.8	737.3	740	+ 2.7
3	1st	683.75	- 19.6	664.2	670	+ 5.8
	2nd	687.5	+202.2	889.7	900	+10.3

4.8 These residuals are quite small when compared to the trend. Even the biggest, 12.4, is only 2% of the trend value of 650. So it looks as if the additive model is a 'good fit' in this case.

Multiplicative model

4.9 Instead of adding or subtracting the seasonal component we could instead increase or decrease the trend by a seasonal percentage. This is a *multiplicative* model.

4.10 Suppose the trend is 650 and the seasonal component is + 10%. That means that on average for the quarter in question, sales are 10% more than the trend. 10% of 650 is 650/10- = 65, so we would expect actual sales of 650 + 65 ie 715.

4.11 You are unlikely to be examined on the multiplicative model but you should be aware of what it means and you should be able to perform simple calculations such as the one above. The multiplicative model is generally found to be better than the additive model when the trend is either increasing or decreasing steeply. This is because the seasonal variations remain proportionate to the level of the trend with this model whereas with the additive model they remain static.

5. FORECASTING

General method

5.1 According to the additive model, the actual value should be given by the trend plus the appropriate seasonal component. If we can predict the trend, then we can predict the actual value by adding the seasonal component.

> Forecast value = trend forecast plus seasonal component

5.2 The problem therefore becomes one of forecasting the trend.

8: TIME SERIES ANALYSIS

Graphical method

5.3 The trend points are graphed and a straight line or a curve is fitted to them. Sometimes trends show sudden jumps or drops and have to be fitted by several lines. See if you can work your own solution to the following problem. You won't get exactly the same answers as ours because fitting a trend line by eye is matter of individual judgement.

5.4 The sales (in £'000) of golf equipment by a large department store is shown for each period of three months as follows.

Quarter	19X4	19X5	19X6	19X7
First		8	20	40
Second		30	50	62
Third		60	80	92
Fourth	24	20	40	

(a) Using an additive model, find the centred moving average trend.
(b) Find the average seasonal variation for each quarter.
(c) Graph the moving averages using a horizontal (time) axis that extends across the whole of 19X8.
(d) Fit a trend line to the points and extend it across 19X8.
(e) Read trend predictions for the four quarters of 19X8 from the line and use them to predict sales for each of the quarters of 19X8.

Solution

5.5

	Quarter	Four quarter moving total	Centred moving total	Moving average(÷8)
19X4	4			
19X5	1			
		122		
	2		240	30
		118		
	3		248	31
		130		
	4		280	35
		150		
19X6	1		320	40
		170		
	2		360	45
		190		
	3		400	50
		210		
	4		432	54
		222		
19X7	1		456	57
		234		
	2			
	3			

(a) The centred moving average trend is shown in the right hand column of the table.

(b) *Seasonal variations*

		Quarter				
		1	*2*	*3*	*4*	*Total*
Year	19X5		0	+29	-15	
	19X6	-20	+5	+30	-14	
	19X7	-17				
	Total	-37	+5	+59	-29	
	Average	-18.5	+2.5	+29.5	-14.5	-1
Adjust total variation to nil		+0.25	+0.25	+0.25	+0.25	+1
Average seasonal variation		-18.25	+2.75	+29.75	-14.25	

(c) and (d)

Golf sales - graph of trend

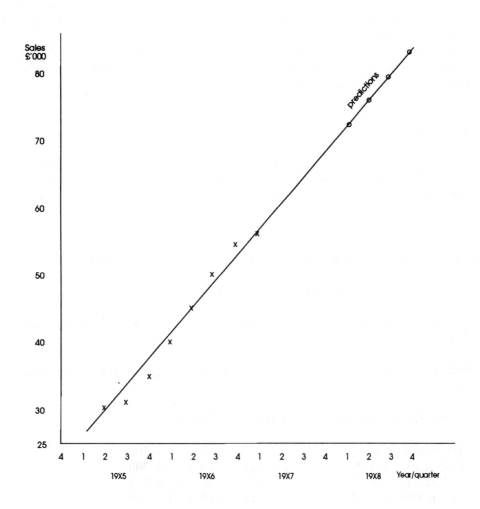

(e)   From the graph the forecasts of the trend for 19X8 are as follows.

	\u00a0	Quarter		
	1	*2*	*3*	*4*
Forecast trend	73	77	81	85

Forecasts of actual sales are given by adding the appropriate seasonal components (or subtracting if they are negative).

	Quarter			
	1	*2*	*3*	*4*
Forecast trend	73	77	81	85
Seasonal component	- 18.25	+ 2.75	+ 29.75	- 14.25
Sales forecast	54.75	79.75	110.75	70.75

Forecast sales for the four quarters of 19X8 are therefore (rounded to nearest £'000).

   £55,000,   £80,000,   £111,000   and £71,000   respectively.

Tutorial note: if there can be said to be a *typical* exam question, the previous example would be that question as far as time series are concerned. Check back carefully if there was anything that you didn't follow. Students often needlessly lose marks in the production of graphs. Did you give your graph a title? Did you label the axes and show the scale clearly? These points might be worth a crucial couple of marks in an exam. Check your graph carefully against ours to see that you missed nothing out.

Regression method

5.6   If the moving average points are reasonably linear, an alternative method of predicting the trend is to find the regression equation as we did in the previous chapter. You could check whether there is a linear trend by finding the correlation coefficient. If it is quite close to 1, this method will give the most reliable predictions.

5.7   For example the data of paragraph 3.20 gives a regression equation

   $y = 644 + 5.39x$ (see workings in paragraph 5.8)

where y is the trend in the volume of sales in 000's units and x is the quarter with the third quarter of 19X5 = 1.

Suppose we want to predict for 19X8. The four quarters of that year correspond to x = 11, 12, 13 and 14.

Trend predictions for 19X8 are therefore as follows.

   1st quarter x = 11 $y = 644 + 5.39 \times 11 = 703$
   2nd quarter x = 12 $y = 644 + 5.39 \times 12 = 709$
   3rd quarter x = 13 $y = 644 + 5.39 \times 13 = 714$
   4th quarter x = 14 $y = 644 + 5.39 \times 14 = 719$

The seasonal components are given in paragraph 3.24 and are - 20, + 202, - 242 and + 60 respectively so predictions of sales for 19X8 are given by

	Quarter			
	1	*2*	*3*	*4*
	'000 units	'000 units	'000 units	'000 units
Trend prediction	703	709	714	719
Seasonal component	- 20	+ 202	- 242	+ 60
Predicted sales	683	911	472	779

5.8 *Detailed workings*. To find the regression equation.

Year	Quarter	x	y	x^2	xy
19X5	3	1	650	1	650
	4	2	657.5	4	1,315
19X6	1	3	660	9	1,980
	2	4	662.5	16	2,650
	3	5	668.75	25	3,343.75
	4	6	677.5	36	4,065
19X7	1	7	683.75	49	4,786.25
	2	8	687.5	64	5,500
		36	5,347.5	204	24,290

$$b = \frac{n\Sigma xy - \Sigma x \Sigma y}{n\Sigma x^2 - (\Sigma x)^2} = \frac{8 \times 24,290 - 36 \times 5,347.5}{8 \times 204 - 36^2}$$

$$= \frac{1,810}{336} = 5.3869$$

$$a = \bar{y} - b\bar{x} = \frac{\Sigma y}{n} - b\frac{\Sigma x}{n} = \frac{5,347.5}{8} - 5.3869 \times \frac{36}{8}$$

$$= 644 \text{ (to three significant figures)}.$$

So the regression equation is

$$y = 644 + 5.39x$$

The rest of the method is shown in the previous paragraph.

Reliability of time series predictions

5.9 The predictions made in the preceding paragraphs are based on the following assumptions.

(a) The trend will continue in future as it has in the past.
(b) The same pattern of seasonal variations will continue.
(c) There will be no unforeseen events that will cause random changes.

5.10 Clearly it is not possible to be sure that these three assumptions will prove correct. At best, time series predictions enable decision makers to say that, all other things being equal, their forecast is what is likely to happen. If unforeseeable events do then occur, decision makers must use their knowledge of the field in question to work out how to modify the predictions.

5.11 Assuming that previous trends and patterns of seasonality do prevail and that there are not unforeseen events, there are two other factors that determine the reliability of results, both of which can be checked statistically.

(a) We can use the correlation coefficient to check that there is in fact a linear trend. If not, there are more sophisticated statistical techniques available that permit the fitting of a curved trend. These are beyond the scope of your syllabus.

(b) We can also check whether or not the additive model really reflects what happens in practice. If the trend is increasing or decreasing, a multiplicative model would generally be better. Models are compared by looking at residuals, the best model being the one that has the smallest residuals.

6. SEASONAL ADJUSTMENT

6.1 One of the problems of time series analysis is that there is a time lag between obtaining the data for a particular quarter and being able to work out the trend for that quarter.

6.2 Consider the data shown in paragraphs 3.20 and 3.21.

	Quarter	Sales	Trend
19X7	1	670	683.75
	2	900	687.5
	3	430	
	4	760	

Although the sales figures are available for the fourth quarter, the most recent trend is located at the second quarter. There is a six month time lag between the two.

6.3 Suppose that a sales promotion had been launched that might have been expected to increase the figures for the fourth quarter. As soon as those figures arrived, we would want to know whether or not it had been effective in increasing the trend. So an instant estimate of the trend would be required. This is given by the process of *seasonal adjustment*.

6.4 We see from paragraph 3.24 that the seasonal component for the fourth quarter is + 60. That means that in this quarter sales are generally 60 more than the trend. We know that the actual sales for the fourth quarter of 19X7 are 760 so it is reasonable to estimate that the trend is 60 less than that value, ie 700.

If sales = trend + seasonal component then trend should be approximately given by trend = sales - seasonal component.

> The seasonally adjusted value is given by actual value - seasonal component and it provides an instant estimate of the trend.

Exercise

Seasonally adjust the sales figures for the final two quarters of 19X1 given the following data. Interpret your results.

	3rd quarter	4th quarter
Value of sales	450	305
Seasonal component	+50	– 100

Solution

The seasonally adjusted figures are given by the actual value minus the seasonal components. Hence they are 450 – 50 = 400 for the third quarter and 305 – (–100) = 305 + 100 = 405 for the fourth quarter.

These values give an instant estimate of the trend for the two quarters concerned.

---

7. CONCLUSION

7.1 This chapter has looked at the components of a time series and how to analyse a time series to determine the trend and seasonal variations.

7.2 We have used an additive model and have shown how residuals can be calculated and used to test if the model fits what happens in reality. When there is not a good fit, a multiplicative model might be used instead.

7.3 We have shown how the trend values and seasonal components can be used to forecast future values, either by fitting a trend line 'by eye' or by using regression.

7.4 Finally we have seen how an instant estimate of the trend can be obtained by the process of seasonal adjustment.

7.5 It is very likely that there will be a question on time series analysis in your exam so it is very important that you should practice these techniques by trying the illustrative questions.

TEST YOUR KNOWLEDGE

The numbers in brackets refer to paragraphs of this chapter

1. Give one example each of a seasonal variation, a cyclical variation and a random variation. (2.1, 2.4, 2.7)

2. Name three ways of isolating the trend in a time series. (3.3)

3. What is a residual? (4.5)

4. Explain the difference between the additive and multiplicative models. (4.9)

5. Under what circumstances is the multiplicative model generally preferred to the additive one? (4.11)

6. How are future values forecast using the additive model? (5.1)

7. What assumptions are made in time series forecasting? (5.9)

8. What is the purpose of seasonal adjustment? (6.3)

Now try illustrative questions 21 to 24

PART D
INDEX NUMBERS

Chapter 9

INDEX NUMBERS

This chapter covers the following topics.

1. Single item index numbers
2. Multi-item price indices
3. Quantity indices
4. Practical problems in constructing an index
5. The limitations of index numbers
6. Published indices

---

1. SINGLE ITEM INDEX NUMBERS

What is an index number?

1.1 A series of values relating to different points in time become *index numbers*, with a particular time point as their *base*, if each value is expressed as a percentage of the value for the base time.

1.2 Most indexed data is annual and so from now on we will refer to 'years' rather than the more clumsy 'time points' but it should be remembered that weekly or quarterly data and so on can also be indexed.

1.3
$$\text{Index for a given year} \quad = \quad \frac{\text{Value for that year}}{\text{Value for base year}} \quad \times \quad 100$$

If, say, 1984 is the base year, we write '1984 = 100'. This is mathematical shorthand for the statement that 'these numbers have been indexed with 1984 as the base year'.

Example

1.4 Index the following data, taken from the Monthly Digest of Statistics, HMSO, November 1982, taking 1976 as the base year.

Sales of potatoes for food in the UK ('000 tonnes)

	1976	1977	1978	1979	1980	1981
Sales	330	382	430	453	460	469

Solution

1.5   The base year is 1976 and the value for that year is 330. Each value in turn must therefore be divided by 330 and multiplied by 100.

	1976	1977	1978	1979	1980	1981
Index of sales (1976 = 100)	100	116	130	137	139	142

Exercise

Index the following data taken from the Monthly Digest, November 1982.

(a)   Sales of sugar (000 tonnes), taking 1976 = 100

	1976	1977	1978	1979	1980
Sales	203.8	203.1	204.9	202.1	191.8

(b)   Sales of eggs (million dozens), taking 1977 = 100

	1977	1978	1979	1980	1981
Sales	96.9	99.6	100.6	94.7	91.6

Solution

(a)   Sugar

	1976	1977	1978	1979	1980
Index of sales (1976 = 100)	100	99.7	100.5	99.2	94.1

(b)   Eggs

	1977	1978	1979	1980	1981
Index of sales (1977 = 100)	100	102.8	103.8	97.7	94.5

Why we use index numbers

1.6   Index numbers enable us to very easily see the change since the base year.

(a)   The percentage increase or decrease is given by subtracting 100.

For example we see from the earlier example that sales of potatoes rose by 16% from 1976 to 1977. Over the two year period 1976 to 1978 they rose by 30%. Over 1976 to 1979 they rose by 37% and so on.

(b)   The ratio of present and base year values is given by dividing by 100 (ie by moving the decimal point two places to the left).

Suppose for instance that an index is a very large figure such as 472. We could subtract 100 and interpret the index as a 372% increase but this might not be very meaningful. Interpretation is easier if we divide by 100 and conclude that values are now 4.72 times what they were in the base year.

1.7   Index numbers enable us to compare very different sets of figures, such as sales of potatoes and sales of sugar, much more easily than if we simply look at the actual sales figures.

1.8   We can see that potato sales rose steadily over the period 1976 to 1980, being 39% up by the end of the period, whilst sugar sales remained very stable until 1980 when they dipped sharply, resulting in an overall drop of approximately 6% since 1976.

Index points

1.9   The potato index rises by three *points* from 139 in 1980 to 142 in 1981. This must not be confused with an increase of three *per cent*.

Three points on an initial value of 139 is actually 3/139 x 100 = 2.2%.

1.10   A points increase in an index is only a percentage increase if it is measured from the base year. For example, the increase of 16 points from 1976 to 1977 is a 16% increase since 1976 is the base year.

1.11   It is important to note that index numbers only show changes relative to the base year. Changes between any other years must be calculated as in paragraph 1.9 above.

The base year

1.12   The choice of a base date or base year is not significant, except that it should be 'representative'. In the construction of a price index, the base year must not be one in which there were abnormally high or low prices for items involved in the index. For example a year in which there is a potato famine or a bread famine would be unsuitable as a base period for the Retail Price Index in the UK.

1.13   *Change of base year*
       We cannot easily compare the sales of sugar and of eggs in the previous exercise because the indices have different base years. We need to recalculate the sugar index with base 1977. This could of course be done using the original sugar data but suppose that data was not available. The recalculation can be done just as well by treating the sugar index numbers as if they were the original data. This will give correct figures except for errors which accumulate due to rounding.

Example

1.14   Using the data from the previous exercise, change the base for sugar sales to 1977.

	1976	1977	1978	1979	1980
Index of sales (1976 = 100)	100	99.7	100.5	99.2	94.1
Index of sales (1977 = 100)	100.3	100	100.8	99.5	94.4

Method. The new base year is 1977 and the value for that year is 99.7. Each other value must therefore be divided by 99.7 and multiplied by 100.

9: INDEX NUMBERS

Exercise

Using the potato sales index in paragraph 1.5 rather than the original data, change the base from 1976 to 1977.

Solution

The new base year is 1977 and the value for that year is 116 so we divide other values by 116 and multiply by 100.

	1976	1977	1978	1979	1980	1981
Index of sales (1976 = 100)	100	116	130	137	139	142
Index of sales (1977 = 100)	86	100	112	118	120	122

1.15 Over a period of time, the fixed base of an index will become rather irrelevant to the decision-making process. In 1991, for example, we would be unlikely to be interested in percentage changes since, say, 1970. The base of the index would need to be changed to a more recent year if the index was to continue to be of value.

1.16 In statistical digests and similar publications, we often encounter series of index numbers in the middle of which a change of base occurs. This is shown by a particular year (19X5 in the following example) having *two* index values instead of the usual *one*.

Example

1.17 A country's retail price index is as follows.

	Year	Index
19X1 = 100	19X3	138.4
	19X4	160.0
	19X5	{193.0
19X5 = 100		{100
	19X6	118.1
	19X7	133.3
	19X8	145.9

Required

(a) Recalculate to give a continuous index with base 19X1.
(b) Recalculate to give a continuous index with base 19X5.

Solution

1.18 (a) The indices for 19X6, 19X7 and 19X8 need to be converted to the base 19X1. This can be done by recognising that they are, respectively, 18.1%, 33.3% and 45.9% greater than the 19X5 index of 193.0 based in 19X1.

To increase a value by 18.1% the easiest method is to multiply it by 118.1% ie by 118.1/100.

Hence the required indices with base 19X1 are as follows.

19X6	193.0	x	$\dfrac{118.1}{100}$	= 227.9
19X7	193.0	x	$\dfrac{133.3}{100}$	= 257.3
19X8	193.0	x	$\dfrac{145.9}{100}$	= 281.6

The continuous index with 19X1 = 100 is therefore as follows.

RPI 19X1 = 100	19X3	19X4	19X5	19X6	19X7	19X8
	138.4	160.0	193.0	227.9	257.3	281.6

(b) The required new base year is 19X5 and the value for that year is 193.0. Divide each value by 193.0 and multiply by 100.

RPI 19X5 = 100	19X3	19X4	19X5	19X6	19X7	19X8
	72	83	100	118	133	146

Notice that we have rounded these final figures to the nearest whole number. This is to avoid spurious accuracy.

1.19 The above process of combining two series of index numbers into a single continuous series is called *splicing* two indices together.

Exercise

Express the following sales index as a single series with base 19X2.

	Year	Sales index
19X0 = 100	19X2	114
	19X3	120
	19X4	{129
19X4 = 100		{100
	19X5	107
	19X6	116

Solution

First convert the entire series to base 19X0 by increasing the 19X4 value of 129 by 7% and 16% respectively, by multiplying by 107/100 and 116/100. Then change the base to 19X2 by dividing throughout by 114 and multiplying by 100.

Sales index	19X2	19X3	19X4	19X5	19X6
19X0 = 100	114	120	129	138.0	149.6
19X2 = 100	100	105	113	121	131

9: INDEX NUMBERS

Chain based index numbers

1.20 All the series of index numbers considered so far have had a fixed base, such as 1976 = 100, and hence percentage changes have always related back to that base. It is often of more interest to know the annual percentage increase. *Chain based* index numbers express each year's value as a percentage of the value for the previous year, and subtracting 100 gives the annual percentage change.

Example

1.21 The following is a chain based index of turnover figures.

	19X1	19X2	19X3	19X4
	105	107	102	108

It shows that from 19X0 to 19X1 turnover rose by 5%, followed by a 7% increase from 19X1 to 19X2 and so on.

1.22 A chain based index can be converted into a fixed base index and vice versa. Suppose in the above example we require the fixed base index with 19X0 = 100.

1.23 We already have the 19X1 value as a percentage of the 19X0 value so the fixed base index for 19X1 remains at 105.

1.24 The 19X2 index is 7% more than 19X1, so we obtain the fixed base index for 19X2 by increasing the index for 19X1 by 7%. We do this by multiplying the 19X1 fixed base index by 107%, ie by 107/100.

1.25 Similarly the 19X3 fixed base index = 19X2 fixed base index multiplied by 102/100 and so on.

Solution

1.26

Year	Index (19X0 = 100)
19X0	100
19X1	105
19X2	$105 \times \dfrac{107}{100} = 112.4$
19X3	$112.4 \times \dfrac{102}{100} = 114.6$
19X4	$114.6 \times \dfrac{108}{100} = 123.8$

Example of conversion from fixed base to chain base

1.27 Convert the potato sales index to a chain based index.

	1976	1977	1978	1979	1980	1981
Potato sales	100	116	130	137	139	142

146

Solution

1.28 We do not know the 1975 figure so we cannot express the 1976 figure as a percentage of it.

For each other year, we express the index for that year as a percentage of the index for the previous year.

Chain index = $\frac{\text{this year's index}}{\text{previous year's index}}$ x 100

	1976	1977	1978	1979	1980	1981
Potato sales chain index	–	116	112	105	101	102

Exercise

(a) Convert the fixed base index to a chain base.

	19X0	19X1	19X2	19X3
Income (19X0 = 100)	100	106	110	117

(b) Convert the chain based index to fixed base 19X2.

	19X2	19X3	19X4	19X5
Sales (chain base)	112	107	110	105

Solution

(a)

	19X0 = 100	Chain base
19X0	100	–
19X1	106	106
19X2	110	104 $\left(= \frac{110}{106} \times 100\right)$
19X3	117	106 $\left(= \frac{117}{110} \times 100\right)$

(b)

	Chain base	19X2 = 100
19X2	112	100
19X3	107	107
19X4	110	118 $\left(= 107 \times \frac{110}{100}\right)$
19X5	105	124 $\left(= 118 \times \frac{105}{100}\right)$

1.29 So far we have dealt with the most simple type of index numbers involving only a single item such as potato sales, although the modifications introduced have been mathematically quite difficult. We must now consider the construction of more complex index numbers which, ironically, is found to be mathematically less demanding.

1.30 The techniques for change of base, splicing and moving between fixed and chain base are equally applicable to multi-item index numbers.

2. MULTI-ITEM PRICE INDICES

2.1 Most practical indices are made up for more than one item. For example suppose that the cost of living index is calculated from only three commodities: bread, tea and caviar, and that the prices for 19X1 and 19X5 were as follows.

	19X1	*19X5*
Bread	20p a loaf	40p a loaf
Tea	25p a packet	30p a packet
Caviar	450p an ounce	405p an ounce

2.2 An examination of these figures reveals three main difficulties.

(a) Two prices have gone up and one has gone down. The index number must be a compromise, produced by averaging.
(b) The prices are given in different units.
(c) There is no indication of the relative importance of each item.

Nothing can be done about difficulty (a), it is a feature of index numbers and must always be borne in mind, but (b) and (c) can be overcome by *weighting*.

Weighted averages

2.3 In an earlier chapter we saw how values (x) occurring with different frequencies (f) could be combined together to produce an average, the mean. The formula for this average is $\Sigma fx/\Sigma f$. Each value is multiplied by its frequency and the results are totalled and then divided by the total frequency.

2.4 Wherever there is a Σ (sigma) in the formula, a column is required which will then be totalled, so the above formula requires a column entitled f and another entitled fx.

2.5 The frequency of a value can be regarded as a measure of its importance, with more frequent values being seen as more important than those which occur less often.

2.6 In constructing index numbers we have to allocate to each item a measure of its importance, which is called the *weight* of that item. In the case of bread, tea and caviar, the weights might be very similar to frequencies. They would probably be the quantities purchased, ie the number of loaves, number of packets of tea and ounces of caviar.

2.7 In other cases quantities would not be a sensible measure of importance. The average household will probably spend its money on only one mortgage whilst it might annually buy 30 tins of baked beans. It would be absurd to weigh baked beans as 30 times more important than mortgages. This problem is overcome in the Retail Price Index by weighting items according to how much the average household spends annually on each item.

2.8   In other cases the importance has to be decided subjectively. For example examiners might feel that a traditional exam was twice as testing as a multichoice exam and they would then allocate a weight of 2 to the traditional exam and 1 to the multichoice exam.

2.9   Whichever way the weights are determined, a weighted average is then calculated in exactly the same manner as an arithmetic mean, with frequencies replaced by weights.

2.10   The formula for the weighted average of values (x) with weights (w) is as follows.

$$\text{Weighted average} = \frac{\Sigma wx}{\Sigma w}$$

Each value is multiplied by its weight and the results are totalled and then divided by the total weight. A column entitled *w* and another entitled *wx* will be required.

Example

2.11   Find a student's weighted average mark over three exams if his results and the weights of the exams are as follows.

Exam	Weight (w)	Result (x)	wx
Statistics	1	60%	60
Law	1	55%	55
Marketing	2	70%	140
$\Sigma w =$	4	$\Sigma wx =$	255

$$\text{Weighted average} = \frac{\Sigma wx}{\Sigma w} = \frac{255}{4} = 63.75\%$$

This is higher than the simple average, $(60 + 55 + 70)/3 = 61.7\%$, because of the larger weight given to the student's high marketing result.

Price indices

2.12   The construction of a price index spanning several items involves two processes.

(a) Weighted averaging.
(b) Indexing.

2.13   There are two different methods of construction depending on the order in which these processes take place.

2.14   *Price relatives indices*
       First the price of each item is indexed relative to the base year and then these individual index numbers are combined by weighted averaging.

2.15 *Aggregative indices*

First the weighted average price is obtained and then the average is indexed relative to the average for the base year.

2.16 *Notation*

The subscript 'o' is used to refer to prices and quantities in the base year and the subscript 'i' refers to the year under consideration.

Thus p_0 = price of an item in the base year
p_1 = price in the year for which the index is being calculated
q_0 = base year quantity bought (or sold)
q_1 = 'current' year quantity

Price relatives indices

2.17 The formula given in the CIM exam is

$$\text{Index} = 100 \times \sum \frac{p_1}{p_0} . w \, / \, \Sigma W$$

Step 1: for each item, find the *price relative* p_1/p_0. This is the same as indexing the price of each item except that multiplication by 100 is left to the end for convenience.

Step 2: multiply each price relative by its weight.

Step 3: total the resulting figures to obtain $\sum \frac{p_1}{p_0} . w$

Step 4: total the weights to obtain ΣW

Step 5: divide as in the formula and multiply by 100 to obtain the overall index.

Example

2.18 Find the price relatives index for bread, tea and caviar using the quantity weights given. The base year is 19X1 and the year under consideration is 19X5.

Item	Quantity	Price in 19X1	Price in 19X5
Bread	6 loaves	20	40
Tea	2 packets	25	30
Caviar	0.067 ounces	450	405

Solution

2.19 First label the prices and quantities in accordance with the formula.

A column entitled W will be required, as will another entitled $\frac{p_1}{p_0} . W$. As an interim step towards calculating the latter we will include a column entitled p_1/p_0.

Item	W	p_0	p_1	p_1/p_0	$\frac{p_1}{p_0}W$
Bread	6	20	40	2	12
Tea	2	25	30	1.2	2.4
Caviar	0.067	450	405	0.9	0.0603
ΣW =	8.067			$\sum \frac{p_1}{p_0}.w$ =	14.4603

Price relatives index for 19X5 with 19X1 = 100

$$= 100 \times \sum \frac{p_1}{p_0}.w \ / \ \Sigma W$$

$$= 100 \times 14.4603 \ / \ 8.067$$

$$= 179$$

This is telling us that the average price of these three items has risen by 79% from 19X1 to 19X5.

Exercise

The Brough Beeton Company manufactures a special sort of cough syrup, made from four secret ingredients, A, B, C and D. For the three years 19X1 to 19X3, the cost of these ingredients varied as follows.

Ingredient		Cost	
	19X1	19X2	19X3
A (per ounce)	10p	12p	11p
B (per packet)	20p	20p	30p
C (per litre)	£1.20p	£1.10p	£1.15p
D (per ounce)	70p	85p	80p

In order to make one bottle of cough syrup, the following ingredients are used.

Ingredient	Quantity in one bottle
A	2 ounces
B	0.5 packets
C	0.2 litres
D	1.5 ounces

Required
Using 19X1 as base year, find the price relatives indices for 19X2 and 19X3 using the quantities as weights.

Solution

Item	W	p_0	19X2 p_1	p_1/p_0	$\dfrac{p_1}{p_0}.W$	19X3 p_1	p_1/p_0	$\dfrac{p_1}{p_0}.W$
A	2	10	12	1.2	2.4	11	1.1	2.2
B	0.5	20	20	1	0.5	30	1.5	0.75
C	0.2	120	110	0.9167	0.1833	115	0.9583	0.1917
D	1.5	70	85	1.2143	1.8215	80	1.1429	1.7144
Totals	4.2				4.9048			4.8561

The price relatives indices (19X1 = 100) are therefore

19X2 $\quad \dfrac{4.9048}{4.2} \times 100 = 117$

19X3 $\quad \dfrac{4.8561}{4.2} \times 100 = 116$

Aggregative price indices

2.20 For an aggregative index the weighted average prices are obtained and then they are indexed relative to the base year.

Average price in current year $\quad = \quad \dfrac{\Sigma w p_1}{\Sigma w}$

Average price in base year $\quad = \quad \dfrac{\Sigma w p_0}{\Sigma w}$

So the index $\quad = \quad \dfrac{\Sigma w p_1/\Sigma w}{\Sigma w p_0/\Sigma w} \times 100$

Readers who are familiar with algebra will see that the Σw cancels, leaving a simplified formula as follows.

Aggregative index $\quad = \quad \dfrac{\Sigma w p_1}{\Sigma w p_0} \times 100$

2.21 In the CIM exam, two different formulae are given for aggregative price indices. Both have quantities as weights but one has base year quantities and the other has current quantities. Both are named after the mathematicians who 'invented' them.

2.22 Laspeyre price index $\quad = \quad 100 \times \dfrac{\Sigma p_1 q_0}{\Sigma p_0 q_0}$ (base weighted)

Paasche price index $\quad = \quad 100 \times \dfrac{\Sigma p_1 q_1}{\Sigma p_0 q_1}$ (current weighted)

Example

2.23 Find (a) the base weighted aggregative price index and (b) the current weighted aggregative price index for 19X5 with 19X1 = 100, for the following data.

Item	19X1		19X5	
	Quantity	Price	Quantity	Price
Bread	6	20	5	40
Tea	2	25	2	30
Caviar	0.067	450	0.074	405

Solution

2.24 First label prices and quantities in accordance with the formulae.

The Laspeyre index requires columns p_1q_0 and p_0q_0 and the Paasche index requires p_1q_1 and p_0q_1.

(a)
Item	q_0	p_0	p_1	p_1q_0	p_0q_0
Bread	6	20	40	240	120
Tea	2	25	30	60	50
Caviar	0.067	450	405	27.135	30.15
				327.135	200.15

$$\text{Laspeyre index} = \frac{327.135}{200.15} \times 100 = 163$$

(b)
Item	p_0	q_1	p_1	p_1q_1	p_0q_1
Bread	20	5	40	200	100
Tea	25	2	30	60	50
Caviar	450	0.074	405	29.97	33.3
				289.97	183.3

$$\text{Paasche index} = \frac{289.97}{183.3} \times 100 = 158$$

2.25 Before we proceed, it is useful to consider our various price indices for bread, tea and caviar. We have so far shown, using three different acceptable methods, that the average price increase was either 58% or 63% or 79%. It has to be admitted that index numbers are very open to misuse and the method selected does tend to be the one which gives the 'best' result. When results vary markedly, as in the above case, the proper course of action is to offer all the results to those involved in decision making.

2.26 There is a second feature of the above results that is worthy of comment. The Laspeyre index is somewhat higher than the Paasche and this is quite common. Base weighted indices do tend to exaggerate price inflation.

2.27 As would be expected, the very high increase in the price of bread has led to a reduction in demand. The Laspeyre index does not reflect the reduction in demand, since it uses the base quantity. It gives a much higher weighting to the big price increase than does the Paasche index and so it results in a higher index number.

Exercise

The wholesale price index in Ruritania is made up from the prices of five items. The price of each item, and the average quantities purchased by manufacturing and other companies each week were as follows, in 19X0 and 19X2.

Item	Quantity '000 units 19X0	Price per unit in roubles 19X0	Quantity '000 units 19X2	Price per unit in roubles 19X2
P	60	3	80	4
Q	30	6	40	5
R	40	5	20	8
S	100	2	150	2
T	20	7	10	10

Calculate the price index in 19X2, if 19X0 is taken as the base year, using:

(a) a Laspeyre index;
(b) a Paasche index.

Comment on your results.

Solution

Workings:

Item	p_0	q_0	p_1	q_1	Laspeyre p_0q_0	p_1q_0	Paasche p_1q_1	p_0q_1
P	3	60	4	80	180	240	320	240
Q	6	30	5	40	180	150	200	240
R	5	40	8	20	200	320	160	100
S	2	100	2	150	200	200	300	300
T	7	20	10	10	140	200	100	70
					900	1,110	1,080	950

19X2 index

(a) Laspeyre index $\frac{1,110}{900} \times 100 = 123.3$

(b) Paasche index $\frac{1,080}{950} \times 100 = 113.7$

The Paasche index for 19X2 reflects the decline in consumption of the relatively expensive items R and T since 19X0. The Laspeyre index for 19X2 fails to reflect this change.

---

3. QUANTITY INDICES

3.1 Just as price indices use quantities as weights, so changes in the quantities bought or sold can be calculated using prices as weights. A change in the quantity of an expensive item clearly is of more significance than a similar change for a cheaper item.

9: INDEX NUMBERS

3.2 The formulae for quantity indices are given by interchanging the p's and q's of price indices. For example look at these two base weighted indices.

Base weighted aggregative price index $= 100 \times \dfrac{\Sigma p_1 q_0}{\Sigma p_0 q_0}$

Base weighted aggregative quantity index $= 100 \times \dfrac{\Sigma q_1 p_0}{\Sigma q_0 p_0}$

Example

3.3 The Falldown Construction Company uses four items of materials and components in a standard production job.

In 19X0 the quantities of each material/component used per job and their cost, were as follows.

	Quantity (units)	Price per unit
Material A	20	£2
Material B	5	£10
Component C	40	£3
Component D	15	£6

In 19X2 the quantities of materials and components used per job were as follows.

	Quantity (units)
Material A	15
Material B	6
Component C	36
Component D	25

Using 19X0 as a base year, calculate the quantity index value in 19X2 for the amount of materials used in a standard job.

Solution

3.4

Item	Price p_0	Quantity used in 19X0 q_0	$p_0 q_0$	Quantity used in 19X2 q_1	$p_0 q_1$
Material A	£2	20	40	15	30
Material B	£10	5	50	6	60
Component C	£3	40	120	36	108
Component D	£6	15	90	25	150
			300		348

Quantity index value $\dfrac{348}{300} \times 100 = 116$

This would be interpreted to suggest that the company is using 16% more materials in 19X2 than in 19X0 on a standard job.

Exercise

Stopwatch Ltd prepares an annual index of productivity of employees in the company. Efficiency is measured in four departments, as a percentage (with 100% efficiency representing standard productivity levels).

The performance of each department is weighted to reflect the volume of output from the department (in standard hours).

Data for 19X0 and 19X2 were as follows.

Dept	Std hours of output per week '000s 19X0	Productivity or efficiency ratio 19X0	Std hours of output per week '000s 19X2	Productivity or efficiency ratio 19X2
A	3	120	4	150
B	6	95	5	98
C	1	140	2	130
D	4	110	3	114

Calculate the productivity index for 19X2 (with 19X0 as the base year) using:
(a) a Laspeyre index;
(b) a Paasche index.

Solution

Laspeyre quantity index $= 100 \times \dfrac{\Sigma q_1 p_0}{\Sigma q_0 p_0}$

Paasche quantity index $= 100 \times \dfrac{\Sigma q_1 p_1}{\Sigma q_0 p_1}$

'p' in this case refers to the weightings given to the quantities measured, ie to the standard hours of output per week in each department.

Workings

Department	"p_0"	q_0	"p_1"	q_1	Laspeyre $p_0 q_0$	$p_0 q_1$	Paasche $p_1 q_1$	$p_1 q_0$
A	3	120	4	150	360	450	600	480
B	6	95	5	98	570	588	490	475
C	1	140	2	130	140	130	260	280
D	4	110	3	114	440	456	342	330
					1,510	1,624	1,692	1,565

Productivity index for 19X2.

(a) Laspeyre method: $\dfrac{1,624}{1,510} \times 100 = 107.5$

(b) Paasche method: $\dfrac{1,692}{1,565} \times 100 = 108.1$

---

4.   PRACTICAL PROBLEMS IN CONSTRUCTING AN INDEX

What items to include

4.1   The purpose to which the index is to be put must be carefully decided. Once this has been done, the items selected must be as representative of the subject as possible, taking into account this purpose. Care must be taken to ensure that the items are unambiguous and readily ascertainable.

4.2   For some indices, the choice of items might be relatively straightforward. For example, the FT Actuaries All-Share Index, compiled jointly by the Financial Times, the Institute of Actuaries and the Faculty of Actuaries, is made up of approximately 750 different types of ordinary shares quoted on the stock exchange. The index is based on the market capitalisation of the 750 types of share (ie number of shares in issue multiplied by market value).

4.3   For other indices, the choice of items will be more difficult. The retail price index is an excellent example of the problem. It would be impossible to include all items of domestic spending (both type of item and company brands) and a selective, representative 'basket of goods' must be found, ranging from spending on mortgages and rents, to cars, public transport, food and drink, electricity, gas, telephone, clothing, leisure activities and so on.

4.4   The sources of statistical data were described earlier in this text; however it is useful to note here that often the government has unique access to sources of business data, and is able to compile a regular national index of prices or quantities which would be outside the resource capabilities of most business organisations.

How to get the data

4.5   Data is required for determining the following.
(a)   The values attached to each item.
(b)   The weights that will be attached to each item.

4.6   Consider as an example a cost of living index. The prices of a particular commodity will vary from place to place, from shop to shop and from type to type. Also the price will vary during the period under consideration. The actual prices used must obviously be some sort of average. The way in which the average is to be obtained should be clearly defined at the outset.

4.7   When constructing a price index, it is common practice to use the quantities consumed as weights; similarly, when constructing a quantity index, the prices may be used as weights. Care must be taken in selecting the data for weighting. For example, in a cost of living index, it may be decided to use the consumption of a 'typical family' as the weights, but some difficulty may be encountered in defining a 'typical family'.

9: INDEX NUMBERS

What weights to use: current or base?

4.8 In the previous paragraph it was mentioned that quantities consumed are often used as weights. Obviously, patterns of consumption change and a decision is necessary on whether to use:

    (a)   the quantity consumed in the base year; or

    (b)   the quantity consumed in the current year.

4.9 The following points should be considered when deciding which type of index to use.

    (a)   A Paasche index requires quantities to be ascertained each year. A Laspeyre index only requires them for the base year.

    (b)   For the Paasche index the denominator $\Sigma p_0 q_1$ has to recalculated each year because the base year quantities must be changed to current year consumption levels.

        For the Laspeyre index, the denominator $\Sigma p_0 q_0$ is fixed.

    (c)   Because of (b) the Laspeyre index for several different years can be directly compared whereas with the Paasche index comparisons can only be drawn directly between the current year and the base year (although indirect comparisons can be made).

    (d)   The weights for a Laspeyre index become out of date, whereas those for the Paasche index are updated each year.

    (e)   The Laspeyre index tends to exaggerate inflation.

Which method to use: relatives or aggregative?

4.10 There is no evident pattern of one method giving consistently higher results than the other, but the following points should be considered when deciding which method to use.

    (a)   A relatives index requires each individual item to be indexed prior to averaging. In the course of calculating it we therefore gain additional information about which items contributed most to the overall price change.

    (b)   Relatives indices can easily be built up in stages. Individual food indices such as meat, bread etc can be combined to give a food index which is then combined with other similar interim indices, such as housing, transport, etc, to give an overall cost of living index. This technique is used in the construction of the retail price index.

    (c)   Aggregative indices also give valuable information in the course of their construction. $\Sigma p_0 q_0$, for instance, gives total expenditure in the base year, while $\Sigma p_1 q_0$ tells us what total expenditure would be, at current prices, if quantities bought had remained static.

    (d)   Probably the most important factor in deciding which method to use is the method which was used in constructing other indices with which yours is to be compared. Like should be compared with like as far as possible.

5. THE LIMITATIONS OF INDEX NUMBERS

5.1 Index numbers are easy to understand and fairly easy to calculate, so it is not surprising that they are frequently used. However, they are not perfect and it is as well to bear in mind the following points.

(a) Index numbers are usually only approximations of changes in price or quantity over time, and must be interpreted with care and reservation.

(b) Weightings become out of date as time passes. Unless a Paasche index is used, the weightings will gradually cease to reflect the current 'reality'.

(c) New products or items may appear, and old ones cease to be significant. For example spending has changed in recent years, to include new items such as colour television, domestic computers and video recorders, whereas demand for large black and white televisions and twin-tub washing machines has declined. These changes would make the weightings of a retail price index for consumer goods out of date and the base of the index would need revision.

(d) Sometimes, the data used to calculate index numbers might be incomplete, out of date, or inaccurate. For example the quantity indices of imports and exports are based on records supplied by traders which may be prone to error or even falsification.

(e) The base year of an index should be a 'normal' year, but there is probably no such thing as a perfectly normal year. Some error in the index will be caused by untypical values in the base period.

(f) The 'basket of items' in an index is often selective. For example the retail price index (RPI) is constructed from a sample of households and, more importantly, from a basket of only about 600 items.

(g) A national index cannot necessarily be applied to an individual town or region. For example if the national index of wages and salaries rises from 100 to 115, we cannot necessarily state the following.

(i) The wages and salaries of people in, say, Glasgow, have gone up from 100 to 115.
(ii) The wages and salaries of each working individual have gone up from 100 to 115.

(h) An index may exclude important items; for example, the RPI excludes payments of income tax out of gross wages.

Misinterpretation of index numbers

5.2 You must be careful not to misinterpret index numbers. Several possible mistakes will be explained using the following example of a retail price index.

19X0		19X1		19X2	
January	340.0	January	360.6	January	436.3
		February	362.5	February	437.1
		March	366.2	March	439.5
		April	370.0	April	442.1

(a) It would be wrong to say that prices rose by 2.6% between March and April 19X2. It is correct to say that prices rose 2.6 points, or

$$\frac{2.6}{439.5} = 0.6\%$$

(b) It would be wrong to say that because prices are continually going up, then there must be rising inflation. If prices are going up, then there must be inflation. But is the *rate* of price increases going up, or is the rate slowing down? In our example, it so happens that although the trend of prices is still upwards, the *rate* of price increase (inflation) is slowing down.

(i) Annual rate of inflation, March 19X1 to March 19X2

$$= \frac{439.5 - 366.2}{366.2} = 20\%$$

(ii) Annual rate of inflation, April 19X1 to April 19X2

$$= \frac{442.1 - 370.0}{370.0} = 19.5\%$$

The rate of inflation has dropped from 20% per annum to 19.5% per annum between March and April 19X2, even though prices went up in the month between March and April 19X2 by 0.6%.

(c) It is also wrong to state that the average annual rate of inflation between January 19X0 and January 19X2 is as follows.

$$\tfrac{1}{2} \text{ of } \frac{436.3 - 340.0}{340.0} = 14.2\% \text{ per annum}$$

The average annual rate of growth is a compound rate and cannot be calculated from just an arithmetic mean.

6. PUBLISHED INDICES

The UK Retail Price Index (RPI)

6.1 This index is compiled and published monthly by the Department of Employment. On a particular day each month some 130,000 separate price quotations are obtained, covering about 600 different goods and services. The prices are obtained from a representative sample of retail outlets.

6.2 Each individual price is indexed relative to the January price of the year in question and then the resulting price relatives are combined by means of weighted averaging into a subgroup index. For example, white sliced bread would form part of a subgroup relating to several types of bread. The subgroup indices are similarly combined into 14 groups, which in turn are combined to give the five broad groups shown in the following table with their weights.

	1962	*1974*	*1987*
Food and catering	33	30	21
Alcohol and tobacco	14	11	11
Housing and household expenditure	26	28	34
Personal expenditure	12	11	11
Travel and leisure	15	20	23
	100	100	100

Note: in the 1914 index the weighting for food was 60%.

6.3 The resulting overall price index is then recalculated with its current fixed base of January 1987 (ie January 1987 = 100).

6.4 The weightings given to each group and subgroup are based on information provided by the *Family Expenditure Survey* which is based on a survey of over 10,000 households, spread evenly over the year. Each member of the selected households (age 16 or over) is asked to keep a detailed record of their expenditure over a period of 14 days, and to provide information about longer term payments (for example insurance premiums, car road tax). Information is also obtained about their income.

6.5 The weights used are as current as is practical. They derive from the Family Expenditure Survey for the previous year and each item's weight is the proportion of expenditure by the average household on that item. The weights are updated annually. They are of special interest in marketing because they show what people currently spend their money on.

6.6 The RPI is therefore a current weighted price relatives index with expenditure weightings. It is obtained with a fixed base by the process of chaining.

6.7 Not all common expenditure is covered by the RPI. For example life insurance and income tax are excluded. Equally not all households are covered. The 4% of households with the highest incomes and pensioner households largely dependent on state benefits are excluded on the grounds that their expenditure patterns differ greatly from most other households. A separate quarterly price index is produced for pensioner households.

6.8 The main uses of the RPI are:

(a) as a cost of living index in wage bargaining;
(b) as an indicator of competitiveness in the international market; and
(c) to enable comparison of financial quantities over the years, by scaling them up or down using the RPI.

6.9 In marketing, the subgroup indices might be of more interest than the overall index since they enable a comparison to be made between the prices charged by a given firm and those prevailing generally in its sector.

9: INDEX NUMBERS

The Index of Industrial Production

6.10 This is a quantity index compiled by the central statistical office in collaboration with other government departments. It measures changes in the volume of production in the major part of the country's industry. The index is used as a measure of the state of the national economy.

6.11 The index covers several major industries, together accounting for over one half of the UK gross domestic product.

    (a) Manufacturing.
    (b) Mining and quarrying.
    (c) Construction.
    (d) Gas, electricity and water supply.

It excludes agricultural, fishing, trade, transport, finance and other industries.

6.12 The items in the index are divided into 20 'industrial orders' which include:

    (a) mining and quarrying;
    (b) construction;
    (c) gas, electricity and water;
    (d) food, drink and tobacco;
    (e) chemicals;
    (f) electrical engineering;
    (g) mechanical engineering;
    (h) vehicles.

Each industrial order is given a weighting.

6.13 Within each industrial order, items are further sub-divided into series (of which there are 890 in total). For example the order for mining and quarrying is sub-divided into natural gas, crude oil, cement, different types of coal mining etc.

Each series is given a weighting within the industrial order.

6.14 The weight given to each series and to each industrial order is based on average monthly production in each of the industries in a *fixed base period*.

7. CONCLUSION

7.1 You should know how to construct the main types of price indices which are either aggregative (Laspeyre and Paasche) or relatives indices with various weightings.

7.2 It is important to be aware of the various problems associated with the construction of index numbers such as what items to include, what weights to use, what sort of method to use and the choice of base year.

7.3 It is important also to be able to manipulate index number series by changing the base, splicing two series together and converting between fixed and chain based series.

7.4 Finally you need to be broadly familiar with the construction and coverage of the RPI and the Index of Industrial Production.

7.5 Before you go on to the next chapter you should try the illustrative questions on index numbers, all of which are CIM examination questions. In this context we want to emphasise how important it is to attempt the discursive sections of the questions as well as the calculations. Index number questions often allocate a high proportion of marks to the discussion of the various problems associated with index numbers and it is particularly important that you are not tempted to skip these sections.

TEST YOUR KNOWLEDGE

The numbers in brackets refer to paragraphs of this chapter

1. What is an index number? (1.1)

2. Why are index numbers used? (1.6, 1.7)

3. What factors should influence the choice of the base year? (1.12)

4. What is a chain based index number? (1.20)

5. State the formula for a weighted average. (2.10)

6. What two processes are involved in the calculation of a multi-item price index? (2.12)

7. What is a price relative? (2.17)

8. Why are base weighted indices 'inflationary'? (2.27)

9. How is a price index formula converted into a quantity index formula? (3.2)

10. List the factors that influence the choice of base or current weights. (4.9)

11. State four limitations of index numbers. (5.1)

12. How is the RPI computed each month? (6.1 - 6.5)

Now try illustrative questions 25 to 28

PART E
PROBABILITY AND STATISTICAL
INFERENCE

Chapter 10

PROBABILITY THEORY

This chapter covers the following topics.

1. Introduction to probability theory
2. Permutations and combinations
3. The rules of probability

---

1. INTRODUCTION TO PROBABILITY THEORY

1.1 Probability is the likelihood or chance of something happening. It is quantified as a percentage or a proportion of the total possible outcomes. Suppose, for instance, that a coin is tossed. There are two possible outcomes, head or tail, and they occur equally often if it is a fair coin. The probability of a head is therefore 1 out of 2 ie 0.5 or 50%.

1.2 If a playing card is selected from a pack of 52 cards, there are four aces in a pack so the probability that the card is an ace is 4 out of 52 ie 4/52.

Definition of probability

1.3 The probability P(A) that an event A will occur is the number of outcomes in which A occurs divided by the total number of possible outcomes.

1.4 In the first example given above, the action or experiment involved is the tossing of a fair coin and the event in which we are interested is the obtaining of a head. In the second example, the action is the selection of a card and the event is the obtaining of an ace.

1.5 In each case we need to work out the number of ways the outcome or event in which we are interested could occur and then divide it by the total number of possible outcomes.

Example

1.6 A letter is chosen at random from the letters CASSOCK. Find the probability that it is

(a) K
(b) C
(c) C or S.

Solution

1.7   CASSOCK has seven letters so there are seven possible outcomes.

   (a)   Only one of those letters is K so P(K) = 1/7
   (b)   There are two Cs so P(C) = 2/7
   (c)   There are two Cs and two Ss so P(C or S) = 4/7.

Example

1.8   A company carries out a survey of the number of outlets each of its 70 customers has. The results are as follows.

Number of outlets	1	2	3	4	5
Number of customers	10	30	20	8	2

If one customer is selected at random, find the probability that the customer has (a) five outlets, (b) more than two outlets, (c) two or less outlets.

Solution

1.9   (a)   Only two customers out of 70 have five outlets so P(5) = 2/70.

   (b)   The number of customers with more than two outlets is 20 + 8 + 2 = 30 so P(more than 2) = 30/70.

   (c)   The number of customers with two or less outlets is 10 + 30 = 40 so P(2 or less) = 40/70.

1.10 In each of the above examples we have left the probability in its original fractional form, in order to illustrate the thinking involved. In general however such fractions should be reduced to their most simple form or written as decimals or percentages. Thus 40/70 would be written either as 4/7 or 0.571 or 57.1%.

Exercise

A box contains two red, three green, one pink and four blue cards. If one card is selected at random find the probability that it is (a) red, (b) pink, (c) green or blue, (d) not red.

Solution

The box contains ten cards so there are ten possible outcomes.
(a)   P(red) = two out of 10 = 2/10 = 0.2
(b)   P(pink) = 1/10 = 0.1
(c)   P(green or blue) = 3 + 4 out of 10 = 7/10 = 0.7
(d)   P(not red) = 3 + 1 + 4 out of 10 = 8/10 = 0.8

1.11 Probability is concerned with *uncertainty* about what will happen. An estimate can be made about the *likelihood* of something happening, but what actually happens afterwards cannot be predicted with certainty. In business, where future events are nearly always uncertain, probability theory has widespread potential applications.

1.12 Since probability is concerned with future events, it is helpful to consider how probability can be quantified. A manager might estimate that if the selling price of a product is raised by 20 pence, there would be 90% probability that demand would fall by 20%, but how would the estimate of 90% probability have been reached? Similarly, if it is expected that a company's products will capture 40% of the total UK market next year, how would this estimate have come about?

1.13 There are several ways of assessing probability which can be broadly categorised as theoretical, empirical or subjective.

1.14 *Theoretical probabilities* can be measured with mathematical certainty. Examples are as follows.

(a) If a coin is tossed, there is a 0.5 probability that it will come down heads, and a 0.5 probability that it will come down tails.

(b) If a dice is thrown, there is a one-sixth probability that a six will turn up.

1.15 *Empirical probabilities* can be estimated from an analysis of past experience.

(a) For example an analysis of the last 300 working days shows that on 180 days there were no machine breakdowns. Given no change in the average life of machinery, we would therefore be able to estimate the probability of there being no machine breakdowns during a day. $\frac{180}{300}$ or 60% (and the probability of at least one breakdown during the day must be 40%).

(b) They can also be estimated from research or surveys. For example a new product might be test-marketed in selected trial areas, and from the results of the test it might be estimated that if the product were sold nationally, there might be a 70% chance that sales demand would be sufficient to earn a satisfactory profit for the company.

1.16 *Subjective probabilities* are estimates of probabilities made without theoretical or empirical support, such as when a manager hazards a guess that there is a 70:30 likelihood that the company will win a contract.

1.17 A final introductory point about probability is that it is a measure of the likelihood of an event happening *in the long run*, or over a large number of times. If we toss a coin eight times, we cannot predict that it will come down heads four times and tails four times. The coin may come down heads eight times, or not once in the eight throws, ie heads may occur any number of times between zero and eight. We *would* say, however, that in the long run heads will occur 50% of the time if a coin is thrown a sufficiently large number of times.

1.18 Similarly, if a sales forecast estimates that there is a 75% chance that sales of a product will exceed 1,000 units per month in the first four months of the year, we cannot say that sales necessarily *will* exceed 1,000 in (75% x 4) = three months, and fall short of 1,000 in one month.

2. PERMUTATIONS AND COMBINATIONS

2.1 Before probability theory is described in more detail, it will be useful to digress for some paragraphs to consider the theory of combinations and permutations, which helps us to calculate the number of ways that events can occur.

2.2 A *combination* is a set of items, selected from a larger collection of items, regardless of the order in which they are selected. We might refer to the number of possible combinations of r items from n unlike items. For example, suppose that five people apply for two vacancies as junior accountants in Combo Limited and these people are called A,B,C,D and E. The different possible combinations of filling the two posts from the five applicants would be AB, AC, AD, AE, BC, BD, BE, CD, CE or DE.

2.3 A *permutation* is a set of items, selected from a larger group of items, in which the order of selection or arrangement is significant. We might refer to the number of possible permutations of r items from n unlike items.

In the previous example, suppose that the two vacancies were for the post of senior accountant and junior accountant. The order of selection would be important and the possible permutations would be as follows.

Senior	Junior	Senior	Junior
A	B	B	A
A	C	C	A
A	D	D	A
A	E	E	A
B	C	C	B ...... and so on

Whereas there were ten combinations of two from five, there would be 20 permutations of two from five.

Combinations and permutations are an important element in probability theory.

The multiplication principle

2.4 If one event can occur in X ways and then a second event can occur in Y ways, the number of ways in which the two can occur, in the specified order, is X times Y.

2.5 For example suppose that there were three main routes from London to Sheffield and two main routes from Sheffield to Leeds. The total number of routes from London to Leeds would be $3 \times 2 = 6$, with each London to Sheffield route being followed by one or other of the Sheffield to Leeds routes.

Permutations

2.6 The number of permutations of N objects means the number of ways they can be placed in order. For example suppose that an investment manager must rank three projects, A, B and C in order of profitability. How many possible ways are there of ordering them first, second and third?

The first can be chosen in three ways (either A or B or C). Only two will then remain, so the second can be selected in only two ways and finally only one way remains of selecting the third.

The number of permutations of three projects is therefore $3 \times 2 \times 1 = 6$.

(The permutations are ABC, ACB, BCA, BAC, CBA, CAB)

2.7 If there are N objects to be placed in order, the first can be selected in N ways, the second in N-1 ways and so on until the last which can be selected in only one way.

2.8

> Number of permutations of N objects
> $= N \times N\text{-}1 \times N\text{-}2 \times ... \times 3 \times 2 \times 1$
> $= N!$

2.9 You may not be familiar with the symbol '!'. N! is pronounced 'N factorial' and means the product of all of the whole numbers from N downwards. For example 5! means $5 \times 4 \times 3 \times 2 \times 1$.

2.10 Your calculator should have a factorial key. On the Casio fx 100C, x! is written in orange, which means $\boxed{\text{SHIFT}}$ must be pressed before the key $\boxed{\text{x!}}$. For example 5 $\boxed{\text{SHIFT}}$ $\boxed{\text{x!}}$ will result in 120 being displayed, because $5! = 5 \times 4 \times 3 \times 2 \times 1 = 120$.

2.11 If we wish to place just R items out of a total of N in order, the thinking is similar to that above. The first can be selected in N ways, the second in N-1 ways and so on until the Rth item has been selected.

2.12 For example in how many ways can two people be selected from five candidates if the jobs differ so that the order of selection is important?

The number of ways $= 5 \times 4 = 20$.

2.13 The number of permutations of R objects from a total of N unlike objects is denoted by $_N P_R$.

> $_N P_R = N \times N\text{-}1 \times ... R \text{ terms}$
>
> $\quad = \dfrac{N!}{(N\text{-}R)!}$

Example

2.14 In the previous example of five candidates for two jobs the number of different permutations would be as follows.

$$_5 P_2 = \frac{5!}{(5\text{-}2)!} = \frac{5 \times 4 \times 3 \times 2 \times 1}{3 \times 2 \times 1} = 5 \times 4 = 20$$

This can be obtained on a calculator with an $_nP_r$ button as follows.

5 [SHIFT] [nPr] 2 [=]

Exercise

50 people take part in a competition. In how many ways can the first three places be filled?

Solution

Method 1: $_{50}P_3 = 117,600$ given by 50 [SHIFT] [$_nP_r$] 3 [=]

Method 2: $\dfrac{50!}{(50-3)!} = \dfrac{50!}{47!}$ given by 50 [SHIFT] [x!] [÷] 47 [SHIFT] [x!] [=]

Method 3: $50 \times 49 \times 48 = 117,600$.

Note: most calculators cannot work out factorials greater than 69! because they do not have enough display space.

Combinations

2.15 A combination is a selection of items with no regard to order. The number of combinations of r items which are possible from a set of n unlike items is given by the formula which follows.

$$nCr = \frac{n!}{(n-r)!\ r!}$$

Examples

2.16 (a) The number of ways of selecting two people from five in no special order

$$= {_5}C_2 = \frac{5!}{3!\ 2!} = 10$$

[Calculator: either 5 [SHIFT] [nCr] 2 [=] or use the [x!] button.]

(b) In how many ways can a shortlist of five be drawn up from 32 candidates?

$$_{32}C_5 = \frac{32!}{27!\ 5!} = 201,376$$

2.17 0! is defined to be equal to 1. For example the number of ways of choosing a work team of four people from a total number of only four people available would be as follows.

$$_4C_4 = \frac{4!}{0!4!} = 1$$

Exercise

A class of 15 BPP students is about to sit a statistics exam. They will subsequently be listed in descending order by reference to the marks scored. Assuming that there are no tied positions with students sharing the same mark, calculate the following figures.

(a) The number of different possible orderings for the whole class.
(b) The number of different possible results for the top three places.
(c) The number of different possible ways of having three people taking the top three places (irrespective of order).

Solution

(a) The number of different possible orderings of the whole class is as follows.

15! (= over 1.3 million millions)

(b) The number of different possible results for the top three places is given by the number of permutations of three out of 15.

$$_{15}P_3 = \frac{15!}{(15-3)!} = \frac{15!}{12!} = 15 \times 14 \times 13 = 2,730$$

(c) The number of ways of having three people taking the top three places is given by the number of combinations of three out of 15.

$$_{15}C_3 = \frac{15!}{(15-3)!3!} = \frac{15!}{12!\ 3!} = 455$$

Scientific or exponential form of numbers

2.18 15! is shown on a calculator as 1.307674368 then a gap and a small 12.

This method of displaying numbers is called either scientific or exponential form and it means $1.307674368 \times 10^{12}$. In other words, the answer is the number displayed multiplied by 10 twelve times.

ie 1,307,674,368,000

Every time we multiply by 10, the decimal point has to be moved one place to the right.

2.19 Later in this text you will encounter probabilities which are very small and these may well also be displayed in scientific form.

If you input 0.002 $\boxed{x}$ 0.004 $\boxed{=}$ into your calculator, the result will be displayed as

8.-06

with the 06 written in small letters.

The negative sign is very important. It tells us that the result is 8×10^{-6} or 8 divided by 10 six times. We have to move the decimal point to the left six times.

ie the result is 0.000008.

3. THE RULES OF PROBABILITY

3.1 Having digressed to consider permutations and combinations, which help to quantify possibilities, we will now return to the evaluation of probabilities. We will illustrate the most elementary rules by reference to the following experiment. One person is to be selected randomly from a group of 20 people of whom 12 have blue eyes, seven have brown eyes and one has green. So, for instance, the probability that the person selected has blue eyes is given by

P(blue) = 12 out of 20 = 12/20 = 0.6

3.2 *Impossible* events have probability equal to zero.

For example P(person selected has red eyes) = 0/20 = 0.

3.3 *Absolutely certain* events have probability equal to one.

For example P(person has some sort of eyes) = 20/20 = 1

3.4 | All probabilities lie between 0 and 1.

3.5 If all possible outcomes are considered, total probability equals one.

P(blue)   = 12/20
P(brown) = 7/20
P(green) = 1/20
Total   = 20/20 = 1

3.6 The probability that something is not true is one minus the probability that it is true.

For example P(person has not got blue eyes) = 8/20
= 1 - 12/20
= 1 - P(blue)

The special rule of addition

3.7 If two events cannot both occur, they are said to be *mutually exclusive*. In the example, blue eyes and green eyes are mutually exclusive.

If events A and B are mutually exclusive, then

$$P(A \text{ or } B) = P(A) + P(B)$$

For example P (either blue or green eyes) = 13/20 = 12/20 + 1/20
= P(blue) + P(green)

Example

3.8 The delivery of an item of raw material from a supplier may take up to six weeks from the time the order is placed. The probability of delivery times is as follows.

Delivery time	Probability
1 week	0.1
2 weeks	0.25
3 weeks	0.2
4 weeks	0.2
5 weeks	0.15
6 weeks	0.1
	1.0

What is the probability that a delivery will take:

(a) two weeks or less?
(b) more than three weeks?

Solution

3.9 (a) P(1 or 2 weeks) = P(1) + P(2) = 0.1 + 0.25
= 0.35

(b) P(4 or 5 or 6 weeks) = P(4) + P(5) + P(6)
= 0.2 + 0.15 + 0.1
= 0.45

The special rule of multiplication

3.10 Two events are said to be *independent* if the occurrence of either one does not in any way change the probability of the other.

3.11 When two events A and B are independent, the probability that they will *both* occur is given by the special rule of multiplication.

$$P(A \text{ and } B) = P(A) \times P(B)$$

P(A and B) might be referred to as the *joint probability* of both A and B occurring.

Example

3.12 A company uses either two or three units of a raw material each week. The probability of demand during the week is as follows.

2 units	0.7
3 units	0.3

Demand in any one week is independent of demand in previous or future weeks.

(a) What is the probability that demand will be two units per week:
   (i)   for two consecutive weeks?
   (ii) for three consecutive weeks?

(b) What is the probability that demand will be three units in week 1 and week 2, and two units in week 3?

Solution

3.13 (a) (i)   P (2 and 2)   =   P (2) x P (2)
                        =   0.7 x 0.7
                        =   0.49

         (ii)   P (2, 2 and 2)   =   P (2) x P (2) x P (2)
                             =   0.7 x 0.7 x 0.7
                             =   0.343

Note: $0.7 \times 0.7 \times 0.7$ can be written as 0.7^3, and it can be obtained by using the x^y button on a calculator as follows: 0.7 $\boxed{x^y}$ 3 $\boxed{=}$.

(b) P (3, 3 and 2)   =   P (3) x P (3) x P (2)
                             =   0.3 x 0.3 x 0.7
                             =   0.063

Example

3.14 Three machines, A, B and C, operate independently and their probabilities of being out of order are 0.01, 0.05 and 0.04 respectively. Find the probabilities of the following.

(a) All three are out of order.
(b) Machine A is operational.
(c) All three are operational.
(d) A is out of order but B and C are operational.
(e) One machine is out of order and the other two are operational.
(f) At least one machine is out of order.

Solution

3.15 (a) P(all out of order)   = P(A) × P(B) × P(C)
                                     = 0.01 × 0.05 × 0.04
                                     = 0.00002

(b) P(A is OK) = 1 - P(A is out of order) = 1 - 0.01
 = 0.99

(c) P(all are operational) = P(A is OK) × P(B OK) × P(C OK)
 P(B is OK) = 1-0.05 = 0.95
 P(C is OK) = 1 - 0.04 = 0.96
 ∴ P(all are OK) = 0.99 × 0.95 × 0.96
  = 0.90288

(d) P(A out of order but B and C are OK)
  = P(A out of order) × P(B is OK) × P(C is OK)
  = 0.01 × 0.95 × 0.96
  = 0.00912

(e) To find the probability that one is broken and the other two are operational, we have to consider all the possibilities. The various possibilities are mutually exclusive so we can then add their probabilities.

Possibility	Probability	
A broken, B and C OK	0.01 × 0.95 × 0.96	= 0.00912
B broken, A and C OK	0.99 × 0.05 × 0.96	= 0.04752
C broken, A and B OK	0.99 × 0.95 × 0.04	= 0.03762
		0.09426

∴ P(one broken and other two operational) = 0.09426.

(f) To find the probability that at least one machine is out of order we could list all the possibilities, namely that any one is broken or any two are broken or all three are broken, and then add up their probabilities. However, there is a much quicker method. Either at least one is broken or all three are operational.

Thus P(at least one is broken) = 1 - P(all 3 are OK)
  = 1 - 0.90288 (from part (c))
  = 0.09712

Exercise

Your company is attempting to win three totally independent contracts A, B and C. The probabilities of success are judged to be 70%, 60% and 48% respectively. Find the probabilities:

(a) that all three contracts will be won;
(b) that exactly two contracts will be won.

Solution

(a) P(all three won) = 0.7 × 0.6 × 0.48
  = 0.2016

(b)

Possibility	Probability	
A and B but not C	0.7 × 0. 6 × 0.52	= 0.2184
B and C but not A	0.6 × 0.48 × 0.3	= 0.0864
C and A but not B	0.7 × 0.48 × 0.4	= 0.1344
P(exactly two will be won) =		0.4392

Note: P(not C) = 1 - P(C) = 1 - 0.48 = 0.52 etc.

The general rule of addition

3.16 If events A and B are *not* mutually exclusive, ie they could both occur at the same time, we cannot find P(A or B) by adding P(A) and P(B) because this double counts situations when they both occur.

3.17 A more general rule of addition must be applied. If A and B are two possible outcomes of an event then the probability of A or B occurring is as follows.

> P (A or B) = P (A) + P (B) - P (A and B)

The word 'or' is used in an inclusive sense, ie either A or B or both. The deduction of P (A and B) is required to eliminate double counting, as the combination A and B will have to be considered in the calculation of both P (A) and P (B).

Example

3.18 If one card is drawn from a normal pack of 52 playing cards, what is the probability of getting an ace or a spade?

There are four aces in the pack, so P (ace) $= \dfrac{4}{52}$

There are 13 spades in the pack, so P (spade) $= \dfrac{13}{52}$

There is only one ace of spades, so P (ace of spades) $= \dfrac{1}{52}$

It follows that P (ace or spade) $= \dfrac{4}{52} + \dfrac{13}{52} - \dfrac{1}{52} = \dfrac{16}{52}$

The same result could, of course, have been obtained more quickly by working as follows.

Number of spades   13
Number of other aces   3
                 16

Therefore P (ace or spade) $= \dfrac{16}{52}$ as before

Exercise

A company sells two products, S and T. The budgeted contribution earned by each product in the coming year is as follows.

	Product S		Product T	
Contribution £	Probability		Contribution £	Probability
0	0.1		0	0.2
5,000	0.4		5,000	0.6
10,000	0.5		10,000	0.2

What is the probability that either S or T (on its own) will make a contribution of £10,000? The sales of either product are not dependent upon sales of the other.

Solution

$\quad$ P(S or T = 10,000)
$= $ P(S = 10,000) + P(T = 10,000) - P(S and T = 10,000)
$= 0.5 + 0.2 - (0.5 \times 0.2)$
$= 0.6$

The general rule of multiplication

3.19 If events A and B are independent, we saw previously that $P(A \text{ and } B) = P(A) \times P(B)$. We must now consider the situation where they are *not* independent, where, for instance, the fact that A occurs has an effect on the likelihood of B.

3.20 We will need to introduce the *conditional* probability, $P_A(B)$ or $P(B/A)$ which is the probability that B will occur, subject to the condition that A has already occurred. Equally $P_B(A)$ is the probability of A conditional on B having occurred.

3.21 If events A and B are not independent then

$$\begin{array}{rl} P(A \text{ and } B) = & P(A) \times P_A(B) \\ \text{or} & P(B) \times P_B(A) \end{array}$$

Example

3.22 If two cards are selected randomly from a pack, what is the probability that both will be Jacks?

Solution

3.23 P(first is a Jack) = 4/52
$\quad$ P(second is a Jack given that the first was a Jack)
$\qquad$ = 3 remaining Jacks out of only 51 remaining cards = 3/51
$\quad$ So P(both are Jacks) = $\dfrac{4}{52} \times \dfrac{3}{51} = 0.0045$

3.24 In the above example, order was not important since both cards were Jacks. When we select different items, we have to consider all possible orders in which they might be selected.

Example

3.25 If two cards are selected randomly from a pack, what is the probability that one is a Jack and the other is an ace?

Solution

3.26

Possibilities	Probability
First a Jack, then an ace	$\frac{4}{52} \times \frac{4}{51}$
First an ace, then a Jack	$\frac{4}{52} \times \frac{4}{51}$

$$\therefore P(\text{a Jack and an ace}) = 2 \times \frac{4}{52} \times \frac{4}{51} = 0.012$$

Exercise

Clothes produced by a fashion house are sold through 15 boutiques and ten large stores. Two outlets are to be selected for a special promotional event. Find the probability:

(a) that both are boutiques;
(b) that one is a boutique and the other a large store.

Solution

(a) $P(\text{both are boutiques}) = \frac{15}{25} \times \frac{14}{24} = 0.35$

(b) $P(\text{one is a boutique and other is a store})$

$= P(\text{boutique then store}) + P(\text{store then boutique})$

$= \frac{15}{25} \times \frac{10}{24} + \frac{10}{25} \times \frac{15}{24}$

$= 0.5$

Examples

3.27 Probabilities often take some getting used to, and a number of examples will now be introduced to give you a chance to get used to the logic behind them.

3.28 *First example*
The independent probabilities that the three sections of a costing department will encounter one computer error are respectively 0.1, 0.2 and 0.3 each week. Calculate the probability that there will be:

(a) at least one computer error;
(b) one and only one computer error;

encountered by the costing department next week.

3.29 *Solution*
(a) The probability of at least one computer error is 1 minus the probability of no errors. The probability of no errors is: 0.9 x 0.8 x 0.7 = 0.504.

(Since the probability of an error is 0.1, 0.2 and 0.3 in each section, the probability of no error in each section must be 0.9, 0.8 and 0.7 respectively.)

Probability of at least one error = 1 - 0.504 = 0.496 or 49.6%.

(b)
Possibilities	Probability	
Error in section 1 only	$0.1 \times 0.8 \times 0.7$	= 0.056
Error in section 2 only	$0.9 \times 0.2 \times 0.7$	= 0.126
Error in section 3 only	$0.9 \times 0.8 \times 0.3$	= 0.216
		0.398

P(one and only one error) = 0.398

3.30 *Second example*
Quality control checks have shown that 2% of wine glasses produced are faulty in some respect. The glasses are sold in packs of six. Find the probability that a pack contains no more than one defective glass.

3.31 *Solution*
We will assume that the quality of each glass in the pack is independent of all others. So in each case P(faulty) = 0.02 and P(satisfactory) = 0.98.

P(no more than 1 defective) = P(0 defectives) + P(1 defective).

$$P(0 \text{ defectives}) = 0.98 \times 0.98 \times \text{ and so on for all 6 glasses}$$
$$= 0.98^6 \quad [0.98 \; \boxed{x^y} \; 6 \; \boxed{=} \;]$$
$$= 0.886$$

To find the probability of just one defective glass in six, we have to consider the order in which the defective glass and the others might be selected.

Possibilities	Probability
First faulty, rest OK	0.02×0.98^5
Second faulty, rest OK	0.02×0.98^5
and so on	.....
Sixth faulty, rest OK	0.02×0.98^5

There are six possible orders so the overall probability requires us to add the six separate probabilities.

P(1 defective) $= 6 \times 0.02 \times 0.98^5$
$= 0.108$

Hence P(no more than one defective) $= 0.886 + 0.108$
$= 0.994$

3.32 *Third example*
A company has four branches in each of five towns A, B, C, D and E. Three branches in total are to be selected at random to test new production methods. Find the probability that the three chosen branches:

(a) are all in town E;
(b) are all in the same town;
(c) are all in different towns.

3.33 *Solution*

(a) P(all in E) $= \dfrac{4}{20} \times \dfrac{3}{19} \times \dfrac{2}{18} = 0.0035$

After the first branch in E has been selected, only three branches in E remain out of 19 remaining branches, so the probability that the second is also in E is 3/19. Similarly the third can be chosen from E in two ways out of the 18 remaining.

(b) Since the three branches can now belong to any one town we want P(all 3 in A or in B or in C etc)
$= $ P(all 3 in A) + P(all 3 in B) + ...and so on
$= 5 \times$ P(all in E) $= 5 \times 0.0035 = 0.0175$

An alternative approach is as follows.

At the first selection, all 20 branches are equally acceptable so the P(1st is acceptable) = 20/20. At the second and third selections the branches must be in the same town as the first and so their probabilities are 3/19 and 2/18 respectively.

Hence P(all in the same town) $= \dfrac{20}{20} \times \dfrac{3}{19} \times \dfrac{2}{18}$
$= 0.0175$

(c) Again all 20 branches are equally acceptable at the first selection so the probability is 20/20. The second must now come from one of the 16 branches in other towns out of a total of 19 remaining and the third must come from yet another town and this can occur in 12 out of the remaining 18 branches.

∴   P(all in different towns) $= \dfrac{20}{20} \times \dfrac{16}{19} \times \dfrac{12}{18} = 0.56$

Expected number of events

3.34 Suppose that the probability that a transistor is defective is 0.02 or 2%. How many defectives would we expect to find in a batch of 4,000 transistors?

Expected number = 4,000 × 0.02
= 80 defectives would be expected.

3.35 In general, if the probability of an event is p and if the situation that might give rise to the event is repeated n times, then the expected number of occurrences is n × p.

Example

3.36 If the probability that a pack of six glasses is totally satisfactory is 0.886 and if the packs are transported in crates each containing 90 packs, what is the expected number of satisfactory packs per crate?

Solution

3.37 Expected number = n × p = 90 × 0.886 = 79.74
= 80 (say).

4. CONCLUSION

4.1 Probability is the likelihood or chance of an event happening. This chapter has dealt with the rules of probability and how they can be applied in a variety of business situations.

4.2 In CIM exam questions, probability theory tends to be combined with sampling theory and together they are a very popular examination topic. We will go on to cover sampling theory in the next chapter.

TEST YOUR KNOWLEDGE
The numbers in brackets refer to paragraphs of this chapter

1. What is the definition of probability? (1.3)

2. What is the difference between a permutation and a combination? (2.2, 2.3)

3. Interpret the calculator display 2.86 - 03. (2.19)

4. What are mutually exclusive events? (3.7)

5. What is the formula for P(A and B) if A and B are independent? (3.11)

6. State the general rule of addition of probabilities. (3.17)

7. What is meant by a conditional probability? (3.20)

Now try illustrative question 29

Chapter 11

SAMPLING THEORY

This chapter covers the following topics.

1. The normal distribution
2. Estimation and significance tests

---

1.   THE NORMAL DISTRIBUTION

1.1   You may recall that earlier in this text we showed how data can be formed into a frequency distribution and how the average and the variability of the distribution can be measured by calculating its mean and its standard deviation.

1.2   The normal distribution is a frequency distribution with special characteristics or properties, which have important statistical implications. The distribution can be represented on a graph by the normal curve. The curve is determined by the values of σ, the standard deviation, and by μ the arithmetic mean of the population.

1.3   The normal curve is a symmetrical bell shape, with the left hand side and right hand side mirror images of each other, either side of the mean.

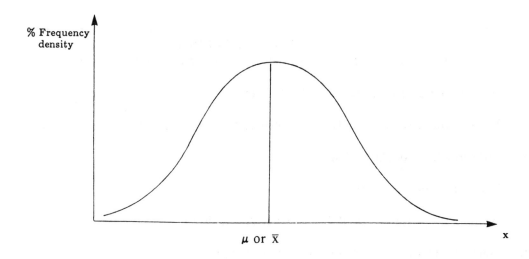

1.4 The normal curve is best thought of as a very smooth histogram. Like a histogram, the x axis represents the values whose frequency is being measured and the y axis shows % frequency density. The area under the curve shows % frequency or probability.

1.5 Very many continuous (ie measured) variables such as weights, speed, sales values, costs etc have distributions which approximate very closely to the normal distribution.

1.6 The most important feature of the normal distribution is that the probability associated with any value can be worked out provided we know how many standard deviations there are between that value and the mean.

1.7 The entire area under the curve represents 100% probability. It is certain that all values lie between A and B in the diagram. Since the curve is symmetrical, 50% of frequencies must lie between A and the mean and another 50% between the mean and B.

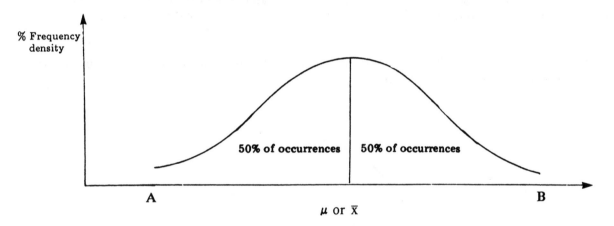

1.8 About 68% of frequencies have a value within plus or minus 1 standard deviation from the mean.

Thus if a normally-shaped frequency distribution has a mean of 80 and a standard deviation of 3, 68% of the total frequencies would occur within the range ± one standard deviation from the mean, ie within the range 77 - 83.

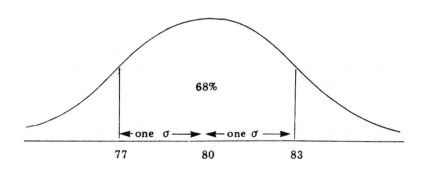

Since the curve is symmetrical, 34% of frequencies must fall in the range 77 - 80 and 34% in the range 80 - 83.

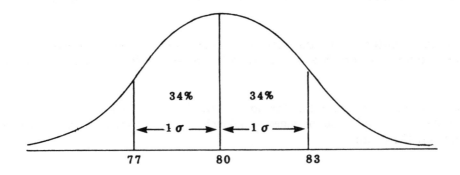

1.9 We can express the above statements in terms of probabilities. Suppose the values being investigated are weights, with an average of 80 kg and standard deviation of 3 kg. The probability that a randomly selected item weighs between 77kg and 80 kg is 0.34.

1.10 Similarly about 95% of the frequencies in a normal distribution occur in the range ± 1.96 standard deviations from the mean.

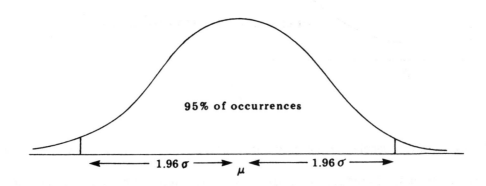

1.11 In our example, 95% of items will have weights lying between 80 - 1.96 × 3 and 80 + 1.96 × 3 ie between 74.12 kg and 85.88 kg. A randomly selected item would have a 0.95 probability of falling into this range.

1.12 We can say further that $47\frac{1}{2}$% will lie between 74.12 and 80 and another $47\frac{1}{2}$% between 80 and 85.88 kg.

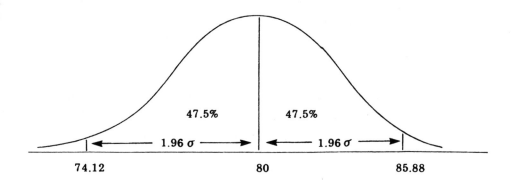

47.5%   47.5%

── 1.96 σ ──→   ←── 1.96 σ ──→

74.12   80   85.88

Percentage points of the normal distribution

1.13 The diagram and table below are provided in the CIM exam.

Percentage points of the normal distribution

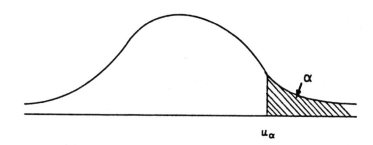

u_α

This table gives the 100 α percentage points and the U_α position of the standardised normal distribution. Thus, U_α is the value of a standardised normal variate which has probability α of being exceeded.

α	u_α	α	u_α	α	u_α
0.5	0.0000	0.05	1.6449	0.025	1.9600
0.4	0.2533	0.01	2.3263	0.005	2.5758
0.3	0.5244	0.001	3.0902	0.0005	3.2905
0.2	0.8416	0.0001	3.7190	0.00005	3.8906
0.1	1.2816	0.00001	4.2649	0.000005	4.4172

1.14 U_α is the number of standard deviations a value is away from the mean, and ∝ (pronounced alpha) is the probability associated with that value. As can be seen from the diagram, ∝ is the area in the tail of the curve. It gives the probability of exceeding the value under consideration. From now on we will omit the subscript ∝ and simply refer to 'U'.

1.15 In the U column we can see the number 1.9600. This represents any value which is 1.96 standard deviations from its mean. The corresponding figure in the ∝ or probability column is 0.025 or 2.5%. This fits in with our previous statement that 95% of frequencies lie within 1.96 standard deviations either side of the mean, as shown in the following diagram.

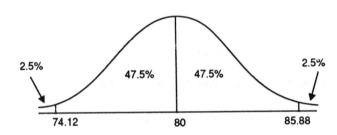

With 2.5% in both the tails, making 5% together, 95% of frequencies fall in the central range.

Example

1.16 What % of frequencies lie more than 1.6449 standard deviations above their mean?

From the table, the number of standard deviations = U = 1.6449 is associated with ∝ = 0.05 or 5%. Five per cent of normal frequencies lie more than 1.6449 standard deviations above the mean.

Exercise

From the table find the probabilities associated with the following values of U and interpret them.

(a) U = 1.2816
(b) U = 2.3263
(c) U = 2.5758

Solution

(a) ∝ = 0.1 or 10%. 10% of frequencies lie more than 1.2816 standard deviations above the mean.

(b) ∝ = 0.01 or 1%. 1% of frequencies lie more than 2.3263 standard deviations above the mean.

(c) ∝ = 0.005 or $\frac{1}{2}$%. $\frac{1}{2}$% of frequencies lie more than 2.5758 standard deviations above the mean.

Example

1.17 If the mean weight is 80kg and the standard deviation is 3 kg, find the range within which the central 99% of weights lie.

Solution

1.18 99% in the central range means that 1% must lie in the two tails taken together, ie $\frac{1}{2}$% = 0.005 in each tail.

If $\propto$ = 0.005, from the table U = 2.5758.

Hence 99% of weights lie in the range 2.5758 standard deviations either side of the mean.

Range is 80 - 2.5758 × 3 to 80 + 2.5758 × 3
        ie 72.3 to 87.7 kg

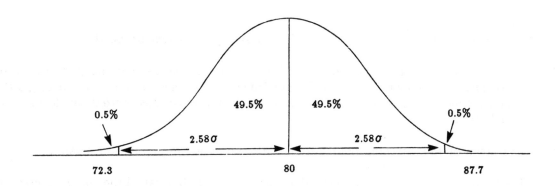

2. ESTIMATION AND SIGNIFICANCE TESTS

2.1 Suppose that we wish to estimate the mean of a population, for example the average weight of an item made in a factory. A sample of, say, 100 units of the product might be taken, and the average weight per unit of the sample might be, say, 5.8 kilograms.

Another sample of 100 units might then be taken and the mean weight might be, say, 6.3 kilograms.

A large number of samples might be taken and the mean of each sample calculated. Obviously these means will not all be the same and they can be plotted as a frequency distribution. This distribution is called a 'sampling distribution of the mean'.

2.2 In our hypothetical example, a frequency distribution of the mean weight per unit in each of 250 samples (of 100 units per sample) might be as follows.

Mean weight per unit $\bar{x}$(kilograms)	Frequency (No of samples)
5.45 and < 5.55	3
5.55 and < 5.65	7
5.65 and < 5.75	16
5.75 and < 5.85	30
5.85 and < 5.95	44
5.95 and < 6.05	50
6.05 and < 6.15	44
6.15 and < 6.25	30
6.25 and < 6.35	16
6.35 and < 6.45	7
6.45 and < 6.55	3
	250 samples

The average weight per unit might thus range from 5.45 to 6.55 kilograms. The true mean of the population - ie the true mean of all units produced - presumably must lie somewhere within this range.

2.3 A sampling distribution of the mean has the following important properties.

(a) It is very close to being normally distributed. This is true even if the distribution of the population from which the samples are drawn is fairly heavily skewed. The larger the sample the more closely will the sampling distribution of the means approximate to a normal distribution.

(b) The mean of the sampling distribution is the same as the population mean.

(c) The sampling distribution has a standard deviation which is called the *standard error of the mean.*

2.4 The theory discussed here only holds in the following situations.

(a) If the samples are taken at random and therefore exclude bias.

(b) If the samples are fairly large (over 30). Small samples give rise to special problems of interpretation, which are outside the scope of your syllabus.

2.5 It is helpful to make a distinction between the mean and standard deviation of a sample, and the mean and standard deviation of the population (which the sample attempts to represent).

> We shall therefore use the following symbols.
>
> $\bar{x}$ is the mean of the sample
> μ (mu) is the true mean of the population
> s   is the standard deviation of a sample
> σ (sigma) is the true standard deviation of the population

Central limit theorem

2.6 The central limit theorem is the name given to the theory of how sample statistics are distributed. It can be shown that the standard deviation of the sampling distribution of the mean, called the *standard error* of the mean, is given by $\sigma/\sqrt{n}$ where σ is the population standard deviation and n is the number of items in each sample.

2.7 We generally do not know the value of σ and so we have to use the sample standard deviation, s, as an estimate of it. This is acceptable as long as the sample size is over 30.

2.8 *Summary of central limit theorem*

For random samples of size greater than 30

> (a) Sample means are normally distributed.
>
> (b) Their mean is μ.
>
> (c) Their standard error is $\dfrac{\sigma}{\sqrt{n}}$ or $\dfrac{s}{\sqrt{n}}$

Confidence limits

2.9 From our knowledge of the properties of a normal distribution, together with the rule that sample means are normally distributed around the true population mean with a standard deviation equal to the standard error, we can predict the following (using normal distribution tables).

(a) 95% of all sample means will be within 1.96 standard errors of the population mean.
(b) 99% of all sample means will be within 2.5758 standard errors of the population mean, etc.

2.10 By looking at it the other way you will see that we can make the following statements.

(a) With 95% certainty the population mean lies within the range: sample mean ± 1.96 standard errors.

(b) With 99% certainty the population mean lies within the range: sample mean ± 2.5758 standard errors.

These ranges are known as *confidence limits* or *bands* or *intervals*.

First example: standard error and confidence limits

2.11 From a random sample of 576 of a company's employees, it was found that the average number of days each person was absent from work due to illness was eight days per annum, with a standard deviation of 3.6 days.

$\bar{x}$ = 8 days
s = 3.6 days

What are the confidence limits for the average number of days' absence through sickness per employee for the company as a whole:

(a) at a 95% level of confidence;
(b) at a 99% level of confidence?

Solution

2.12 We must first calculate the standard error, which is estimated as $\dfrac{s}{\sqrt{n}}$

(because we do not know σ, the standard deviation of the entire population).

$$se = \frac{3.6}{\sqrt{576}} = 0.15 \text{ days}$$

(a) At a 95% level of confidence, the mean number of days' absence per employee per annum is in the range $8 \pm 1.96 \times 0.15$
$$= \quad 8 \pm 0.294$$
$$= \quad 7.706 \text{ days to } 8.294 \text{ days, (say 7.7 days to 8.3 days).}$$

(b) At a 99% level of confidence, the true average number of days' absence per employee per annum is in the range of $8 \pm 2.5758 \times 0.15$
$$= \quad 8 \pm 0.386$$
$$= \quad 7.614 \text{ days to } 8.386 \text{ days, (say 7.6 days to 8.4 days).}$$

2.13 It is useful to ask why it was necessary to calculate confidence limits. If the sample mean was eight days would it not be sufficient to use eight days as a *point estimate* of the population mean? Such an estimate would be 'common sense' and practical. How does it help to know a range of possible values for the population mean?

2.14 In practice, a sample mean might indeed be used as a 'point estimate' of the population mean. However, we could not be sure how reliable the estimate might be, without first considering the size of the standard error.

2.15 The sample mean might be above or below the true population mean.

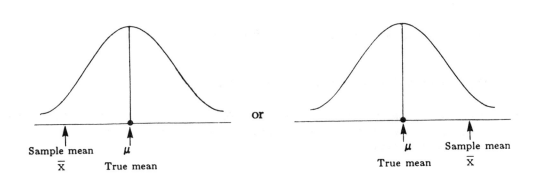

2.16 With 95% confidence, we could say that the sample mean is no further than 1.96 standard errors above or below the true population mean.

2.17 If the confidence limits cover a wide range of values, a point estimate of the population mean from the sample would not be considered reliable. On the other hand, if the confidence limits cover a narrow range of values, a point estimate of the population mean, using the sample mean, would be regarded as reliable.

Second example: standard error and confidence limits

2.18 The cost of assembling an item of equipment has been estimated by obtaining a sample of 144 jobs. The average cost of assembly derived from the sample was £4,000 with a standard deviation of £1,500.

Estimate confidence limits for the true average cost of assembly. Use the 95% level of confidence.

Solution

2.19 The standard error is estimated as $\dfrac{s}{\sqrt{n}} = \dfrac{1,500}{\sqrt{144}} = £125$

At a 95% level of confidence, the population mean is £(4,000 ± 1.96 × 125) = £(4,000 ± 245), ie in the range of £3,755 - £4,245.

The possible range of values for the population mean is 2(245) = £490. This is quite a large range, so that an average of £4,000 would not be considered to be sufficiently reliable for use by management in cost estimations.

Exercise

In a survey of 80 contracts, the average value was found to be £24,520 and the standard deviation was £5,260. Find the 95% confidence interval for the mean.

Solution

n = 80, s = 5260

Standard error = $\dfrac{s}{\sqrt{n}} = \dfrac{5,260}{\sqrt{80}} = 588.09$

The 95% confidence interval for the true mean is

    24,520 - 1.96 × 588.09 to 24,520 + 1.96 × 588.09
ie 24,520 - 1,152.66 to 24,520 + 1,152.66
ie £23,367 to £25,673

Estimating a proportion

2.20 The arithmetic mean is a very important statistic, and sampling is often concerned with estimating the mean of a population. Many surveys, however, attempt to estimate a *proportion* rather than an arithmetic mean, especially those concerned with the following.

(a) Human attitudes or opinions about an issue.

(b) The percentage of times an event occurs (for example the proportion of faulty items out of the total number of items produced in a manufacturing department).

2.21 The central limit theorem applies equally to proportions estimated from large random samples.

> (a) Sample proportions are normally distributed.
>
> (b) Their mean is the population proportion, π.
>
> (c) Their standard error is $\sqrt{\dfrac{p(1-p)}{n}}$

where p is the proportion of the sample with the characteristic being investigated, and n is the sample size.

The Greek capital letter π is used to denote the true population proportion and the true standard error is $\sqrt{\dfrac{\pi(1-\pi)}{n}}$. Since we do not know the value of π, we must use the approximation $\sqrt{\dfrac{p(1-p)}{n}}$.

2.22 The formulae for the standard errors of the mean and of the proportion are both given in your exam.

Example: the standard error of a proportion

2.23 In a random sample of 500 employees, 320 were members of a trade union. Estimate the proportion of trade union members in the entire organisation at the 95% confidence level.

Solution

2.24 Sample proportion $= \dfrac{320}{500} = 0.64$

Standard error $= \sqrt{\dfrac{0.64 \times (1 - 0.64)}{500}} = \sqrt{\dfrac{(0.64)(0.36)}{500}} = 0.0215$

An estimate of the population proportion at the 95% confidence level is the sample proportion $\pm$ 1.96 standard errors.

The population proportion = 0.64 ± (1.96) (0.0215) = 0.64 ± 0.04 (approx) ie the percentage of employees who are trade union members is between 60% and 68% at the 95% level of confidence.

Exercise

A survey of 200 clients has shown that 75% are happy with the service being given. Estimate the true proportion of satisfied clients at 95% confidence level.

Solution

n = 200
p = 0.75   1 - p   =   0.25

standard error $= \sqrt{\dfrac{p(1-p)}{n}} = \sqrt{\dfrac{0.75 \times 0.25}{200}} = 0.0306$

95% confidence limits are
   $0.75 - 1.96 \times 0.0306$ and $0.75 + 1.96 \times 0.0306$
ie   0.6900 and 0.8100
ie   between 69% and 81%

2.25 *Summary*

95% confidence limits are given by mean (or proportion) ± 1.96 × appropriate standard error.

99% confidence limits are given by mean (or proportion) ± 2.5758 × standard error.

Significance tests

2.26 We have seen how samples can be used to estimate the true average or proportion. The other major purpose of sampling is to test theories. For example to test whether sales have in fact risen following the introduction of new packaging or whether a new product does in fact perform better than those of competitors.

2.27 The problem in answering such questions is that a sample might well show improved sales or improved performance even though in fact there has really been no change. The very randomness of the sampling process means that results do vary from the true values. The question in interpreting sample results becomes one of whether our results are sufficiently different from those that prevailed previously or elsewhere to mean that we are justified in claiming that a genuine change has taken place.

2.28 We work on the assumption that no change has occurred. This is called the *null hypothesis*, 'null' meaning no change or no difference etc. On that basis we know what the sampling distribution of the mean or the proportion ought to be and we know, for instance, that 95% of sample means should lie within a certain range if the 'no change' hypothesis is correct. If our sample mean falls outside that range, it could of course simply be a freak result and the null hypothesis could still be true, but it is more likely that a genuine change has occurred.

2.29 The *significance level* adopted in a test is the probability level at which we will undergo a change of mind and reject the null hypothesis. The levels generally adopted are either 5% (if we are fairly ready to change our minds) or 1% (if we are hard to convince). Using central limit theorem, the probability of the particular sample result can be calculated and if it falls below the significance level we reject the null hypothesis and decide that a change has in fact occurred.

First example

2.30 Suppose that a company's management accountant has estimated that the average direct cost of providing a certain service to a customer is £40.

A sample has been taken, consisting of 150 service provisions, and the mean direct cost of each service in the sample was £45 with a standard deviation of £10.

Is the sample consistent with the estimate of an average cost of £40?

Solution

2.31 *Null hypothesis* (H_0): the true average is still £40

Alternative hypothesis (H_1): the true average is different from £40

Significance level: 5%

Standard error $\dfrac{s}{\sqrt{n}} = \dfrac{10}{\sqrt{150}} = 0.8165$

If the null hypothesis is true, sample means should be normally distributed with an average of £40 and standard error of 0.8165.

Decision rule: we will reject the null hypothesis if our sample mean has a probability below 5% ie if it is more than 1.96 standard errors away from £40.

The critical values of U are ± 1.96

The sample value of U = number of standard errors between £40 and £45 = $\dfrac{45-40}{0.8165}$ = 6.1

The sample value of U is outside the critical range ± 1.96, hence its probability is (considerably) less than 5% and we reject the null hypothesis.

Conclusion. The true average cost is different from £40 at 5% significance level.

Second example

2.32 Over the years the proportion of faulty goods has been quite steady at 3%, but a recent sample of 50 items had 4% faulty. At 5% significance level, can we conclude that a change has occurred?

Solution

2.33 H_0: true proportion is still 3% ie $\pi = 0.03$

H_1: true proportion is different from 3% ie $\pi \neq 0.03$

Significance level: 5%

Standard error if H_0 is true $= \sqrt{\dfrac{\pi(1-\pi)}{n}} = \sqrt{\dfrac{0.03 \times 0.97}{50}}$

$$= 0.0241$$

Critical values of U are ± 1.96

Sample value of $U = \dfrac{0.04 - 0.03}{0.0241} = 0.41$

The sample U is between ± 1.96 so we cannot reject the null hypothesis.

Conclusion. At 5% significance level, the results are compatible with the true proportion still being 3%.

One-tail and two-tail tests

2.34 Both the examples so far have asked whether the true mean or proportion is significantly *different* from a presumed value. It could have been either above or below that value and so we performed a *two-tail* test. We would have rejected H_0 if the sample U had been greater than 1.96 or equally if it had been less than - 1.96.

2.35 Sometimes the question is whether the true value is significantly *greater* than a presumed value. In this case we reject H_0 only if the sample U exceeds the critical U and this is called a *one tail* test since the 5% probability must all lie in just one tail. The opposite would apply if the question suggests that the truth is *less than* a presumed value.

2.36 If we return to the normal table in paragraph 1.13, it can be seen that the critical U values for two-tail tests are either ± 1.96 (at 5% significance level) or ± 2.5758 (at 1% level). The first of these values cuts off 2.5% in each of two tails, making 5% altogether, and the second cuts off $\frac{1}{2}$% in each tail, making 1% altogether.

Summary for two-tail tests

Significance level	Accept H_0 if sample U is in range
5%	- 1.96 to + 1.96
1%	- 2.5758 to + 2.5758

2.37 For one-tail tests, the critical U values are 1.6449 (cutting 5% off in one tail) or 2.3263 (cutting 1% off in one tail).

Summary for one-tail tests

Significance level	*Accept H_0 if sample U is less than*
5%	1.6449
1%	2.3263

If the question suggests that the true value is *less than* a presumed level, we accept H_0 if the sample U is greater than -1.6449 or -2.3263.

Example of a one-tail test

2.38 It is believed that 90% of potential customers are familiar with a firm's trademark but a sample of 100 consumers showed that only 70% recognised the trademark. Is this significantly less than the expected proportion at 1% significance level?

Solution

2.39 H_0: π is 0.9
H_1: π is less than 0.9. One-tail test required.

Significance level : 1%
If H_0 is true, then

$$\text{standard error} = \sqrt{\frac{\pi(1-\pi)}{n}} = \sqrt{\frac{0.9 \times 0.1}{100}} = 0.03$$

Critical U = -2.3263

Sample U = $\dfrac{0.7 - 0.9}{0.03}$ = -6.67 which is less than the critical value.

We reject the null hypothesis.

Conclusion. The proportion of consumers familiar with the trademark is significantly less than 90% at 1% significance level.

3. CONCLUSION

3.1 In this chapter we have introduced the normal distribution which enables probabilities to be associated with the values taken by a wide range of measured variables.

3.2 The central limit theorem enables us to apply the normal distribution to making estimates and testing theories on the basis of sample results.

3.3 Probability and sampling theory is one of the most difficult topics on your syllabus but there is a question on it in virtually every CIM exam paper. We strongly urge you to try the illustrative questions for this chapter, all of which are taken from past CIM exam papers.

TEST YOUR KNOWLEDGE

The numbers in brackets refer to paragraphs of this chapter

1. Interpret the statement that, from the Normal table, $\propto = 0.3$ corresponds to $U = 0.5244$. (1.14)

2. What conditions must be met if the central limit theorem is to apply? (2.4)

3. What is meant by the expression '95% confidence interval for the mean'? (2.10)

4. Describe how significance tests are carried out. (2.28, 2.29)

5. What is the difference between a one-tail and a two-tail test? (2.34, 2.35)

Now try illustrative questions 30 to 33

ILLUSTRATIVE QUESTIONS AND
SUGGESTED SOLUTIONS

ILLUSTRATIVE QUESTIONS

1   **COMPUTER GAMES** (20 marks)

A company which designs and manufactures computer games has decided that it wishes to conduct a survey to find the views of users of its computer games. The company wishes to obtain some factual information: make and age of computer; whether a television set or monitor is used; whether a disk drive or cassette is used for storing programs; age and sex of main user(s) of games; whether the computer is used for writing games programs; whether the computer is used for business purposes. The company is particularly interested to find the preference of users for arcade games, adventure games, simulation games, educational games etc.

Required

(a)   Briefly explain how you would try to obtain a sample of computer games users. (8 marks)

(b)   Draw up a questionnaire for use with the survey.   (12 marks)

2   **HYPERSTORE** (20 marks)

The annual sales in £'00,000 of three departments of a hyperstore from 1975 to 1984 are shown in the following table.

Year	Department A	Department B	Department C
1975	15	27	19
1976	19	28	25
1977	21	27	20
1978	24	31	26
1979	22	30	20
1980	25	33	27
1981	20	31	24
1982	16	36	28
1983	19	37	29
1984	14	32	25

(a)   Draw the following.
    (i)   A band chart to show the information in the table.   (8 marks)
    (ii) A pie chart to show the figures for 1984.   (6 marks)

(b)   What are the advantages of presenting statistical information in diagrammatic form?
                                                                    (6 marks)

CIM June 1986

3   **SORBETS** (20 marks)

Construct two different types of chart that would suitably illustrate the data below.

	1986	1987	1988	1989
Vanilla	280	301	300	450
Strawberry	125	153	107	110
Lemon	50	96	158	269
Banana	25	31	31	35

CIM December 1990

4   ADVERTISING EXPENDITURE (20 marks)

A company has spent the following amounts in £'s on advertising for each of the months of 19X7 and 19X8.

	January	February	March	April	May	June
19X7	410	380	420	430	480	390
19X8	420	390	410	450	500	410

	July	August	September	October	November	December
19X7	430	370	390	450	510	480
19X8	450	370	400	480	540	490

(a) Display the necessary calculations and draw accurately a Z chart for advertising expenditure during 19X8.   (12 marks)

(b) Explain the interpretation and use of each part of the chart.   (8 marks)

CIM June 1989

5   UTOPIAN RETAILERS (20 marks)

The following figures relate to the annual turnover of retail outlets in Utopia in the years 19X1 and 19X9.

Turnover per outlet over dollars	Turnover per outlet not over dollars	19X1 Number of outlets	19X1 Total turnover of outlets in each class m dollars	19X9 Number of outlets	19X9 Total turnover of outlets in each class m dollars
-	1,000	3,500	2.0	5,200	2.6
1,000	3,000	4,900	7.4	5,400	8.6
3,000	5,000	2,900	13.1	3,100	14.0
5,000	8,000	3,800	24.9	2,200	14.3
8,000	12,000	1,500	14.7	1,200	11.8
12,000	16,000	700	9.9	600	8.4
16,000	25,000	500	11.2	300	6.0
25,000	50,000	200	7.4	100	3.8
50,000	100,000	100	7.5	100	7.5
100,000	-	0	0	100	1.5
		18,100	98.1	18,300	78.5

Required

Present the information in the form of a Lorenz curve and comment on the results.

6   ANNUAL TURNOVER (10 marks)

Represent the following information on a semi-logarithmic graph. Explain also the various purposes for which this form of graphical presentation is chosen.

Annual turnover of the Apex Company

Year	£'000	Year	£'000
1975	12.4	1981	126.3
1976	26.7	1982	158.7
1977	45.6	1983	171.5
1978	62.5	1984	203.0
1979	78.7	1985	238.4
1980	97.1	1986	221.8

CIM December 1988

7   DISHWASHERS (25 marks)

Over a period of 55 days, the following number of dishwashers were sold.

0	2	5	6	2	3	1	2	4	3	0
2	1	2	2	3	2	3	1	2	4	2
3	2	3	3	1	2	5	2	4	1	3
4	3	4	1	2	4	3	5	2	2	1
2	3	2	2	3	0	2	1	3	3	2

(a)   Form the data into a frequency distribution.

(b)   Display the data by means of a frequency polygon.

(c)   Find the mean, mode, median, standard deviation, coefficient of variation and range.

(d)   Compare these results with those of a similar period a year previously for which the mean number of dishwashers sold per day was 2.25 and the standard deviation was 1.12.

(e)   Check your results in (c) by using your calculator in SD mode.

8   COACH EXPORTS (20 marks)

Two competing companies manufacture and export passenger vehicles. The following table records the number of 54 seater coaches each company exported to the European market in twelve successive four-week trading periods.

ILLUSTRATIVE QUESTIONS

Trading period	No of coaches exported Company X	Company Y
1	26	20
2	12	28
3	34	24
4	18	23
5	20	19
6	37	26
7	16	22
8	23	29
9	28	18
10	39	25
11	14	30
12	17	21

(a) Calculate the standard deviation of coaches exported for each of companies X and Y.

(12 marks)

(b) In the light of your results compare the two companies interpreting the marketing implications of this measure of dispersion.

(8 marks)

CIM June 1986

9 TELEPHONE CALLS (25 marks)

British Telecom have monitored the lengths of telephone calls from a customer and the results are shown below giving the times in seconds.

47	141	43	293	104	82	24	84	41	86
100	29	211	28	16	18	24	157	209	28
194	41	318	49	194	212	19	140	16	120
105	116	29	58	167	163	29	88	302	101
186	155	106	153	69	105	23	88	97	64
49	203	170	218	18	313	307	219	111	71

(a) Tabulate the times in the form of a frequency distribution, grouping by suitable intervals.

(b) Find the mean, the standard deviation and the coefficient of variation for the grouped distribution.

(c) Display the data by means of a histogram and hence estimate the mode.

(d) Display the data by means of an ogive and hence estimate the median and quartile deviation.

Data taken from CIM June 1990

10 CHAIN STORE (20 marks)

A chain store monitors its level of daily sales in two different locations over a common period of 100 trading days. The distribution of sales for both outlets is shown in the accompanying table.

ILLUSTRATIVE QUESTIONS

Sales £'000	Number of days Outlet P	Outlet Q
2 but less than 4	14	18
4 but less than 6	16	45
6 but less than 8	17	17
8 but less than 10	19	9
10 but less than 12	18	7
12 but less than 14	16	4
	100	100

(a) Calculate the arithmetic mean and standard deviation of daily sales for each of the two outlets. (14 marks)

(b) In the light of these results discuss the significant differences revealed about the nature of the sales pattern in the two locations. (6 marks)

CIM June 1987

11 REPS' MILEAGES (20 marks)

Weekly distance travelled by company's sales representatives is as follows.

Miles travelled	No of representatives
under 100	12
100 and under 140	39
140 and under 180	25
180 and under 220	17
220 and under 260	11
260 and under 300	8
300 and under 340	5
340 and under 380	3
380 and under 420	1

(a) Find, arithmetically, the mode, median and arithmetic mean of miles travelled in the above frequency distribution. (12 marks)

(b) Explain the meaning of these three measures and their different uses as representative values of the distribution. (8 marks)

CIM June 1986

12 STAMPS (20 marks)

To encourage sales in its chain of supermarkets a company introduced a bonus-stamp scheme. Stamps were given according to purchases made and could be saved and redeemed against other goods within the store. To examine the progress of the scheme after three months' operation a random sample of customers was asked to state how many stamps they had so far obtained. The results are given in the cumulative table that follows.

Number of stamps saved	Number of customers
Less than 500	46
Less than 1,500	118
Less than 2,500	207
Less than 3,000	259
Less than 3,500	299
Less than 4,000	332
Less than 4,500	350

(a) Rearrange this information in the form of a grouped frequency table and construct a histogram to illustrate the distribution. (6 marks)

(b) Hence, calculate the arithmetic mean and standard deviation for the number of stamps saved by a customer. (10 marks)

(c) Explain the meaning of the results you have obtained. (4 marks)

CIM June 1989

13 CORRELATION (18 marks)

Calculate the correlation coefficient for the following sets of data. From your solution, comment on the apparent degree of correlation between the two variables.

(Ignore the low value of n.)

(a)

x	y
10	38
40	86
30	70
50	102
20	54

(b)

x	y
2	3
5	4
3	0
7	1
4	10
2	8

(c)

1981	10
1982	10
1983	7
1984	7
1985	6
1986	5

14   SCATTER DIAGRAMS (12 marks)

Draw scatter diagrams of about ten points to illustrate the following degrees of linear association.

(a)   Weak, positive correlation.

(b)   Approximately zero correlation.

(c) $r = -1$.

(d)   Fairly strong negative correlation.

15   COMPLETIONS (20 marks)

Calculate the product moment coefficient of correlation between the orders and completion figures shown below for nine successive weeks.

The information is derived from a company marketing and fitting kitchen units. Comment on both the result and any time lag that might be looked for in studying the correlation between orders and completions.

Orders under construction	Completions
26	29
14	15
22	24
17	16
15	21
23	18
28	19
19	20
13	25

CIM June 1986

16   RANK CORRELATION (20 marks)

(a)   Describe the difference between the product moment and the rank coefficients of correlation and explain the circumstances in which one might prefer to use each of them.

(10 marks)

(b)   Research has been conducted into the percentage recall of advertising material amongst a panel of readers of daily newspapers. Members of the panel have also been asked to indicate their liking for each newspaper by placing them in order of preference. From the summary data that follows calculate the rank coefficient of correlation and comment upon the result.

Newspaper	Order of preference	% recall of advertisements
A	9	7.2
B	3	9.8
C	10	6.8
D	1	11.5
E	6	9.3
F	4	10.3
G	12	4.6
H	2	10.7
I	7	6.4
J	11	5.3
K	5	8.7
L	8	7.2

CIM June 1987

17 ADVERTISING (20 marks)

The marketing director of Sell It has been asked by the managing director to justify his advertising budget. The marketing director has collected the following information in an effort to satisfy this request.

Product area	Advertising expenditure £	Sales £
1	15	200
2	18	240
3	18	260
4	21	290
5	23	300
6	23	320
7	26	380
8	28	370
9	32	400
10	37	470

(a) Calculate the least squares regression line between advertising expenditure and sales revenue. (12 marks)

(b) How should the managing director interpret the result? (8 marks)

CIM June 1990

18 PLANNING EXERCISE (20 marks)

You are involved in a planning exercise, part of which requires an assessment of the financial implications of future output levels. As part of the preliminary work you have been asked to investigate the production of product A for a whole industry. Since 19X1, production (million tonnes) of A for the industry has been as follows.

Year	Production Million tonnes
19X1	19
19X2	24
19X3	28
19X4	33
19X5	35
19X6	41
19X7	45
19X8	47
19X9	52

Required

(a) Find the least squares regression equation of production on time.

(b) Predict production for 19Y1, explaining any assumptions or limitations.

19 EIGHT EMPLOYEES (25 marks)

A sample of eight employees is taken from the production department of a light engineering factory. The data below relate to the number of weeks' experience in the wiring of components, and the number of components which were rejected as unsatisfactory last week.

Employee	A	B	C	D	E	F	G	H
Weeks of experience(X)	4	5	7	9	10	11	12	14
Number of rejects (Y)	21	22	15	18	14	14	11	13

$\Sigma X = 72$, $\Sigma Y = 128$, $\Sigma XY = 1,069$, $\Sigma X^2 = 732$, $\Sigma Y^2 = 2,156$

(a) Draw a scatter diagram of the data.
(b) Calculate the product moment correlation coefficient for these data and interpret its value.
(c) Find the least squares regression equation of rejects on experience. Predict the number of rejects you would expect from an employee with one week of experience.

20 STANDARD SIZE BOXES (20 marks)

A cost accountant has derived the following data on the weekly output of standard size boxes from a factory.

Week	Output (X) thousands	Total cost (Y) £'000
1	20	60
2	2	25
3	4	26
4	23	66
5	18	49
6	14	48
7	10	35
8	8	18
9	13	40
10	8	33

$\Sigma X = 120$, $\Sigma Y = 400$, $\Sigma X^2 = 1,866$ $\Sigma Y^2 = 18,200$ $\Sigma XY = 5,704$

Required

(a) Plot a scatter diagram of the data.

(b) Which weekly outputs, if any, appear to be different from the rest of the data?

(c) State the co-ordinates of a point which must lie on a regression line fitted to the data above.

(d) Find the least squares regression of total cost on output, and plot the line on the graph.

(e) What is the fixed cost of the factory?

(f) In a given week it is planned to produce 25,000 standard size boxes. Use your regression equation to estimate the total cost of producing this quantity.

21 EARTHWORM GARDEN CENTRE (20 marks)

The cash sales of the Earthworm Garden Centre for the four weeks of February 19X3 were as follows.

	Week No 1 £	Week No 2 £	Week No 3 £	Week No 4 £
Wednesday	510	500	540	550
Thursday	360	380	390	410
Friday	570	580	580	600
Saturday	800	820	830	850
Sunday	850	840	870	900

The centre is closed on Mondays and Tuesdays.

Required

(a) From this data, calculate the trend, the average 'seasonal' (ie daily) variations and the residuals.

(b) Forecast sales for the next week if the trend is forecast to be as follows.

	Wednesday	Thursday	Friday	Saturday	Sunday
Trend forecast	670	673	676	679	681

(c) Comment on the likely reliability of your forecasts.

22 SEASIDE CAFE (20 marks)

A seaside cafe is to be sold. In advertising the sale it is intended to give the 'probable annual turnover for 19X9'. The following data are available showing quarterly turnover in thousands.

Quarters	I	II	III	IV
19X5	20	35	26	18
19X6	18	36	24	15
19X7	14	34	25	14
19X8	15	32	23	12

(a) Analyse this series by moving averages and find the seasonal variations.   (10 marks)

(b) Plot the data on a time series graph and insert the estimated trend curve.   (5 marks)

(c) State the information you would provide for the advertisement commenting on the validity of this figure.   (5 marks)

CIM June 1989

23 LAWNMOWERS (20 marks)

The following data represents the number of lawnmowers sold by a local garden shop.

Year	1st quarter	2nd quarter	3rd quarter	4th quarter
6	14	26	7	4
7	15	28	7	5
8	15	29	8	5
9	17	34	9	5

(a) Smooth this time series by means of a centred moving average.   (6 marks)

(b) Calculate the average seasonal variations.   (6 marks)

(c) Explain how your calculations could be used for forecasting lawnmower sales during year 10. What factors should be considered in assessing the accuracy of such a forecast?
                                                                            (8 marks)

CIM June 1990

24 FORECASTS (15 marks)

(a) If the trend in sales (y) is related to time (x) by the regression equation

$$y = 217 + 2.7x$$

where x = 1 for the first quarter of 19X2, predict the trend for the quarters of 19X4.

(b) If the average seasonal variations using the additive model are given by

	Quarter		
1	2	3	4
− 13	− 112	+ 103	+ 22

forecast the actual quarterly sales for 19X4.

(c) If the average seasonal variations using the multiplicative method are given by

	Quarter		
1	2	3	4
− 5%	− 45%	+ 42%	+ 9%

forecast the actual quarterly sales for 19X4.

ILLUSTRATIVE QUESTIONS

25 COFFEE BEANS (20 marks)

An importer of coffee beans notes the following changes in the prices and relative quantities for the five leading varieties marketed through his company. Results are quoted for the three year period 19X3 to 19X5.

Variety	19X3		19X4		19X5	
	Price £	Quantity	Price £	Quantity	Price £	Quantity
A	3.65	7	4.00	6	4.13	5
B	2.14	9	2.37	11	2.35	12
C	2.85	8	2.89	10	2.98	8
D	3.29	12	3.38	15	3.52	18
E	4.06	6	4.23	6	4.11	7

Using 19X3 as the base year.

(a) Calculate the overall base weighted price index for 19X4 and also for 19X5. (8 marks)

(b) Calculate the overall current weighted price index for 19X4 and also for 19X5. (8 marks)

(c) Using the results obtained in (a) and (b) to illustrate your answer, contrast the Laspeyre and Paasche methods for obtaining price index numbers. (4 marks)

CIM June 1988

26 COMPONENTS (20 marks)

A company produces certain machine components by assembling bought-in parts. The cost of the parts have been changing as shown in the following table.

Part number	Total cost in 19X6 £	Unit price in 19X6 £	Unit price in 19X8 £
A19043	465	3.00	3.12
B25467	1,200	2.50	2.65
E53692	798	1.20	1.17
B49628	600	2.40	2.46
C38571	2,100	6.00	6.24
A42975	900	4.50	4.86
C24847	1,400	2.80	3.08

(a) Deduce the 19X6 quantity weights that may be adopted for each part. (4 marks)

(b) Calculate the all-item price relative index for 19X8 using 19X6 = 100 and the weights deduced in (a). (8 marks)

(c) During the previous five years the company's purchasing costs have varied according to the following index series.

19X3	19X4	19X5	19X6	19X7
100	103	107	112	115

Extend this series to include the 19X8 index maintaining the 19X3 base. (3 marks)

(d) Recalculate the index series given in (c) so that it is based on 19X7 = 100. (5 marks)

CIM June 1989

27 BATTERIES (20 marks)

The following data represents the sales of batteries at a local garage.

Category of battery	Quantities		Price £	
	19X7	19X8	19X7	19X8
Economy	10	6	10	15
Standard	8	8	27	29
De luxe	9	25	47	32
Super	14	16	48	53

Required

(a) Calculate an all items base weighted price index for 19X8 using 19X7 as the base period.
(8 marks)

(b) Explain the relative advantages of base and current weighted index numbers. (6 marks)

(c) Explain the effects of changing the base weighted index calculated in (a) to a current weighted index.
(6 marks)

CIM June 1990

28 ITEMS FOR INCLUSION (20 marks)

What is an index number?

Describe the problems that might arise in choosing items for inclusion in a price index and explain how these problems might be overcome.

Calculate a total Laspeyre price index for October 19X9 from the following information, using January 19X2 as a base.

Commodity	January 19X2		October 19X9
	Price (£)	Quantity	Price (£)
A	1.62	37	1.98
B	3.57	25	4.52
C	0.94	11	2.65
D	5.60	6	9.23
E	2.83	20	3.71

CIM December 1989

29 DEEFEX LIMITED (20 marks)

Deefex Limited operates two factories, at Staines and at Scratchwood. At each location, the factory manager wishes to obtain some information about defective items of production.

(a) At the Staines factory, product P is susceptible to two types of defect. There is a 0.15 probability of inspected output having defect X, and a 0.14 probability of it having defect Y. The defects occur independently.

What is the probability that an item of product P has the following.

(i)   At least one defect?
(ii)   Both defects, X and Y?
(iii) One defect only?
(iv)   No defects at all?

(b) Also made at the Staines factory is another product, Q, which is susceptible to three types of defect, X, Y and Z. The probability that product Q has defect Z depends on whether it contains any other defect, X or Y.

The probability of having defect X is	0.15
The probability of having defect Y is	0.14
The probability of having defect Z if it has neither X nor Y is	0.3
The probability of having defect Z if it has one of X or Y, but not both is	0.2
The probability of having defect Z if it has both defects X and Y is	0.1

What is the probability that an item of product Q has the following.

(i)   None of the three defects?
(ii)   One of the three defects?

(Note: you should use your solution to part (a) to help in the calculation of the solution to (b)).

(c) At the Scratchwood factory, Product R goes through five consecutive operations before it is completed. Information about production which you are given, and which is thought to be typical of normal operations, is as follows.

Units of product R started in process 1	7,500
Rejects	
Process 1	660
Process 2	520
Process 3	430
Process 4	290
Process 5	80

(i)   What is the probability that a unit, once started, will become a completed unit of finished product?

(ii)   What is the probability that a unit will get beyond the second process?

30 SIGNIFICANCE TESTS (20 marks)

(a) In a certain city 60% of the families own their own homes. A survey made among the subscribers to a magazine asked whether or not the family owned the home in which they were living. A random sample of 1,200 was taken and 62% of the subscribers reported that they owned their home.

Is it correct to conclude that the proportion of subscribers who owned their home is significantly different from the percentage in the population of the city? Explain your reasoning.   (10 marks)

(b) A life insurance salesman with a great deal of experience believes that the peak earning age of businessmen is reached at age 52. A random sample of 26 retired businessmen was studied and the age at which they received their highest salary was found to be an arithmetic mean of 56.8 years and the standard deviation of the sample was 8.9 years. What does this information suggest about the insurance salesman's theory that the peak age of earning is 52 years? Explain your conclusion.   (10 marks)

CIM November 1986

31 CAMERA BATTERIES (20 marks)

(a) A simple random sample of 425 camera batteries from a given production run shows that the mean life was 150 hours under normal use. If the sample standard deviation was 15 hours, what is the 95% confidence interval of the mean life of all batteries in the production run? Could the true mean be as high as 160 hours? Explain your answer. Also, test the hypothesis that the true mean is 148 hours or less, using the 1% level of significance.
                                                                                                          (12 marks)

(b) One manufacturer of the camera batteries has seven factories in the UK and five in other parts of the world. A second manufacturer has four factories in the UK and ten in other parts of the world. To conduct a survey one factory is chosen at random from each of the two manufacturers. What is the probability of the two chosen factories being:

(i)   one from the UK and one from outside the UK;
(ii)   both from the UK; and
(iii) neither from the UK.   (8 marks)

CIM November 1987

32 DEPARTMENTAL STORE (20 marks)

(a) The national mean delivery time for goods to be dispatched from a particular chain of retail departmental stores to their customers is 5.62 working days.

From a sample of 15 orders selected at random from a certain store in the chain during the first week of March last, the arithmetic mean delivery time was found to be 5.79 working days with a standard deviation of 0.32 days. Is the company justified, at the 5% level of significance, in maintaining that delivery time at this store is worse than their national average? What conclusion would you give at the 1% significance level? You must explain the interpretation of your conclusions.

(b) In the same store the goods inward department decides to carry out a check on the quality of a large consignment of small electrical fuses. Fifty samples of six fuses are drawn from a large bulk in which the proportion of faulty fuses is estimated at 12%. Calculate the number of samples that can be expected to contain no more than one defective component by using the basic rules of probability.

CIM June 1986

33 SURVEYS (20 marks)

(a) Three companies are to be sampled for study of their marketing methods by selection from a list of twenty.

There are five companies in each of four different sales regions A, B, C and D. The selection is made entirely at random without knowing in advance the address of each company. Find the probability that the three companies chosen are:

(i)   all from region A;   (3 marks)
(ii) all from any one region;   (2 marks)
(iii) each from a different region.   (5 marks)

(b) A company manufacturing a certain brand of cat food claims that at least eight out of ten cat owners prefer its brand to another.

A random sample of 450 owners contains 345 who state that they do indeed prefer this brand. Using the 5% level of significance, does this sample result suggest that the claim made by the manufacturers is justified?   (10 marks)

CIM December 1988

SUGGESTED SOLUTIONS

1   COMPUTER GAMES

(a)   A sample of computer game users could be obtained by contacting the following users:

- schools
- businesses
- computer clubs
- computer manufacturers' users clubs
- past customers who have already bought games from the company
- stopping people at random, either in houses or in the street

Schools may well have their own computer clubs, as well as formal classroom tuition being given in computer studies. This will give a biased sample in that the users will all be of a young age, will probably prefer the more trivial arcade games to serious business applications, and may well all be using the same make of computer as selected by the teacher in charge. However schools offer a cheap and convenient method of meeting a large section of the possible customer base.

Businesses suffer from the reverse problem, in that they will be biased towards serious applications and will not be interested in leisure games. However they may comprise another large section of the market (at least in share of turnover) so should not be ignored.

Computer clubs generally offer the opportunity of meeting numbers of 'ordinary users' who will be interested in all forms of games amongst their members. Manufacturers' clubs will comprise users of their type of computer only, but still provide a valuable means of meeting new and prospective customers.

Sales records for the company's past customers will show the historical split of sales between the different forms of games, and will provide a database of names and addresses to be contacted in the future.

People at large will offer an additional unstructured set of opinions, free from any particular manufacturer or club.

One sensible approach to obtaining the sample of users would be to 'stratify' the population into divisions as above in agreed proportions, and then to select a random sample from each stratum, the number in each sample being proportional to the size of the stratum.

(b)   A suggested questionnaire for use with the survey is shown on the following page.

TICK AS APPROPRIATE

	Never	Sometimes	Often
Do you use computer games?	☐	☐	☐

Make of computer ....

Age of computer (years) ....

	TV	Monitor
TV/Monitor used	☐	☐

	Disk	Cassette	Other
Storage medium used	☐	☐	....

	Yes	No
Used for *writing* programs?	☐	☐

	Yes	No
Used for business purposes?	☐	☐

Tick types of games used	Never	Sometimes	Often
Arcade	☐	☐	☐
Adventure	☐	☐	☐
Simulation	☐	☐	☐
Educational	☐	☐	☐
Other	☐	☐	☐

Who are main users?

	Male	Female
(1) Sex	☐	☐
Age		
(2) Sex	☐	☐
Age		
(3) Sex	☐	☐
Age		

Name ....

Address ....

Phone .... (Home) ....
(Work)

THANK YOU FOR YOUR TIME

2 HYPERSTORE

(a) (i)

| | | *Subtotals* | |
Year	A	A + B	A + B + C
1975	15	42	61
1976	19	47	72
1977	21	48	68
1978	24	55	81
1979	22	52	72
1980	25	58	85
1981	20	51	75
1982	16	52	80
1983	19	56	85
1984	14	46	71

Annual departmental sales (£'00,000)

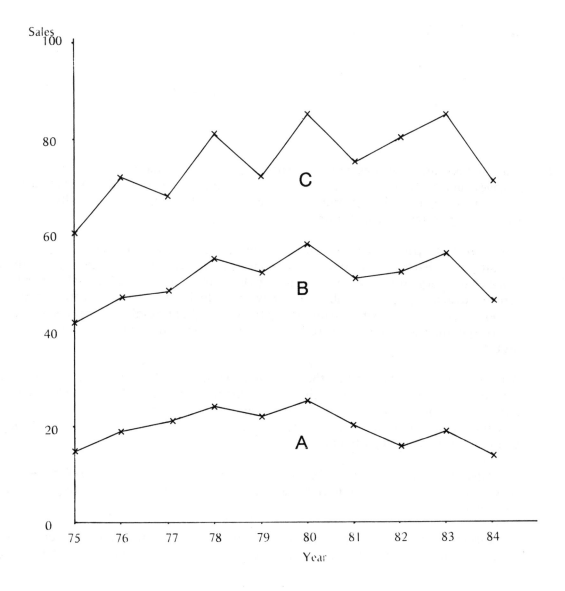

(ii)

Department	Sales	%	Angle
A	14	20	72
B	32	45	162
C	25	35	126
	71	100	360

Departmental sales for 1984

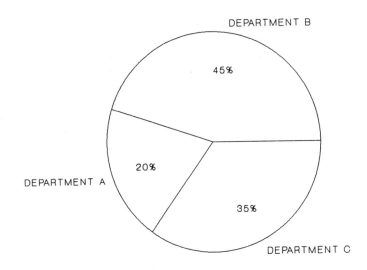

(b) The chief advantage of presenting statistical information in diagrammatic form is that it removes numbers from the text, thereby rendering the text more readable whilst at the same time conveying numerical information to the reader. Many readers will totally omit text which is numerical and this problem is overcome by the use of charts.

Data displayed separately from text may be tabulated or represented by charts. The second advantage of charts is that rather innumerate readers may even be deterred by tables. Since charts very largely *represent* numbers (by bars or angles or pictures) rather than actually displaying them as tables do, they are valuable for communicating with *all* readers, including those who are put off by the very sight of numbers. There is of course a corresponding disadvantage here in that some readers might find the actual figures useful.

A third major advantage is that there is a wide variety of charts and the type of chart used can be selected in order to highlight particular aspects of the data. Thus the pie chart shown above illustrates the relative sales of the three departments in a given year whilst the band chart highlights the trend in total sales as well as the contribution made to the total by each department.

The final important advantage of charts is that they add variety, and therefore interest, to written material. This helps to encourage the reader as well as communicating numerical information.

For the above reasons, diagrammatic representation is an essential means of conveying statistical information to all but the most committed and numerate of readers.

3   SORBETS

Note: in order to provide titles for the charts, we have assumed that the data relates to sales, but this was not explicit in the question.

Calculations

	Cumulative subtotals			
	1986	*1987*	*1988*	*1989*
V	280	301	300	450
V + S	405	454	407	560
V + S + L	455	550	565	829
V + S + L + B	480	581	596	864

(a)   *Component bar chart*

Sales of sorbets 1986 to 1989

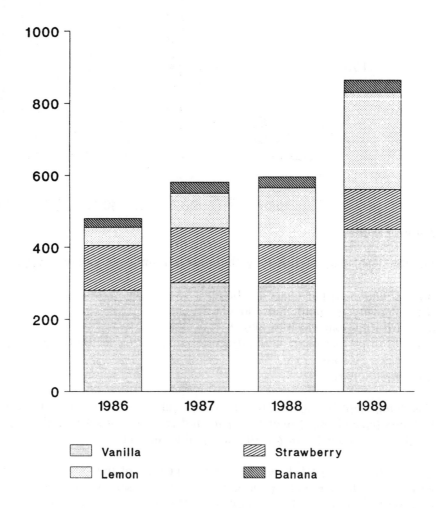

Vanilla   Strawberry

Lemon   Banana

SUGGESTED SOLUTIONS

(b) *Multiple bar chart*

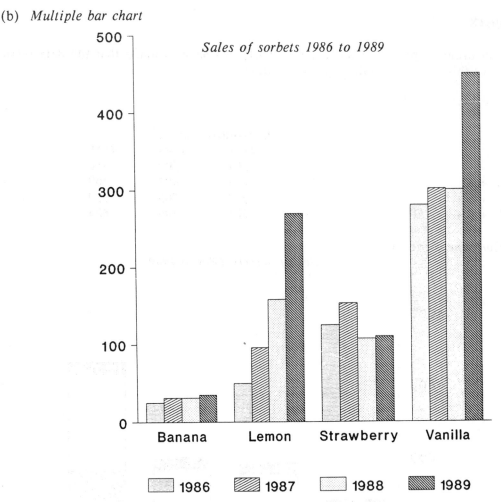

Sales of sorbets 1986 to 1989

1986   1987   1988   1989

Tutorial note

For tabulated data of this type there are a number of possible types of chart.

(a)   Component bar chart as above.
(b)   Percentage component bar chart.
(c)   Multiple bar chart as above.
(d)   Multiple bar chart with adjacent bars relating to the same years rather than the same flavours.
(e)   Band chart.

The component bar chart shows how total sales have risen, how the sales of individual flavours have changed over the years and the relative sales of the various flavours. A band chart would be an equally acceptable alternative.

The multiple bar chart shows the trend in the sales of the various flavours over the years and to a much lesser extent compares the relative sales of the flavours. The alternative multiple bar chart would have emphasised the relative sales of flavours, which has already been well displayed by the component bar chart.

A percentage component bar chart would probably have been acceptable to the examiners but it would have involved the calculation of percentages which is time consuming and, more importantly, it would have meant that neither of our selected charts showed the increase in total sales over the years.

4   ADVERTISING EXPENDITURE

(a)

	Monthly	Cumulative monthly total	Annual moving total
January	420	420	5,150
February	390	810	5,160
March	410	1,220	5,150
April	450	1,670	5,170
May	500	2,170	5,190
June	410	2,580	5,210
July	450	3,030	5,230
August	370	3,400	5,230
September	400	3,800	5,240
October	480	4,280	5,270
November	540	4,820	5,300
December	490	5,310	5,310

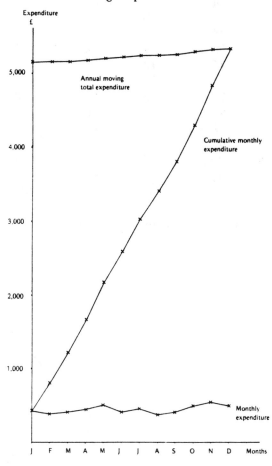

Advertising expenditure 19X8

(b)   The lower section of the chart shows the monthly expenditure over 19X8. Expenditure is fairly steady throughout the year with a slight peak in April and May and another more marked peak in October, November and December. These could be regular seasonal peaks relating to seasonality in the market or they may indicate special sales campaigns at those times. The 'cross bar' section of the chart shows the total expenditure in 19X8 at each stage of the year. It is a very smooth line, reflecting the steadiness of the monthly figures. This section of the chart would mainly be used to check whether expenditure was on target at each stage of the year. A target line could be superimposed on the chart for comparative purposes, if required.

The upper section of the chart shows the total expenditure for the twelve months up to and including each month in turn. It shows the trend in expenditure and its slope illustrates changes compared to 19X7. There is a slight but very steady upwards slope, showing that expenditure in 19X8 exceeds that in 19X7 when each month in turn is compared with the corresponding month of the previous year. In this Z chart the upper section is very smooth and does not seem to be affected by the steady increase in monthly expenditure from the dip in August to the peak in November. This would lead to the conclusion that a similar increase occurred in 19X7 (as indeed the figures show it did) and hence that it is likely to be a seasonal process.

5 UTOPIAN RETAILERS

Workings (percentages are mostly calculated to the nearest whole number)

	19X9				19X1			
	No of outlets		Turnover		No of outlets		Turnover	
		Cum		Cum		Cum		Cum
Range Not over	%	%	%	%	%	%	%	%
1,000	28	28	3	3	19	19	2	2
3,000	30	58	11	14	27	46	8	10
5,000	17	75	18	32	16	62	13	23
8,000	12	87	18	50	21	83	25	48
12,000	7	94	15	65	8	91	15	63
16,000	3	97	11	76	4	95	10	73
25,000	1.5	98.5	8	84	3	98	11	84
50,000	0.5	99	5	89	1	99	8	92
100,000	0.5	99.5	9	98	1	100	8	100
Open ended	0.5	100	2	100	0	100	0	100
	100.0		100		100		100	

The number of outlets is here taken as the x axis.

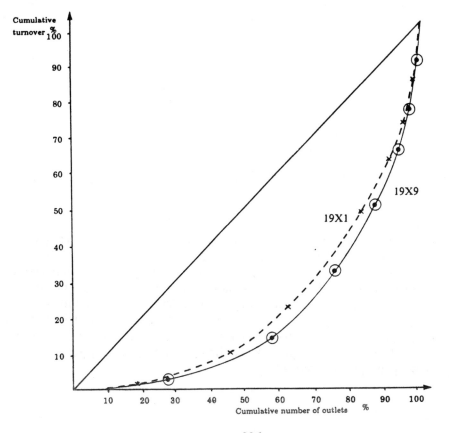

Comment

In both years turnover is very unevenly distributed with a small number of large outlets accounting for a disproportionately high proportion of total turnover. For example, in 19X1, the largest 1% of outlets accounted for 8% of total turnover whilst the smallest 19% accounted for only 2% of total turnover.

From 19X1 to 19X9 this tendency has increased, with an increasing disparity between small and large retail outlets.

Note

If your x axis was the cumulative turnover your curves would have been shaped as follows.

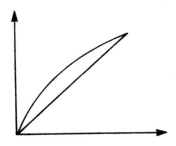

Your conclusions and comments would have been the same.

6 ANNUAL TURNOVER

Year	Turnover £'000	Log (turnover)
75	12.4	1.093
76	26.7	1.427
77	45.6	1.659
78	62.5	1.796
79	78.7	1.896
80	97.1	1.987
81	126.3	2.101
82	158.7	2.201
83	171.5	2.234
84	203.0	2.307
85	238.4	2.377
86	221.8	2.346

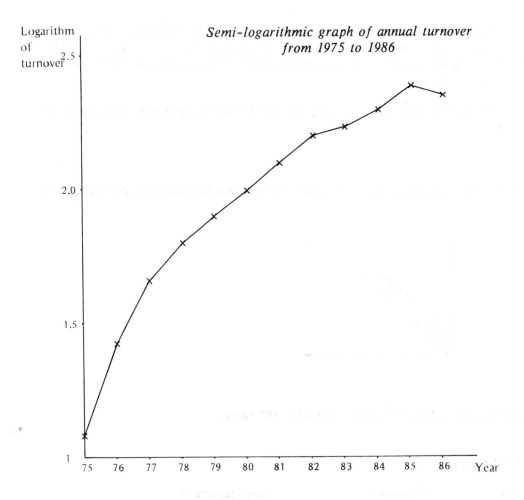

Semi-logarithmic graph of annual turnover from 1975 to 1986

If the growth rate is constant from one year to the next, a semi-logarithmic graph will result in a straight line. If the growth rate varies, a high growth rate will be shown by a relatively high slope and a low growth rate by a relatively low slope. A reduction in the quantity being studied will result in a downwards slope.

In this example, turnover increases at a very fast rate from 1975 to 1977 and then at a somewhat slower, fairly steady rate until 1982. From 1982 to 1985 the rate of growth reduces and then begins to pick up but from 1985 to 1986 there is an actual drop in turnover.

Semi-logarithmic graphs are too technical to be understood by a wide range of readers and their use tends to be limited to the financial press.

7 DISHWASHERS

(a)

No sold per day (x)	Frequency (f)	fx	fx²	Cumulative frequency
0	3	0	0	3
1	8	8	8	11
2	20	40	80	31
3	14	42	126	45
4	6	24	96	51
5	3	15	75	54
6	1	6	36	55
	55	135	421	

(b) *Frequency polygon showing sales of dishwashers per day*

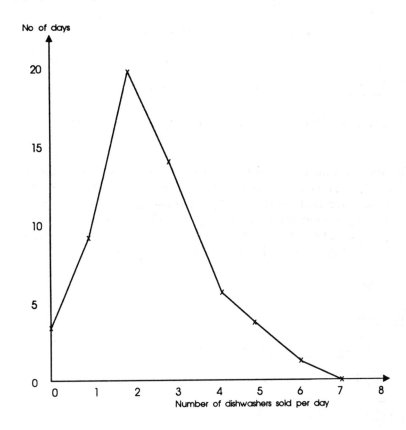

(c) Please note that for convenience the fx, fx² and cumulative frequency columns needed for part (c) have been included with the frequency distribution shown in part (a).

Mean = $\dfrac{\Sigma fx}{\Sigma f}$ = $\dfrac{135}{55}$ = 2.45 dishwashers (to 2 decimal places)

Mode = value with biggest frequency = 2 dishwashers.

Median = middle value = $\dfrac{55 + 1}{2}$th = 28th. From the cumulative frequencies we see that the median = 2 dishwashers.

$$\text{Standard deviation} = \sqrt{\frac{\Sigma fx^2}{\Sigma f} - \left(\frac{\Sigma fx}{\Sigma f}\right)^2}$$

$$= \sqrt{\frac{421}{55} - 2.4545^2}$$

$$= \sqrt{7.6545 - 6.0246} = \sqrt{1.6299}$$

$$= 1.28 \text{ dishwashers (to 2 decimal places)}$$

$$\text{Coefficient of variation} = \frac{1.28}{2.45} \times 100 = 52\%.$$

Range = number of values from 0 to 6
      = 7 dishwashers.

(d)

	This year	*Last year*
$\bar{x}$	2.45	2.25
s	1.28	1.12
Coefficient of variation	52	50*

* Coefficient of variation last year = $\frac{1.12}{2.25} \times 100 = 50\%.$

The average number of dishwashers sold per day, as shown by the means, has increased from 2.25 to 2.45. However, sales now vary more from one day to the next, as shown both by the increased standard deviations and also by the coefficients of variation. The increased variability of sales might lead to increased storage costs or to the loss of customers due to running out of stock and this might somewhat offset some of the increased profits resulting from increased average sales.

(e) [MODE][3]

[SHIFT][AC]

0 [x] 3 [M+] 1 [x] 8 [M+] and so on.

[K out][3] n = 55 = Σf

[K out][2] Σfx = 135

[K out][1] Σfx^2 = 421

[SHIFT][1] $\bar{x}$ = 2.45

[SHIFT][2] s = 1.28

SUGGESTED SOLUTIONS

8 COACH EXPORTS

No of coaches exported

x	y	x^2	y^2
26	20	676	400
12	28	144	784
34	24	1,156	576
18	23	324	529
20	19	400	361
37	26	1,369	676
16	22	256	484
23	29	529	841
28	18	784	324
39	25	1,521	625
14	30	196	900
17	21	289	441
284	285	7,644	6,941

$$\text{Standard deviation} = \sqrt{\frac{\Sigma x^2}{n} - \left(\frac{\Sigma x}{n}\right)^2}$$

n = 12

[*Tutorial note:* the formula given in the exam incorporates frequencies but in this case each frequency equals 1 so the formula simplifies to that given above.]

Company X

$$\text{Standard deviation} = \sqrt{\frac{7,644}{12} - \left(\frac{284}{12}\right)^2}$$

$$= \sqrt{637 - 23.6666^2} = \sqrt{637 - 560.1111}$$

$$= \sqrt{76.8889}$$

$$= \underline{8.77 \text{ coaches}} \text{ (to 2 decimal places)}$$

Company Y

$$\text{Standard deviation} = \sqrt{\frac{6,941}{12} - \left(\frac{285}{12}\right)^2}$$

$$= \sqrt{578.4167 - 23.75^2}$$

$$= \sqrt{578.4167 - 564.0625}$$

$$= \sqrt{14.3542}$$

$$= \underline{3.79 \text{ coaches}} \text{ (to 2 decimal places)}$$

(b) The standard deviations measure variability from one year to the next and show that coach exports by company X are a great deal more variable than those of company Y. This would be perhaps understandable if the average level of exports by X was also greater than those of Y. However, this is not the case since average exports are $\frac{284}{12}$ = 23.7 for X and $\frac{285}{12}$ = 23.8 for Y.

The situation is therefore one which should greatly concern company X. Either its sales effort is not consistent or its markets are unstable. Company Y can apparently rely on a very steady level of export sales and can plan accordingly.

Despite the fact that the companies have the same average level of sales, X is likely to have lower profits than Y. This is because X would have to make special efforts to deal with unexpectedly high demand and to find alternative markets for its coaches when demand is unexpectedly low.

9 TELEPHONE CALLS

Tutorial note: the data ranges from 16 to 318, a range of approximately 300. This will give seven intervals of width 50 and we shall group the data accordingly.

(a)

Length of call (seconds)	Frequency (f)	Interval	Midpoint (x)	fx	fx²
0 - 49	19	0 and less than 50	25	475	11,875
50 - 99	10	50 and less than 100	75	750	56,250
100 - 149	11	100 and less than 150	125	1,375	171,875
150 - 199	9	150 and less than 200	175	1,575	275,625
200 - 249	6	200 and less than 250	225	1,350	303,750
250 - 299	1	250 and less than 300	275	275	75,625
300 - 349	4	300 and less than 350	325	1,300	422,500
	60			7,100	1,317,500

(b) For convenience we have shown the columns required for (b) in the table of (a).

Mean $= \frac{\Sigma fx}{\Sigma f} = \frac{7,100}{60} = 118.3333 = 118$ seconds.

Standard deviation $= \sqrt{\frac{\Sigma fx^2}{\Sigma f} - \left(\frac{\Sigma fx}{\Sigma f}\right)^2} = \sqrt{\frac{1,317,500}{60} - 118.3333^2}$

$= \sqrt{21,958.3333 - 14,002.7770}$

$= \sqrt{7,955.5563} = 89$ seconds

Coefficient of variation $= \frac{s}{\bar{x}} \times 100 = \frac{89}{118} \times 100 = 75\%$

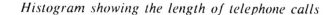

Histogram showing the length of telephone calls

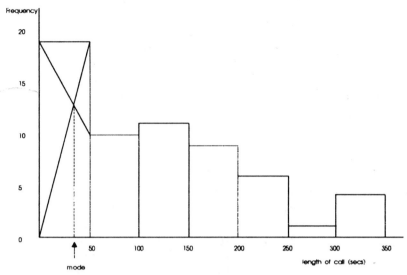

The data has several modes in the strict sense of points at which frequency peaks. However the primary mode, at which frequency peaks for the entire distribution, is given by mode = 34 seconds.

Tutorial comment: this average is very different from the mean of 118 seconds obtained in part (a). This is because the data is extremely skewed.

(d)

Interval	f	cum f		value
0 and less than 50	19	19	less than	50
50 and less than 100	10	29	less than	100
100 and less than 150	11	40	less than	150
150 and less than 200	9	49	less than	200
200 and less than 250	6	55	less than	250
250 and less than 300	1	56	less than	300
300 and less than 350	4	60	less than	350

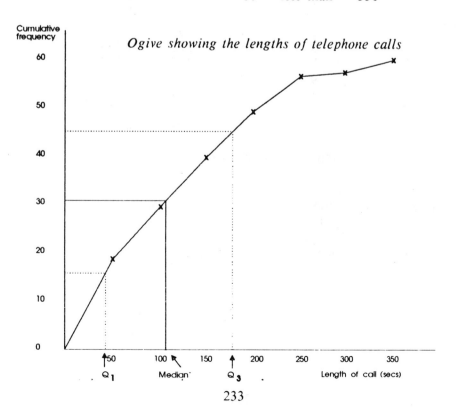

Ogive showing the lengths of telephone calls

SUGGESTED SOLUTIONS

cum f of median = $\dfrac{n}{2} = \dfrac{60}{2} = 30$

∴ From ogive, median = 105 seconds.

Cum f of Q_1 = n/4 = 60/4 = 15 ∴ Q_1 = 40 seconds
Cum f of Q_3 = 3n/4 = 45   ∴ Q_3 = 178 seconds

Quartile deviation = $\dfrac{Q_3 - Q_1}{2} = \dfrac{178 - 40}{2} = \dfrac{138}{2} = 69$ seconds.

10 CHAIN STORE

(a) *Outlet P*

Midpoint (x)	f	fx	fx²
3	14	42	126
5	16	80	400
7	17	119	833
9	19	171	1,539
11	18	198	2,178
13	16	208	2,704
	100	818	7,780

Mean = $\Sigma fx/\Sigma f$ = 818/100 = 8.18 ie £8,180

Standard deviation = $\sqrt{\dfrac{\Sigma fx^2}{\Sigma f} - \left(\dfrac{\Sigma fx}{\Sigma f}\right)^2}$ = $\sqrt{\dfrac{7,780}{100} - 8.18^2}$

= $\sqrt{77.80 - 66.9124}$ = $\sqrt{10.8876}$

= 3.29 ie £3,290

Outlet Q

Midpoint (x)	f	fx	fx²
3	18	54	162
5	45	225	1,125
7	17	119	833
9	9	81	729
11	7	77	847
13	4	52	676
	100	608	4,372

Mean = $\Sigma fx/\Sigma f$ = 608/100 = 6.08 ie £6,080

Standard deviation = $\sqrt{\dfrac{4,372}{100} - 6.08^2}$ = $\sqrt{43.72 - 36.9664}$

= $\sqrt{6.7536}$ = 2.60 ie £2,600

234

SUGGESTED SOLUTIONS

(b) Coefficient of variation for P $= \dfrac{s}{\bar{x}} \times 100 = \dfrac{3{,}290}{8{,}180} \times 100$

$= 40\%$

Coefficient of variation for Q $= \dfrac{2{,}600}{6{,}080} \times 100 = 43\%$

The arithmetic mean shows the average or typical level of daily sales and is given by the total sales being shared out equally over the 100 days.

Outlet P has markedly higher average daily sales than does Q, with £8,180 compared to £6,080.

The standard deviation is a measure of variability around the mean. It enables us to see the likely variation from one day to the next. The standard deviation at P is £3,290 which is considerably greater than £2,600 at Q. This is a matter of some concern since it means that storage costs and probably overtime payments at P will be high, in order to meet unexpectedly high demand whilst quite often demand will be very low and staff will be idle. If stock is perishable, there will be additional costs in this way too. Outlet Q would not be expected to experience these problems.

However, the coefficients of variation conflict with the above remarks about variability, which is best measured in relation to the expected sales level. Outlet Q will actually experience more variability relative to its average level of sales (43%) than will outlet P (40%). On the basis of the coefficient of variation, it is outlet Q which, in addition to having a generally lower level of sales, will suffer the problems of rather greater variability.

11 REPS' MILEAGES

(a)

Miles travelled	Frequency (f)	Midpoint(x)	fx	Cum f
60 and under 100	12	80	960	12
100 and under 140	39	120	4,680	51
140 and under 180	25	160	4,000	76
180 and under 220	17	200	3,400	93
220 and under 260	11	240	2,640	104
260 and under 300	8	280	2,240	112
300 and under 340	5	320	1,600	117
340 and under 380	3	360	1,080	120
380 and under 420	1	400	400	121
	121		21,000	

Mean $= \Sigma fx / \Sigma f = 21{,}000/121 = 173.6$ miles.

Median $= L_1 + (L_2 - L_1)\left(\dfrac{n/2 - \Sigma f_1}{\Sigma f_2 - \Sigma f_1} \right)$

$n = 121 \therefore n/2 = 60.5$ and median class is 140 - 180
$L_1 = 140, L_2 = 180$
$\Sigma f_1 = 51, \Sigma f_2 = 76$

$$\therefore \text{Median} = 140 + (180 - 140)\left(\frac{60.5 - 51}{76 - 51}\right)$$

$$= 140 + \left(40 \times \frac{9.5}{25}\right) = 140 + 15.2$$

$$= 155.2 \text{ miles}$$

Modal class is 100 - 140.

not drawn to scale

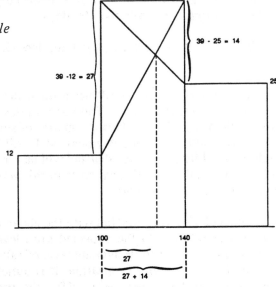

Mode is $100 + \dfrac{27}{27 + 14} \times (140 - 100)$

$$= 100 + \frac{27 \times 40}{41} = 100 + 26.3$$

$$= 126.3 \text{ miles.}$$

(b) The mean gives the total mileage shared out equally amongst the 121 sales representatives. Where data is skewed, as in this example, the mean is distorted by the extreme values and does not provide a good indication of average or typical mileages. It can be seen that the four sales representatives with very high mileages have more impact on the mean than the twelve who travel the least. The mean does however take account of all the information available and if the averages were being calculated in order to inform a discussion about total mileage or its cost, the mean would be the most relevant average despite its exaggerating the travelling of individual sales representatives.

The median gives the best indication of typical weekly mileage in this case, because of the skewness of the data. Half the sales representatives travel less and half travel more than this value of 155 miles and hence it provides a good measure of the average travelling experienced by individual sales representatives.

The mode is the most common single value and with positively skewed data it tends to underestimate the average level. The largest single group of representatives have weekly mileages of only 126 miles. In considering, say, the stress of travelling experienced by sales representatives it would be important to be aware of this figure although the median would also be very relevant.

12 STAMPS

(a)

Number of stamps	Frequency	Interval width	Frequency density
0 and less than 500	46	500	46
500 and less than 1,500	72	1,000	36
1,500 and less than 2,500	89	1,000	44.5
2,500 and less than 3,000	52	500	52
3,000 and less than 3,500	40	500	40
3,500 and less than 4,000	33	500	33
4,000 and less than 4,500	18	500	18
	350		

(Tutorial note: frequencies are obtained by subtracting successive cumulative frequencies, thus 72 = 118 - 46, 89 = 207 - 118 and so on. Taking the standard interval as 500, the two intervals of width 1,000 are twice the standard width and their frequencies must be halved to give the frequency density.)

Histogram showing number of stamps collected

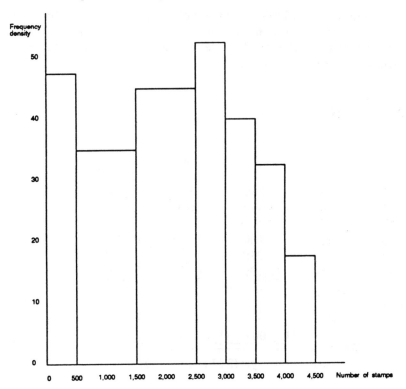

(b)

Midpoint (x)	f	fx	fx²
250	46	11,500	2,875,000
1,000	72	72,000	72,000,000
2,000	89	178,000	356,000,000
2,750	52	143,000	393,250,000
3,250	40	130,000	422,500,000
3,750	33	123,750	464,062,500
4,250	18	76,500	325,125,000
	350	734,750	2,035,812,500

Mean $= \Sigma fx / \Sigma f = \dfrac{734,750}{350} = 2,099.29 = \underline{\underline{2,099 \text{ stamps}}}$

$$\text{Standard deviation} = \sqrt{\frac{\Sigma f x^2}{\Sigma f} - \left(\frac{\Sigma f x}{\Sigma f}\right)^2}$$

$$= \sqrt{\frac{2,035,812,500}{350} - 2,099.29^2}$$

$$= \sqrt{5,816,607.1 - 4,407,018.5}$$

$$= \sqrt{1,409,588.6}$$

$$= \underline{1,187 \text{ stamps}}$$

(c) The arithmetic mean tells us that typically customers have saved 2,099 stamps. It gives an indication of the number of stamps that the company can expect a customer to have saved and is given by sharing out all the stamps equally amongst the 350 customers.

The standard deviation is a measure of variability around the mean level. It indicates the variation from one customer to the next in the amount of stamps saved. Since the average is 2,099 stamps and the standard deviation is 1,187 stamps there is clearly a good deal of variability between customers.

13 CORRELATION

(a)

x	y	xy	x^2	y^2
10	38	380	100	1,444
40	86	3,440	1,600	7,396
30	70	2,100	900	4,900
50	102	5,100	2,500	10,404
20	54	1,080	400	2,916
150	350	12,100	5,500	27,060

$n = 5$

$$r = \frac{5(12,100) - (150)(350)}{\sqrt{[5(5,500) - (150)^2][(5(27,060) - (350)^2]}}$$

$$= \frac{60,500 - 52,500}{\sqrt{(27,500 - 22,500)(135,300 - 122,500)}} = \frac{8,000}{\sqrt{64,000,000}} = 1$$

There appears to be a perfect positive correlation between x and y.

(b)

x	y	xy	x^2	y^2
2	3	6	4	9
5	4	20	25	16
3	0	0	9	0
7	1	7	49	1
4	10	40	16	100
2	8	16	4	64
23	26	89	107	190

$n = 6$

$$r = \frac{6(89) - (23)(26)}{\sqrt{[6(107) - (23)^2][6(190) - (26)^2]}}$$

$$= \frac{534 - 598}{\sqrt{(113)(464)}} = \frac{-64}{229} = -0.28$$

There is no significant correlation between x and y.

(c)

Let $1981 = x = 1$

x	y	xy	x^2	y^2
1	10	10	1	100
2	10	20	4	100
3	7	21	9	49
4	7	28	16	49
5	6	30	25	36
6	5	30	36	25
21	45	139	91	359

$n = 6$

$$r = \frac{6(139) - (21)(45)}{\sqrt{[6(91) - (21)^2][6(359) - (45)^2]}} = \frac{834 - 945}{\sqrt{(105)(129)}} = \frac{-111}{116.4} = -0.95$$

There appears to be a high degree of negative correlation between x and y. In other words there is a downward trend in the value of y over time which is very nearly a straight line trend.

14 SCATTER DIAGRAMS

(a)

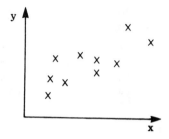

There is a hint of an upward trend in the crosses, but the trend/correlation is not strong.

(b)

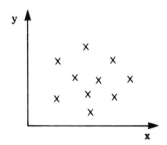

There is no indication whatsoever of a trend up or down in the crosses.

(c)

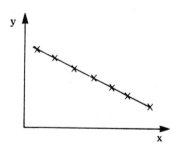

All crosses lie on a straight downward sloping trend line.

SUGGESTED SOLUTIONS

(d)

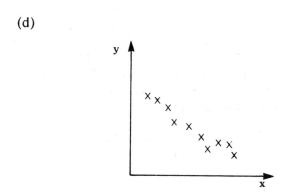

There is a clear downward trend, but the crosses do not lie exactly in a line.

15   COMPLETIONS

$$r = \frac{n \, \Sigma xy - \Sigma x \, \Sigma y}{\sqrt{(n\Sigma x^2 - (\Sigma x)^2)(n\Sigma y^2 - (\Sigma y)^2)}}$$

Tutorial note: from the formula it is clear that we need columns entitled x, y, x^2, y^2 and xy. We should expect the number of completions to depend on the number of orders so the number of completions is called y.

| Orders | Completions | | | |
x	y	x^2	y^2	xy
26	29	676	841	754
14	15	196	225	210
22	24	484	576	528
17	16	289	256	272
15	21	225	441	315
23	18	529	324	414
28	19	784	361	532
19	20	361	400	380
13	25	169	625	325
177	187	3,713	4,049	3,730

$$r = \frac{9 \times 3{,}730 - 177 \times 187}{\sqrt{(9 \times 3{,}713 - 177^2)(9 \times 4{,}049 - 187^2)}}$$

$$= \frac{471}{\sqrt{2{,}088 \times 1{,}472}} = \frac{471}{1{,}753.15} = 0.27$$

This value of r is close to zero and indicates only a very weak, positive linear relationship between the number of orders under construction and the number of completions.

This result is rather surprising since one would expect a very strong relationship between the number of orders and the number of completions. It seems likely therefore that orders take more than one week to complete and that completions in any given week will reflect the number of orders under construction in the previous few weeks. An examination of the data leads one to suspect that completions relate very closely to the orders under construction two weeks previously as shown by the following reorganisation of the data.

Orders under construction	Completions two weeks later
26	24
14	16
22	21
17	18
15	19
23	20
28	25

Tutorial note: were you to check the above data using your calculator in LR mode, you would find that r = 0.94 when the two week time lag is allowed for. As expected this shows a very strong relationship. You would not however have been required to make this additional calculation in the exam.

16   RANK CORRELATION

(a) This is dealt with fully in the text so we will list only the key points that an answer should contain.

   (i) Both correlation coefficients measure the strength of the linear relationship between two variables and both show whether the variables increase together or whether one decreases as the other increases.

   (ii) The product moment correlation coefficient uses the actual values whilst the rank coefficient measures only the relationship between the rankings of those values.

   (iii) The circumstances in which they should be used are described fully in paragraphs 3.11 to 3.14 of chapter 6.

(b)

Newspaper	Order of preference	Ranked % recall	$\|d\|$	d^2
A	9	7.5	1.5	2.25
B	3	4	1	1
C	10	9	1	1
D	1	1	0	0
E	6	5	1	1
F	4	3	1	1
G	12	12	0	0
H	2	2	0	0
I	7	10	3	9
J	11	11	0	0
K	5	6	1	1
L	8	7.5	0.5	0.25
				16.50

SUGGESTED SOLUTIONS

Tutorial note: you will see that we have ranked the largest % recall number 1 and the smallest number 12. This is because, where preference is concerned, the convention is to rank the biggest score as number one. In an exam it would be perfectly acceptable to rank according to numerical magnitude but R would then be negative. The interpretation would be the same, namely that preference and % recall are strongly linked and increase together. The negative would arise from the allocation of the lowest numerical rank to the most preferred newspaper.

Note also that A and L have tied rankings. If they had been different they would have been 7th and 8th so we rank them both 7.5.

$$R = 1 - \frac{6\Sigma d^2}{n(n^2-1)} \quad n = 12 \quad \Sigma d^2 = 16.5$$

$$= 1 - \frac{6 \times 16.5}{12 \times 143}$$

$$= 1 - \frac{99}{1,716} = 1 - 0.06$$

$$= 0.94$$

The value of R indicates that there is a very strong relationship between ability to recall advertising material and preference for a newspaper. As preference increases, so does % recall.

17   ADVERTISING

Tutorial note: the first essential task is to decide which variable to call x and which to call y. It seems reasonable to suppose that sales will depend on advertising and hence we call sales y.

(a)

Advertising expenditure (£) x	Sales (£) y	x^2	xy
15	200	225	3,000
18	240	324	4,320
18	260	324	4,680
21	290	441	6,090
23	300	529	6,900
23	320	529	7,360
26	380	676	9,880
28	370	784	10,360
32	400	1,024	12,800
37	470	1,369	17,390
$\Sigma x = 241$	$\Sigma y = 3,230$	$\Sigma x^2 = 6,225$	$\Sigma xy = 82,780$

$n = 10$

$$b = \frac{n\Sigma xy - \Sigma x \Sigma y}{n\Sigma x^2 - (\Sigma x)^2} = \frac{10 \times 82,780 - 241 \times 3,230}{10 \times 6,225 - 241^2}$$

$$= \frac{827,800 - 778,430}{62,250 - 58,081} = \frac{49,370}{4,169}$$

$$= 11.8422$$

$$a = \bar{y} - b\bar{x} = \frac{\Sigma y}{n} - b\frac{\Sigma x}{n} = \frac{3,230}{10} - 11.8422 \times \frac{241}{10}$$

$$a = 323 - 285.3970 = 37.6030$$

Rounding a and b to three significant figures gives the regression equation

$$y = 37.6 + 11.8x$$

or sales = 37.6 + 11.8 × advertising expenditure.

(b) The value 37.6 gives the value of sales if nothing is spent on advertising. The 'b' value of + 11.8 indicates that sales will be expected to increase as advertising increases and a £1 increase in advertising should correspond to an £11.8 increase in sales.

We would however have to make a number of additional points to the managing director. Firstly we have not calculated the correlation coefficient and, whilst a cursory examination of the data leads one to guess that there is a very strong linear relationship between advertising and sales, we cannot rely on the regression equation until correlation has been checked.

Secondly, the figure of £37.6 sales achievable if there is no expenditure on advertising was obtained by extrapolation and therefore cannot be considered reliable.

Thirdly we must say that a sample of only ten pairs of values would lead us to hesitate about placing much reliance on the results.

18   PLANNING EXERCISE

Year	x	y	xy	x²	y²
19X1	1	19	19	1	361
19X2	2	24	48	4	576
19X3	3	28	84	9	784
19X4	4	33	132	16	1,089
19X5	5	35	175	25	1,225
19X6	6	41	246	36	1,681
19X7	7	45	315	49	2,025
19X8	8	47	376	64	2,209
19X9	9	52	468	81	2,704
	Σx 45	Σy 324	Σxy 1,863	Σx² 285	Σy² 12,654

$n = 9$

When y = a + bx

$$b = \frac{9(1,863) - (45)(324)}{9(285) - (45)(45)} = \frac{2,187}{540}$$

$$= 4.05$$

$$a = \frac{324}{9} - \frac{(4.05)(45)}{9} = 15.75$$

The least squares regression equation is y = 15.75 + 4.05x

where x = 1 is 19X1, x = 2 is 19X2 and so on.

(b) The prediction for 19Y1 (x = 11) is y = 15.75 + 4.05(11) = 60.3

The assumptions are as follows.

(i) Production has increased at a linear rate over time, and so production is positively correlated with time.
(ii) The same rate of increase will continue in the future.

19 EIGHT EMPLOYEES

(a)

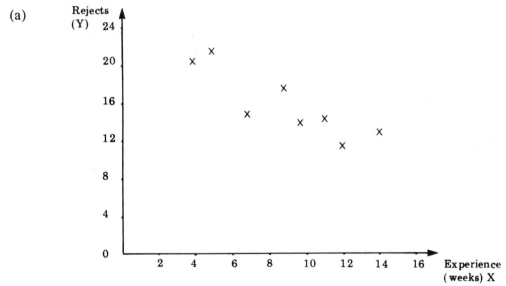

(b) $$r = \frac{8(1069) - (72)(128)}{\sqrt{[8(732) - (72)^2][8(2,156) - (128)^2]}}$$

$$= \frac{-664}{\sqrt{(672)(864)}} = \frac{-664}{762.0}$$

$$= -0.871$$

This value indicates that there is a negative correlation between x and y, which is fairly strong. As experience becomes greater, the number of rejects gets less. The coefficient of determination $r^2 = 0.759$, which indicates that 75.9% of variations in the number of rejects (y) can be predicted from variations in the weeks of experience in the employee (x).

(c) If $y = a + bx$

$$b = \frac{8(1,069) - (72)(128)}{8(732) - (72)(72)}$$

$$= \frac{-664}{672} = \underline{\underline{-0.988}}$$

$$a = \frac{128}{8} - \frac{(-0.988)(72)}{8}$$

$$= \underline{\underline{+24.892}}$$

Tutorial note: remember that when we subtract a negative number it is the same as adding the number without the negative sign.

When x =1, the number of rejects is
$$y = 24.892 - 0.988 (1)$$
$$= \underline{\underline{23.904}}, \text{ say 24}$$

It is worth remarking, however, that a value x = 1 lies outside the range of data used to calculate the line of best fit, and so the formula might not be suitable for predicting the number of rejects for an employee with so little experience.

20 STANDARD SIZE BOXES

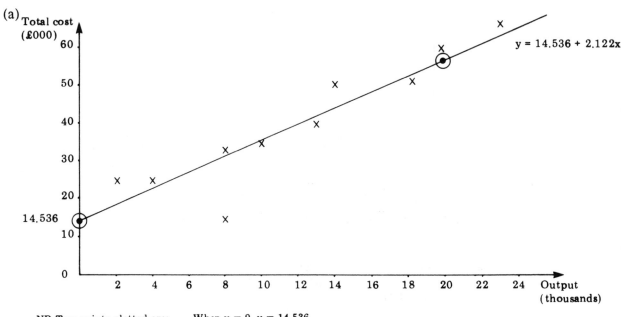

(a)

NB Two points plotted are: When x = 0, y = 14.536
When x = 20, y = 14.536 + 2.122(20)
= 56.976

(b) The output in week 8 appears to be significantly different from the rest of the data because costs in week 8 appear to be much lower than would be expected, in view of cost and output data in the other weeks.

(c) A point that must be on the line of best fit is $(\bar{x}, \bar{y})$

$$\bar{x} = \frac{120}{10} \qquad \bar{y} = \frac{400}{10}$$

ie $\bar{x} = 12$, $\bar{y} = 40$.

(d) When $y = a + bx$

$$b = \frac{10(5,704) - (120)(400)}{10(1,866) - (120)(120)} = \frac{9,040}{4,260}$$

$$= 2.122$$

$$a = 40 - 2.122(12) = 14.536$$

The least squares regression line is therefore:

y $= 14.536 + 2.122x$

where x is output in thousands of boxes, and y is total cost in thousands of pounds.

This line is shown in the diagram in the solution to (a) above.

(e) The fixed cost of the factory is £14,536 per week. This is the cost when output is zero.

(f) When $x = 25$

$$y = 14.536 + (2.122)(25)$$

$$= 67.586$$

Total cost predicted = £67,586

21 EARTHWORM GARDEN CENTRE

(a) We must calculate a moving average of five days' sales to obtain the trend.

Week No	Day	Sales	Moving total of 5	Moving average of 5	Actual sales minus moving average
1	Wednesday	510			
	Thursday	360			
	Friday	570	3,090	618	- 48
	Saturday	800	3,080	616	+184
	Sunday	850	3,100	620	+230
2	Wednesday	500	3,110	622	-122
	Thursday	380	3,130	626	-246
	Friday	580	3,120	624	- 44
	Saturday	820	3,160	632	+188
	Sunday	840	3,170	634	+206
3	Wednesday	540	3,170	634	- 94
	Thursday	390	3,180	636	-246
	Friday	580	3,210	642	- 62
	Saturday	830	3,220	644	+186
	Sunday	870	3,240	648	+222
4	Wednesday	550	3,260	652	-102
	Thursday	410	3,280	656	-246
	Friday	600	3,310	662	- 62
	Saturday	850			
	Sunday	900			

Calculate the average daily variation.

	Wed	Thurs	Fri	Sat	Sun	Total
Week 1			- 48	+184	+230	
2	-122	-246	- 44	+188	+206	
3	- 94	-246	- 62	+186	+222	
4	-102	-246	-62			
Average	-106	-246	- 54	+186	+219	- 1
Adjustment, say					+ 1	1
Adjusted average	-106	-246	- 54	+186	+220	0

Tutorial note: strictly speaking we should have adjusted the average daily variations by adding $1/5 = 0.2$ to each of them. This would however result in spurious accuracy and we have chosen instead to make the entire adjustment to the largest positive value.

SUGGESTED SOLUTIONS

Week	Day	Trend £	Seasonal variation £	Predicted sales £	Actual sales £	Residual £
1	Friday	618	- 54	564	570	+ 6
	Saturday	616	+186	802	800	- 2
	Sunday	620	+220	840	850	+10
2	Wednesday	622	-106	516	500	-16
	Thursday	626	-246	380	380	0
	Friday	624	- 54	570	580	+10
	Saturday	632	+186	818	820	+ 2
	Sunday	634	+220	854	840	-14
3	Wednesday	634	-106	528	540	+12
	Thursday	636	-246	390	390	0
	Friday	642	- 54	588	580	- 8
	Saturday	644	+186	830	830	0
	Sunday	648	+220	868	870	+ 2
4	Wednesday	652	-106	546	550	+ 4
	Thursday	656	-246	410	410	0
	Friday	662	- 54	608	600	- 8

(b) Forecast = trend forecast + daily component

	Wednesday	Thursday	Friday	Saturday	Sunday
Trend forecast	670	673	676	679	681
Daily component	- 106	- 246	- 54	+ 186	+ 220
Sales forecast	564	427	622	865	901

(c) The above forecasts assume that the trend and daily variation will continue in the future as they have in the past and that there are no unforeseen events, such as bad weather. A further assumption is that the additive model adequately describes the factors that determine sales levels. With a rapidly increasing trend, we might expect a multiplicative model to provide a better 'fit' but examination of the residuals shows a maximum random variation of only 16, which is very small compared to the level of sales. It therefore seems quite reasonable to use the additive model.

The techniques used will not necessarily provide accurate forecasts, but on the whole they are likely to provide more reliable estimates than guesswork or rule-of-thumb. Techniques cannot eliminate uncertainty about the future, but they can help to ensure that managers take due consideration of all currently-known facts in the preparation of their forecasts.

22 SEASIDE CAFE

(a) *Tutorial note:* when you tabulate quarterly data, remember to leave a blank line between each entry for the moving totals.

Year	Quarter	Turnover £'000	Moving total £'000	Moving average £'000	Variation £'000
19X5	1	20			
	2	35			
			99		
	3	26		24.50	1.50
			97		
	4	18		24.38	- 6.38
			98		
19X6	1	18		24.25	- 6.25
			96		
	2	36		23.63	12.37
			93		
	3	24		22.75	1.25
			89		
	4	15		22.00	- 7.00
			87		
19X7	1	14		21.88	- 7.88
			88		
	2	34		21.88	12.12
			87		
	3	25		21.88	3.12
			88		
	4	14		21.75	-7.75
			86		
19X8	1	15		21.25	- 6.25
			84		
	2	32		20.75	11.25
			82		
	3	23			
	4	12			

Quarterly variations

	1 £'000	2 £'000	3 £'000	4 £'000	
19X5			1.50	- 6.38	
19X6	- 6.25	12.37	1.25	- 7.00	
19X7	- 7.88	12.12	3.12	- 7.75	
19X8	- 6.25	11.25			Total
Average	- 6.79	11.91	1.96	- 7.04	0.04
Adjustment	- 0.01	- 0.01	- 0.01	- 0.01	- 0.04
Seasonal	- 6.80	11.90	1.95	- 7.05	

(b)

Seaside cafe turnover

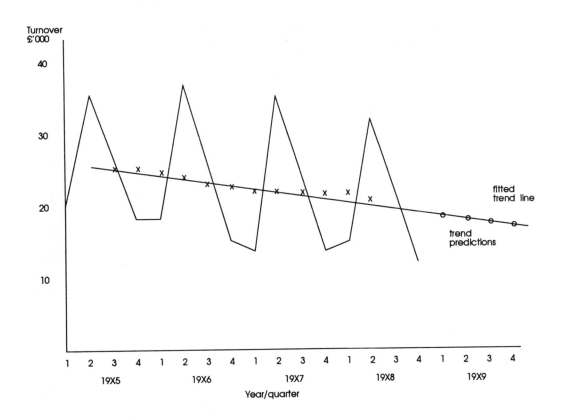

(c)

	19X9			
Quarter	*1*	*2*	*3*	*4*
	£'000	£'000	£'000	£'000
Forecast trend	19.00	18.50	18.00	17.50
Seasonal variation	- 6.80	+ 11.90	+ 1.95	- 7.05
Forecast turnover	12.20	30.40	19.95	10.45

We could provide forecast quarterly turnover for the advertisement of £12,200, £30,400, £19,950 and £10,450 respectively. If required we could also forecast total turnover for 19X9 of £73,000.

The above forecasts will be reliable only if the previous trend and pattern of seasonal variability continue and if there are not unforeseen events. There is a decreasing trend and generally a multiplicative model would be preferred to the additive model we have used. However, the rate of decline is only slight and so it seems likely that the additive model will provide reasonable forecasts.

SUGGESTED SOLUTIONS

23 LAWNMOWERS

(a)

Year	Quarter	Number sold	Moving total	Centred moving average	Variation
6	1	14			
	2	26			
			51		
	3	7		12.9	- 5.9
			52		
	4	4		13.3	- 9.3
			54		
7	1	15		13.5	1.5
			54		
	2	28		13.6	14.4
			55		
	3	7		13.8	- 6.8
			55		
	4	5		13.9	- 8.9
			56		
8	1	15		14.1	0.9
			57		
	2	29		14.3	14.7
			57		
	3	8		14.5	- 6.5
			59		
	4	5		15.4	- 10.4
			64		
9	1	17		16.1	0.9
			65		
	2	34		16.3	17.7
			65		
	3	9			
	4	5			

	Seasonal variations				
Year	1	2	3	4	
6			- 5.9	- 9.3	
7	1.5	14.4	- 6.8	- 8.9	
8	0.9	14.7	- 6.5	- 10.4	
9	0.9	17.7			Total
Average	1.1	15.6	- 6.4	- 9.5	0.8
Adjustment	- 0.2	- 0.2	- 0.2	- 0.2	- 0.8
Average seasonal variation	0.9	15.4	- 6.6	- 9.7	0

(b) The trend for year 10 could be forecast by extrapolating the moving average trend. This could be done either graphically or by fitting a regression line. If a graphical method is used, the moving average values should be graphed against time and a trend line or curve fitted to those points 'by eye'. This should then be extended across year 10 and trend predictions could be read from it.

If regression is used the moving averages give the y values and time gives the x values with x = 1 for the third quarter of year 6. The resulting equation could then be used, taking x = 15 to 18, to give trend predictions.

The sales forecast is then given by adding the appropriate average seasonal variation to the trend forecasts.

The accuracy of the forecasts will depend on the trend and the pattern of seasonal variability continuing in future as it has in the past and on there being no unforeseen events.

24 FORECASTS

(a)

19X4 *Quarter*	*x*	*Trend in sales (rounded)*
1	9	$217 + 2.7 \times 9 = 241$
2	10	$217 + 2.7 \times 10 = 244$
3	11	$217 + 2.7 \times 11 = 247$
4	12	$217 + 2.7 \times 12 = 249$

(b)

	Quarter			
	1	*2*	*3*	*4*
Forecast trend	241	244	247	249
Seasonal component	- 13	- 112	+ 103	+ 22
Sales forecast	228	132	350	271

(c)

	Quarter			
	1	*2*	*3*	*4*
Forecast trend	241	244	247	249
Seasonal component	- 5%	- 45%	+ 42%	+ 9%
ie	- 12	- 110	+ 104	+ 22
Sales forecast	229	134	351	271

Tutorial note: 5% of 241 is given by $241 \times \dfrac{5}{100} = 12$. Hence for the first quarter we subtract 12 and so on for the other quarters.

25   COFFEE BEANS

(a)   Laspeyre index $= \dfrac{\Sigma p_1 q_0}{\Sigma p_0 q_0} \times 100$

Columns entitled $p_1 q_0$ and $p_0 q_0$ are required for each year.

		19X4	*19X5*
Variety	$p_0 q_0$	$p_1 q_0$	$p_1 q_0$
A	25.55	28.00	28.91
B	19.26	21.33	21.15
C	22.80	23.12	23.84
D	39.48	40.56	42.24
E	24.36	25.38	24.66
	131.45	138.39	140.80

Index $= \dfrac{138.39}{131.45} \times 100 = 105.3$ for 19X4

Index $= \dfrac{140.80}{131.45} \times 100 = 107.1$ for 19X5

(b)   Paasche index $= 100 \times \Sigma p_1 q_1 \,/\, \Sigma p_0 q_1$

Columns entitled $p_1 q_1$ and $p_0 q_1$ are required for each year.

	19X4		*19X5*	
Variety	$p_0 q_1$	$p_1 q_1$	$p_0 q_1$	$p_1 q_1$
A	21.90	24.00	18.25	20.65
B	23.54	26.07	25.68	28.20
C	28.50	28.90	22.80	23.84
D	49.35	50.70	59.22	63.36
E	24.36	25.38	28.42	28.77
	147.65	155.05	154.37	164.82

Index $= \dfrac{155.05}{147.65} \times 100 = 105.0$ for 19X4

Index $= \dfrac{164.82}{154.37} \times 100 = 106.8$ for 19X5

(c)   *Tutorial note:* see the solution to illustrative question 27 *Batteries* for a full answer to this part of the question. What follows is a brief list of the points to be made.

Base weights need to be calculated only once
   the denominator $\Sigma p_0 q_0$ is constant from year to year
   indices are comparable from year to year
but   base weights get out of date
   base year needs frequently updating
   indices exaggerate inflation

Current weights are the complete opposite, ie

they are costly and time consuming to recalculate each year
the denominator $\Sigma p_0 q_1$ changes each year
indices are not strictly comparable year to year

but they stay up to date

indices give a true measure of inflation as experienced by consumers

In this particular example the results of the two methods are remarkably similar and the Laspeyre method would be preferred on the grounds of convenience.

26   COMPONENTS

(a)   Total cost for each part   =   number of items purchased x unit price
So the number of items   =   total cost/unit price

The quantities are shown in the table below, in the column entitled q_0

(b)   Price relative index   = $100 \times \dfrac{\Sigma \frac{p_1}{p_0}.w}{\Sigma w}$

In this case the weights are q_0 for each part so the formula becomes

= $100 \times \dfrac{\Sigma \frac{p_1}{p_0}.q_0}{\Sigma q_0}$

To compute it we therefore need columns entitled $\dfrac{p_1}{p_0} q_0$ and q_0

Part	Cost	p_0	p_1	$q_0 = \dfrac{Cost}{p_0}$	$\dfrac{p_1 . q_0}{p_0}$
A1	465	3.00	3.12	155	161.2
B2	1,200	2.50	2.65	480	508.8
E5	798	1.20	1.17	665	648.375
B4	600	2.40	2.46	250	256.25
C3	2,100	6.00	6.24	350	364.0
A4	900	4.50	4.86	200	216.0
C2	1,400	2.80	3.08	500	550.0
				2,600	2,704.625

∴ Price relative index   = $100 \times \dfrac{2,704.625}{2,600}$ =   104.02

(c)   The index for 19X8 needs to be recalculated with base 19X3 instead of its present base 19X6.

Costs in 19X8 are 4.02% greater than in 19X6.

So the index for 19X8   =   112 increased by 4.02%

= $112 \times \dfrac{104.02}{100}$

=   116.5

(d) Series with base 19X3 is

19X3	19X4	19X5	19X6	19X7	19X8
100	103	107	112	115	116.5

The new base year is to be 19X7 and the value for that year is 115. All values must therefore be divided by 115 and multiplied by 100.

This series with base 19X7 is

19X3	19X4	19X5	19X6	19X7	19X8
87	90	93	97	100	101

27   BATTERIES

(a)   Laspeyre price index $= 100 \times \dfrac{\Sigma p_1 q_0}{\Sigma p_0 q_0}$

Category	q_0	p_0	p_1	$p_1 q_0$	$p_0 q_0$
Economy	10	10	15	150	100
Standard	8	27	29	232	216
De Luxe	9	47	32	288	423
Super	14	48	53	742	672
				1,412	1,411

Index for 19X8 $= \dfrac{1,412}{1,411} \times 100 = 100.1$

(b)   Base weights are calculated only once whereas current weights need to be obtained every year. This makes current weighting very costly and often impractical. The production of a current weighted index might well be delayed by the difficulty in obtaining current weights.

The denominator $\Sigma p_0 q_0$ will not need to be recalculated each year if base weights are used but with current weights the denominator $\Sigma p_0 q_1$ must be recalculated each year.

With base weights the basket of goods and services remains constant over the years, so each year's index measures the price of the same basket and indices can be compared from one year to the next. With current weights the basket changes slightly each year and so strictly speaking comparisons can only be made between the current year and the base. In practice however this is not regarded as a problem, because with current weights each year's basket accurately reflects what people are actually spending their money on. Therefore it can be argued that this makes the various, slightly different baskets more comparable than if the weights had been kept artificially static.

The very big advantage of current weights is that they remain up to date and accurately reflect the market.

Two significant disadvantages of base weights are as follows.

(i)   Since they get out of date the base of the index will need changing more often than with a current weighted index.

SUGGESTED SOLUTIONS

(ii) Base weighted indices tend to exaggerate inflation. Consumers reduce the quantities they buy of items subject to big price increases and base weights do not reflect these reductions.

(c) The change to current weights will tend to reduce the index for the reason given above. In this example the economy model has undergone a very high price increase and reducing its weight from 10 to 6 will reduce the index. The same effect on the index will result from increasing from 9 to 25 the weight of the de luxe model which has undergone a very large price cut. In this instance, we would expect the Paasche index to be quite markedly less than the Laspeyre.

28 ITEMS FOR INCLUSION

A series of values relating to different points in time become index numbers, with a particular time point as their base, if each value is expressed as a percentage of the value for the base time. Most price indices involve a range of items and so, in addition to indexing, a process of weighted averaging is also required which may take place either before or after the indexing process.

The choice of items to include in a price index depends very much on the purpose of the index. A manufacturer indexing the prices of the items he sells would almost certainly include all such items in the index since this would present no great practical problems. However the construction of a retail price index aimed at measuring the cost of living for consumers will involve difficult decisions about which items to include. Clearly it is not possible to include all items (both in terms of types of items and company brands) that households buy. The aim must be to select a 'basket' of goods and services which is broadly representative of household expenditure, taking care that the items are unambiguous and readily ascertainable. In the UK the retail price index utilises the results of the family expenditure survey to obtain information about what households spend their money on. On the basis of this information some 600 items called price indicators are selected, in the probably reasonable hope that if, say, the selected brand shows a certain price increase then other similar brands' prices will change in a similar fashion.

Laspeyre index $= 100 \times \dfrac{\Sigma p_1 q_0}{\Sigma p_0 q_0}$

Columns entitled $p_1 q_0$ and $p_0 q_0$ are required.

Commodity	p_0	q_0	p_1	$p_0 q_0$	$p_1 q_0$
A	1.62	37	1.98	59.94	73.26
B	3.57	25	4.52	89.25	113.00
C	0.94	11	2.65	10.34	29.15
D	5.60	6	9.23	33.60	55.38
E	2.83	20	3.71	56.60	74.20
				249.73	344.99

Price index $= 100 \times \dfrac{344.99}{249.73} = 138.1$

29 DEEFEX LIMITED

(a) (i) Probability of a defect, P(X or Y) = P(X) + P(Y) - P(X and Y)

Probability of having both defects, X and Y = P(X and Y) = P(X) × P(Y)
$$= 0.15 × 0.14$$
$$= 0.021$$

$$\text{P(X or Y)} = 0.15 + 0.14 - 0.021$$
$$= 0.269$$

(ii) Probability of having both defects is 0.021, as calculated in (i)

(iii) Probability of one defect only is the solution to (i) minus the solution to (ii), ie 0.269 - 0.021 = 0.248

The calculations should perhaps be shown more fully, as follows.

P (X, not Y)	= 0.15 × 0.86	= 0.129
P (Y, not X)	= 0.85 × 0.14	= 0.119
P (X, not Y) or P(Y, not X)		0.248

(iv) Probability of no defects at all = 0.85 × 0.86 = 0.731

(b) From (a), we know the probabilities of product Q having defects X and Y are as follows.

		Probability of defect Z
Both X and Y	0.021	0.1
X or Y, but not both	0.248	0.2
Neither	0.731	0.3
	1.000	

(i) The probability of having no defect at all is as follows.
P (neither X nor Y, not Z) = P (neither X nor Y) × P(not Z)
$$= 0.731 × 0.7$$
$$= 0.5117$$

(ii) The probability of having one defect only is the sum of:
P (X or Y but not both, not Z) plus
P (neither X nor Y, but defect Z)

The probability of defect X or Y, but not both, without defect Z
$$= 0.248 × 0.8$$
$$= 0.1984$$

The probability of defect Z, but not X or Y
$$= 0.731 × 0.3$$
$$= 0.2193$$

The probability of one defect
$$= 0.1984 + 0.2193$$
$$= 0.4177$$

(c) (i)   Total number of rejects   = 1,980

Total number of successfully completed units   = (7,500 - 1,980)

= 5,520

Probability of successful completion $= \dfrac{5,520}{7,500}$

= 0.736

(ii)   Rejects in processes 1 and 2   = 1,180

Number successfully getting through to Process 3   = (7,500 - 1,180)

= 6,320

Probability of completing process 2 $= \dfrac{6,320}{7,500}$

= 0.8427

30 SIGNIFICANCE TESTS

(a) Population proportion = 60% = 0.6
Sample proportion = 62% = 0.62   n = 1,200

H_0: $\pi = 0.6$
H_1: $\pi \neq 0.6$ 2 tail test

If H_0 is correct, standard error $= \sqrt{\dfrac{\pi(1-\pi)}{n}} = \sqrt{\dfrac{0.6 \times 0.4}{1,200}} = 0.0141$

At 5% significance level,
Critical value of U = 1.96

Sample value of $U = \dfrac{0.62 - 0.6}{0.0141} = 1.4184$

The sample value of U is less than the critical value so we can accept the null hypothesis.

Conclusion
At 5% significance level the proportion of subscribers who owned their home is not significantly different from the percentage in the population of the city.

Explanation
We would assume that there was a real difference between the general population and the magazine subscribers only if the gap between the two proportions was so great as to have occurred by chance with a probability less than 5%. In the event, the gap was quite small and its probability was greater than 5%. We assume therefore that the difference arose as a result of the randomness of the sampling process rather than as a result of a real difference between the two groups.

(b) Presumed average = 52 years
Sample average = 56.8 years, n = 26, s = 8.9

H_0: $\mu = 52$
H_1: $\mu > 52$ 1 tail test

Standard error $= \dfrac{s}{\sqrt{n}} = \dfrac{8.9}{\sqrt{26}} = 1.7454$

The sample size is rather small for normal distribution to be used but no other distribution is available to us. We will consequently adopt a stringent 1% significance level.

Critical value of U = 2.3263

Sample value of U $= \dfrac{56.8-52}{1.7454} = 2.7501$

The sample value of U is greater than the critical value so we reject the null hypothesis.

Conclusion
At 1% significance level, the peak earning age appears to be significantly greater than 52 years.

Explanation
If the peak earning age really is 52 years, it is possible that a sample could show an average as high as 56.8 but it is extremely unlikely. In fact the probability of such a high value occurring, as a result of the random sampling process, is less than 1%. It is therefore reasonable in the circumstances to adopt the alternative viewpoint that the peak earning age is in excess of 52 years.

Tutorial comments
(1) In part (a) the question asks whether there is a significant *difference* in the proportions and therefore a two-tail test is required. In part (b) the question is not so clear. We are given no hints as to whether, prior to taking the sample, the alternative hypothesis was that the peak age might differ from 52 (requiring a two tail test) or might be greater than 52 (requiring a one-tail test). We have opted for the latter but believe that either should have been acceptable to the examiners.

(2) Where the sample size is less than 30, the normal distribution is not strictly applicable, In such circumstances it seems advisable to use a 1% rather than a 5% significance level unless the question specifies that a 5% level should be used.

31 CAMERA BATTERIES

(a) n = 425, $\bar{x} = 150$, s = 15

Standard error $= \dfrac{s}{\sqrt{n}} = \dfrac{15}{\sqrt{425}} = 0.7276$

95% confidence interval for the mean for all batteries is

$\bar{x}$ ± 1.96 × standard error

ie   150 ± 1.96 × 0.7276

ie   between 148.6 and 151.4 hours.

The true mean could be 160 hours but the probability of that being the case is less than 5% since 160 is outside the 95% confidence interval.

Testing the hypothesis that the true mean is 148 hours or less

H_0: $\mu = 148$
H_1: $\mu > 148$ 1 tail test
At 1% significance level,
the critical value of U = 2.3263

the sample value of U = $\dfrac{150 - 148}{0.7276}$ = 2.7488

The sample value of U exceeds the critical value and so we reject the null hypothesis.

Conclusion
At a 1% significance level, we reject the hypothesis that the true mean is 148 hours or less and adopt the viewpoint that the true mean exceeds 148 hours.

(b)

	UK	Other	Total
I	7	5	12
II	4	10	14

(i) P(one from UK, other not from UK)
    = P(I from UK, II not) + P(I not from UK, II from UK)

    = $\dfrac{7}{12} \times \dfrac{10}{14} + \dfrac{5}{12} \times \dfrac{4}{14}$ = 0.5357

(ii) P(both from UK) = $\dfrac{7}{12} \times \dfrac{4}{14}$ = 0.1667

(iii) P(neither from UK) = $\dfrac{5}{12} \times \dfrac{10}{14}$ = 0.2976

[Alternately the probability in (iii) could be obtained by subtracting the other two probabilities from 1 ie 1 − 0.5357 − 0.1667 = 0.2976.]

32 DEPARTMENTAL STORE

(a) National average = 5.62
    Sample average $\bar{x}$ = 5.79, s = 0.32, n = 15

H_0: $\mu = 5.62$
H_1: $\mu > 5.62$ 1 tail test

Standard error = $\dfrac{s}{\sqrt{n}}$ = $\dfrac{0.32}{\sqrt{15}}$ = 0.0826

The sample size is very low for a normal distribution to be used but no other distribution is available to us.

At 5% significance level, critical value of U = 1.6449

Sample value of $U = \dfrac{5.79 - 5.62}{0.0826} = 2.058$

The sample U is greater than the critical U and so we reject the null hypothesis and conclude, at 5% significance level, that this store's average delivery time is greater than the national average.

At 1% significance level, critical value of U = 2.3263 and the sample U is less than this value. Hence we accept the null hypothesis that this store is no worse than the national average.

Explanation
The gap between the sample average and the national average could have arisen simply as a result of the randomness of the sampling process or it could reflect a real difference. If there is no real difference, a gap as large as that observed would occur with a probability of between 5% and 1%. Its occurrence therefore casts doubt on the hypothesis of 'no difference' and inclines one to the view that this store is in fact worse than the average. However, the sample size is very small and the 1% significance level is best in these circumstances. At this level, there is not strong enough evidence to enable us to assert that this store is worse than the national average.

(b) P(faulty) = 0.12   P(satisfactory) = 1-0.12 = 0.88
Number of fuses per sample = 6
Number of samples = 50

P(no more than one faulty fuse per sample) = P(0) + P(1)
$P(0) = P(\text{all 6 satisfactory}) = 0.88^6 = 0.4644$

To find P(1) we have to allow for the fact that there are six ways in which a single faulty fuse can occur. It can be the first or the second or the third and so on. These ways are mutually exclusive and so we add their probabilities. Each such probability = 0.12×0.88^5.

Hence $P(1) = 6 \times 0.12 \times 0.88^5$
$= 0.3800$

And so P(no more than one faulty)
$= P(0) + P(1)$
$= 0.4644 + 0.3800 = 0.8444$ or 84.44%

Expected number of samples with no more than one faulty
$= 84.44\%$ of $50 = 50 \times 0.8444 = 42.22$ ie 42 samples.

33 SURVEYS

(a)

Regions	A	B	C	D	
No of companies	5	5	5	5	Select any three.

(i) $P(\text{all from A}) = \dfrac{5}{20} \times \dfrac{4}{19} \times \dfrac{3}{18} = 0.0088$

[*Tutorial note:* at the first selection, 5 out of 20 companies are in region A. At the second selection only 4 of the remaining 19 companies are in region A etc.]

(ii) $P(\text{all from any one region}) = \dfrac{20}{20} \times \dfrac{4}{19} \times \dfrac{3}{18} = 0.0351$

[*Tutorial note:* at the first selection any of the 20 companies is acceptable. At the second selection the company must belong to that same region and so only 4 of the remaining 19 are acceptable etc. The same result can be obtained by multiplying P(all from A) by 4 since P(all from B) = P(all from A) = P(all from C) etc].

(iii) $P(\text{each from a different region}) = \dfrac{20}{20} \times \dfrac{15}{19} \times \dfrac{10}{18}$

$$= 0.4386$$

[*Tutorial note:* at the first selection any of the 20 companies is acceptable but at the second selection the region must be different so only 15 of the remaining 19 are acceptable and so on.]

(b) Proportion claimed = 8/10 = 0.8

Sample proportion = $\dfrac{345}{450}$ = 0.7667   n = 450

H_0: $\pi = 0.8$
H_1: $\pi < 0.8$ 1 tail test

If H_0 is correct, standard error $= \sqrt{\dfrac{\pi(1-\pi)}{n}} = \sqrt{\dfrac{0.8 \times 0.2}{450}}$

$$= 0.0189$$

At 5% significance level,
critical value of U = -1.6449

sample value of U = $\dfrac{0.7667 - 0.8}{0.0189}$ = -1.76

The sample value of U is less than the critical value and therefore we reject the null hypothesis.

Conclusion
At 5% level of significance, the sample proportion is significantly less than that claimed and the sample therefore suggests that the manufacturer's claim is not justified.

APPENDIX: STATISTICAL FORMULAE FOR USE IN CIM EXAMINATIONS

Given A = assumed mean

C = class interval

d = deviation from A in multiples of C

1.   Arithmetic Mean, $\bar{x} = \dfrac{\Sigma fx}{\Sigma f}$ or $A + C \times \dfrac{\Sigma fd}{\Sigma f}$

2.   Standard Deviation, $s = \sqrt{\dfrac{\Sigma fx^2}{\Sigma f} - \left(\dfrac{\Sigma fx}{\Sigma f}\right)^2}$ or $C \times \sqrt{\dfrac{\Sigma fd^2}{\Sigma f} - \left(\dfrac{\Sigma fd}{\Sigma f}\right)^2}$

3.   Median, $M = L_1 + (L_2 - L_1)\left(\dfrac{n/2 - \Sigma f_1}{\Sigma f_2 - \Sigma f_1}\right)$

       where L_1 = lower boundary of median class

L_2 = upper boundary of median class

n = total number of items

Σf_1 = cumulative frequency below median

Σf_2 = cumulative frequency above median

4.   Product-moment correlation coefficient:

$$r = \frac{n\Sigma xy - \Sigma x\Sigma y}{\sqrt{[n\Sigma x^2 - (\Sigma x)^2][n\Sigma y^2 - (\Sigma y)^2]}}$$

5.   Rank correlation coefficient:

$$R = 1 - \frac{6\Sigma d^2}{n(n^2 - 1)}, \qquad \text{where } d = \text{difference in ranks}$$

6.   Regression Line coefficients:

$$b = \frac{n\Sigma xy - \Sigma x\Sigma y}{n\Sigma x^2 - (\Sigma x)^2}, \qquad a = \bar{y} - b\bar{x}$$

7.   Price relative index $= 100 \times \sum \dfrac{p_1}{p_0} . w \bigg/ \sum w$

8.   Laspeyre price index $= 100 \times \dfrac{\Sigma p_1 q_0}{\Sigma p_0 q_0}$

9.   Paasche price index $= 100 \times \dfrac{\Sigma p_1 q_1}{\Sigma p_0 q_1}$

10.   Standard Error of the Mean $= \dfrac{\sigma}{\sqrt{n}} \simeq \dfrac{s}{\sqrt{n}}$

11.   Standard Error of the Proportion $= \sqrt{\dfrac{\pi(1-\pi)}{n}} \simeq \sqrt{\dfrac{p(1-p)}{n}}$

PERCENTAGE POINTS OF THE NORMAL DISTRIBUTION

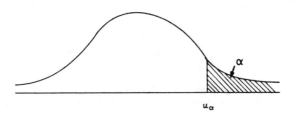

u_α

This table gives the 100α percentage points and the u_α position of the standardised Normal distribution. Thus, u_α is the value of a standardised Normal variate which has probability α of being exceeded.

α	u_α	α	u_α	α	u_α
0.5	0.0000	0.05	1.6449	0.025	1.9600
0.4	0.2533	0.01	2.3263	0.005	2.5758
0.3	0.5244	0.001	3.0902	0.0005	3.2905
0.2	0.8416	0.0001	3.7190	0.00005	3.8906
0.1	1.2816	0.00001	4.2649	0.000005	4.4172

INDEX

FURTHER READING

You may like to test your grasp of *Quantitative Studies* by tackling short questions in multiple choice format. BPP publish the *Password* series of books, each of which incorporates a large collection of multiple choice questions with solutions, comments and marking guides. The Password titles most relevant to this paper are *Foundation Business Mathematics* and *Advanced Business Mathematics*. Each is priced at £6.95 and contains about 300 questions.

To order your *Password* books, ring our credit card hotline on 081-740 6808 or tear out this page and send it to our Freepost address.

To: BPP Publishing Ltd, FREEPOST, London W12 8BR   Tel: 081-740 6808

Forenames (Mr / Ms) _____

Surname: _____

Address: _____

_____

Post code: _____

Please send me the following books:	*Quantity*	*Price*	*Total*
Password: Foundation Business Mathematics		£6.95	
Password: Advanced Business Mathematics		£6.95	

Please include postage:

UK: £1.50 for the first plus £0.50 for each extra book ....

Overseas: £3 for first plus £1.50 for each extra book ....

I enclose a cheque for £_____ or charge to Access/Visa

Card number ☐☐☐☐☐☐☐☐☐☐☐☐☐☐☐☐

Expiry date _____ Signature _____

If you are placing an order, you might like to look at the reverse of this page. It's a Review Form, which you can send in to us with comments and suggestions on the text you've just finished. Your feedback really does make a difference: it helps us to make the next edition that bit better. So if you're posting the coupon, do fill in the Review Form as well.

CIM - QUANTITATIVE STUDIES (STATISTICS)

Name: _____

How have you used this text?

Home study (book only) ☐

On a course: college_____ ☐ Other _____

How did you obtain this text?

From us by mail order ☐ From us by phone ☐

From a bookshop ☐ From your college ☐

Where did you hear about BPP texts?

At bookshop ☐ Recommended by lecturer ☐

Recommended by friend ☐ Mailshot from BPP ☐

Advertisement in _____ ☐ Other _____

Your comments and suggestions would be appreciated on the following areas.

Syllabus coverage

Illustrative questions

Errors (please specify, and refer to a page number)

Presentation

Other (index, cross-referencing, price - whatever!)